The
MEANEST
MAN
in
TEXAS

1-6-75

The MEANEST MAN in TEXAS

A true story based on
the life of Clyde Thompson

by

Don Umphrey

THOMAS NELSON PUBLISHERS
Nashville • Camden • New York

Published in Nashville, Tennessee, by Thomas Nelson, Inc. and distributed in Canada by Lawson Falle, Ltd., Cambridge, Ontario.

Printed in the United States of America.

Scripture quotations are from the King James Version of the Bible.

Library of Congress Cataloging in Publication Data

Umphrey, Don.
   The meanest man in Texas.

   1. Thompson, Clyde, d. 1979.   2. Crime and criminals
—Texas—Biography.   3. Prisoners—Texas—Biography.
4. Murder—Texas—Case studies.   I. Title.
HV6248.T425U46   1984   364.1'523'0924 [B]   84-3383
ISBN 0-8407-5870-7

Dedicated to those who are reading these words from behind bars.

Acknowledgements

There are many whom I wish to thank for their part in this project.

First, there are people connected with the motion picture industry who have encouraged me with their interest in the story. These include Erwin Hearne, Elaine Suranie, Ballard Cabaniss, Earl Miller, Francine Rudine, Peter Wittman, Susan Robinson Fife, Tom Palmer, the late Vera Culwell, and my literary representatives, Paul Gerard and Helen Ruth of the Paul Gerard Agency in Newport Beach, California.

Jan Proctor and Chris Bondurant were good friends who encouraged me in many ways in the beginning stages of the project.

Jay Byrd and Rick Hartley, both of the Texas Department of Corrections, gave me access to prison records and allowed me to tour "The Walls." Much of my secondary research was conducted at the Southwest Collection at Texas Tech University, a repository for artifacts and records of west Texas. There I was able to gain an account of Clyde's trials through looking at microfilm of old newspapers, particularly *The Eastland Telegram* and *Cisco Press*. Don Walker, who was completing his Ph.D. dissertation on the old leased labor system in Texas prisons, assisted greatly.

Several people read the manuscript and made helpful suggestions. These include my mother, Mary Evelyn Umphrey, my sister, Jan Sutherland, Debbie Freshour, Ted Rose, Karen

Randolph, Ray and Mary LaFontaine, Jim Marra, Bob Woodard, E. L. "Luke" Curtis, Marilyn Young, Faye Kennedy, Dr. Bill I. Ross, DeWayne Freshour, Dr. Byron Chesbro, Don White, Ron Bailey, and Dr. Bill Rogers and his wife, Pauline.

Others encouraged me in other ways. These include my many students at Texas Tech University, friends at the Broadway Church of Christ in Lubbock, and many other friends who often asked, "How's the book coming?" Others include my father, Earl D. Umphrey, Maurice and Marie Hall, Mauri and Pat Evans, Jeff and Jim Sale, Lynn and Nina Webb, Joey Cope, Meg Bremer Jones, Frank Beaumont, Jim Stout, Bob Merrifield, Mrs. James Ray, Wes Whitt, the late Max Harper, Dr. Dennis Harp, Dr. Alex Tan, Tim and Becky Talley, and James Bynum.

Most of all, I thank God, from whom I have received daily direction; I continue to learn about grace and have come to understand a little bit about infinite love.

Don Umphrey
November, 1983

Preface

It has been my privilege to chronicle the story of Clyde Thompson. I have gone to great lengths to be as historically accurate as possible. This process started with extensive interviews with Clyde from 1977 to 1979, and with Julia from 1977 to 1983. I also relied heavily upon approximately three hundred hand-written pages of Clyde's notes. I have interviewed many others who knew him. Where possible, the interviews were verified by secondary sources, including prison records, old newspaper accounts, and a variety of books detailing various aspects of Texas history. Clyde's notoriety is exemplified by the fact that the *Fort Worth Star Telegram* had a file that contained fifty different stories about him.

Of course, I could not record actual conversations or probe into the minds of those involved in this story. In some instances, Clyde or others I interviewed recalled actual conversations. But in the majority of cases, dialogue and thoughts have been constructed as they might have occurred, given the particular circumstances.

Two previously unsolved murders from the 1930s are solved in these pages, and other sensitive details are described. For these reasons, I have changed the names of some of the characters. Though many of them are now dead, it is not the purpose of this book to reopen old wounds of those who were involved, or of their loved ones. As a reader, however, you can be confident that all the people described in this book did exist, and that in the majority of cases the names are true.

Chapter
1

THE BLACK CLOUDS rolled in from the west, and lightning streaked across the darkening west Texas sky. The inevitable pounding thunder followed, momentarily drowning out the thirty or so voices singing "Rock of Ages." One of the horses tied outside the small cemetery whinnied and pawed uneasily at the dusty ground. A sudden wind peppered the mourners with blowing dirt.

Closing his eyes to screen out the dirt, seventeen-year-old Clyde Thompson wondered if they were going to get his grandfather properly buried before the summer storm hit. He opened his eyes to look at the brown wooden coffin. He hated to see the old man go. Clyde could remember sitting on his grandfather's knee and listening to stories about west Texas in the 1880s. Grandpa moved to Texas from Alabama, and he worked as a horse trader most of his life. He made horse-trading trips to Missouri and claimed he had been a personal friend of Jesse James. Grandpa told of the time he'd chased down an Indian and threatened to cut his throat unless the Indian gave him some information. After the red man talked, Grandpa cut his throat anyway. Altogether, Grandpa claimed to have killed twenty men, most of them Indians. He had outlived three wives, and Clyde guessed it was about Grandpa's time to go. But Clyde knew he would miss him and his stories. He had really admired the old man.

Though it was 1928, there was still a rugged, pioneer spirit in the part of Texas that lay west of Fort Worth. The people there took pride in being able to survive often bitterly cold winters, harsh, hot summers, and violent tornadoes that came in between. Cowboys and oil field roughnecks came into west Texas towns on Saturday nights to whoop it up. In both distance and culture, this part of the country was a long way from the long-settled cities farther east and along the West Coast. Cowtown, as Fort Worth was called, was very different culturally from Dallas just thirty-three miles to the east.

Clyde figured that, inwardly, he wore the same brand as his grandfather. He too was tough, even by west Texas standards.

There was the time that the .22 caliber rifle had blown up in his face. A bullet had lodged in the dirty barrel, and Clyde and his brothers tried unsuccessfully to poke the bullet through. Finally, Clyde got the idea that it would come out if he fired another bullet through the barrel. Though the exploding barrel had knocked him out and blinded him for two or three days, he had never visited a doctor.

Fights—Clyde had been in plenty of them. He could remember the boys in Oklahoma pulling on his shoulder-length blond hair and calling him a girl. With the long hair, Clyde looked like a miniature Buffalo Bill, and Clyde's folks hoped that he would be able to tour with Buffalo Bill. But in the meantime, the hair caused him a lot of hassles in town. Each time someone pulled on his hair, he would get in a fight. He won quite a few and lost some, but he learned to use his fists.

Once, a boy named Cletus accused Clyde of stealing his gloves after the two had played marbles together. Cletus demanded that Clyde return the gloves. Since Clyde insisted he hadn't stolen them and didn't have them to return, a fight

10

seemed the only way to settle the matter. Cletus already had a swollen and infected right eye, and in the early stages of the fight Clyde had aimed his punches away from it. But when Cletus started getting the better of him, Clyde ended the fight by landing a solid blow to Cletus's right eye. Pus had flown all over the place, and Cletus had gone home crying.

Then there were the fights between the Boy Scouts and non-Scouts, including Clyde, in Graham, Texas. A brawl between the two factions broke out on the school playground, and after it was over, sixty-two boys were marched to the principal's office for a paddling. A few days later Clyde was walking in the downtown area, and some Scouts motioned for him to come over to the shoeshine parlor they operated. It was located between two brick buildings that were about eight feet apart.

"We're going to teach you to respect the Scouts," one of the boys told him. Clyde was escorted behind the shine parlor, where he was forced to square off with Johnny Grant, a Scout known to be a pretty fair scrapper. Clyde had started to win, but several boys grabbed him from behind and Johnny let loose a barrage of punches to his face. The same thing happened a second time. Clyde's eyes had swollen shut, but he kept on fighting. He swung at Johnny and hit one of the brick walls, breaking two knuckles. When the Scouts left him there, the only way Clyde could see to get home was by holding open an eye with his fingers.

Clyde was so beaten up that he missed a week of school. But on the way to school his first day back, he encountered Johnny Grant walking through the park. This time the odds were even, and Clyde beat the tar out of him.

"Education," Grandpa had told him, "is when you're not surprised at anything that happens."

If that's what education really is, thought Clyde, *maybe I had a pretty good one because I've seen quite a bit.* When he was ten, Clyde was selling newspapers in the street at Oil City, the boom town. As Clyde watched, the deputy sheriff staggered out of the saloon and dropped dead in the dust. It was the first time Clyde had seen a man die, and it was a sickening sight that stayed with him. But now that he was older, he assumed it was the way of west Texas. It hadn't bothered him to see two dying lawmen on the streets of Cisco just before Christmas of the previous year. In fact, that caused more excitement than he'd ever seen in Cisco.

The wind gusted again, and larger droplets of water hit the mourners. Within seconds, the rain was pouring down. The preacher concluded the service hastily; then he and the others ran for their automobiles or horses just outside the cemetery gate. Clyde watched them, then looked over at his rain-soaked father and brothers. Clyde knew they couldn't leave yet. They had to lower the wooden coffin into the hole and cover it up.

Chapter
2

FOURTEEN-YEAR-OLD Ruth Welsey watched from the front porch as two of her brothers and Clyde Thompson walked toward the road. Reuben, her eighteen-year-old brother, carried a shotgun loosely in his right hand. Mark, thirteen, held a kerosene lantern. Ruth knew that Clyde, at first just a friend of her brothers but now becoming her first real sweetheart, had her father's .45 caliber Remington pistol tucked in his belt. The three planned to hunt the plentiful wild game among the mesquite, scrub oak, and occasional cactus dotting the surrounding hills. It was Friday, September 7, 1928.

Ruth called out, "Hey, y'all forgot the dogs."

All three looked back. "Naw, don't need 'em tonight," Reuben answered. "Besides," he said, now looking at Clyde as they continued walking, "I don't want our dogs showin' up your dog Jack again."

Clyde chuckled. He knew that Reuben's father had paid good money for their two hunting dogs. But on previous trips Jack had always outhunted the Welseys' dogs. Tonight they were leaving all the dogs at home to do their own tracking.

Hunting was more than just a sport for Clyde. He supplemented his father's income by selling possum skins. In the previous year he had bagged and sold seventy-two of them. This money was in addition to what he earned working as a farmhand and woodchopper during the day or helping his father with his newly formed roof resealing business.

But besides making money by hunting, Clyde enjoyed it. Sometimes he hunted by himself, sometimes with his brothers or stepbrother or the Welsey boys, with whom he had been acquainted since his family moved to a rented house in the Leeray community at the first of the year.

Leeray was already being called a ghost city. Although sparsely populated now, it contained the remnants of dwellings hastily built during the Ranger oil boom of ten years earlier. The discovery of oil near Ranger in Eastland County some eighty miles west of Fort Worth had come following projections that United States oil reserves were dwindling and being used up quickly by the automobiles that were taking over from the horse and buggy. Newspapers reported that the British were trying to gain control of American petroleum. Ranger, a hamlet with a population of eight hundred, quickly grew to thirty thousand and became the center of oil exploration for a forty-mile radius. The boom also skyrocketed the population of the county seat, Eastland, ten miles west of Ranger along the Texas and Pacific Railroad, and of Cisco, ten miles still farther west. Leeray, little more than a crossroad north of Cisco, suddenly became a town of several thousand people. Other boom towns, Gunsight and Frankell, sprang up just as suddenly, with soldiers of fortune and war veterans who wanted to make their own fortunes before settling down. Oil was selling for as high as $4.15 a barrel, compared to $.10 during the earlier Spindletop days. It was estimated that it would take 174,400 wells to pump the $95 billion worth of oil in what became known as the Ranger Oil Field.

But oil prices dropped, and the demand was not what it was projected to be. Some men became overnight millionaires.

Others added to their millions. But the majority returned home to be farmers or storekeepers, with nothing to show for their efforts but tales of wide-open boom towns where dice-throwing took place on the streets and murder was commonplace.

By the time Clyde and his family moved to Ranger in 1926, the days of making a quick fortune had long since passed. There were still producing oil wells, but the derricks that had earlier risen toward the sky in quest of new oil below were now rusting in fields. The population of Ranger had dropped to around seven thousand, and Rees Thompson, Clyde's father, had a difficult time making a living there. Then they moved to Leeray with its deserted buildings and the crumbling foundations of homes and shops that had never been completed. One of Clyde's uncles farmed near Leeray.

The three hunters saw nothing after about thirty minutes. They had gone about two miles from the Welsey home. "Let's make a circle over to Web O'Dell's place and shoot 'im, just to see if he kicks like a dyin' animal after he's been shot," said Reuben suddenly. Clyde laughed at the joke.

Reuben pressed it. "I really do want to go over there and beat the tar outta him. He needs to be taught a lesson."

Clyde knew of Web O'Dell but had never met him. Web was in his late twenties and lived by himself in a cabin in the hills. An employee of an oil company, he maintained some pumping oil wells in the area.

Clyde was still chuckling to himself at Reuben's earlier remark, but now he could see that Reuben was serious. "How come?" he asked.

"He's been talkin' 'round town about Ruthie, said some insultin' things about her," Reuben answered.

"Yeah," Mark chipped in. "Daddy told 'im to quit talkin' 'bout her that way, but he just keeps it up. Daddy's real mad."

"I figure that if I go over there and beat 'im up, everyone'll

15

be satisfied," Reuben continued. "Except maybe Web O'Dell," he added with a smile.

"Sure," answered Clyde. "If ya wanna beat 'im up, I'll go over there with ya to make sure ya get a fair fight."

The trio turned left toward Web's cabin and walked up a dry creek bed. As they walked, Reuben talked of how he could get Web to come out of the cabin. He would say they needed a shovel to dig out a bobcat that their dogs had holed-up.

The cabin was built on the side of a hill, about one hundred yards up from the creek bed. There were no lights on inside the cabin. Reuben walked up to the door and called out for Web. In a moment, a light came on, and a shirtless Web came to the door. From where he stood below, Clyde sized up the man. He was shorter than Clyde's five feet seven inches and probably weighed less than Clyde's 135 pounds. He didn't think Reuben would have any trouble with O'Dell, but if Reuben did, Clyde knew he could handle O'Dell.

Reuben told Web of the fictitious holed-up bobcat about a mile up the creek bed. Web seemed surprised by the visitors after sundown. He stood in silence for a moment before he spoke. Sure, he'd go along with them, as would his younger brother who was visiting for the weekend.

Web closed the door to the cabin while he and his brother dressed inside. Reuben turned around with a surprised look on his face and walked down the stairs to where Clyde and Mark were standing. "I didn't know Jake was here, too," he said quietly, with a note of fear in his voice. "I don't think we'll be able to whip both of 'em."

Reuben paused for a minute, thinking. "I'll tell you what. We'll go along with this holed-up cat story and then take 'em out in the woods. We'll pretend we can't find the place where we got the cat holed up. Later on we'll catch Web alone and give 'im his due. Okay?"

Clyde and Mark nodded in agreement.

Web and Jake emerged from the cabin in a moment. Web

16

carried a brass hunting horn to use for calling the dogs, a pickax, and a large lantern. Jake carried a shovel. Clyde and the two pairs of brothers walked down a trail through the brush to the creek bed and then headed in the direction from which the three had come earlier. After about a quarter of a mile, Web wondered out loud why he couldn't hear dogs baying. "Dogs are probably restin'," replied Reuben.

The five continued to walk, but Reuben dropped back beside Clyde. "Shoot 'em both," Reuben whispered anxiously to Clyde.

Clyde looked quickly at Reuben. "Why should I? You've got a gun. Do it yourself."

"Web insulted your girl, didn't he?" insisted Reuben.

"I didn't hear him," Clyde answered.

Walking in the lead, Web became suspicious of the whispering behind him. He turned around. "What's goin' on?"

Reuben snapped back, "You b——! You insulted my sister!"

That triggered the O'Dells into action. "So that's it," growled Web. "There ain't no bobcat." To his brother, Web said, "You take him!" as he pointed at Reuben.

Swinging the shovel, Jake rushed at Reuben, but Reuben rebuffed the attack with the barrel of the shotgun. The two grappled, steel against steel.

At the same time, Web threw the hunting horn at Clyde. Clyde ducked as it flew over his head and landed in the bushes. Web then rushed Clyde, swinging the lantern. In panic, Clyde pulled the pistol from his belt and fired twice, first at the charging Web and then at Jake, who was still fighting with Reuben. Clyde was unsure whether either of the bullets had found its mark, but Web staggered momentarily. Mark had already backed away from the action, and as the booms from the .45 echoed through the valley, Reuben joined his brother off to the side. Regaining his balance, Web threw the lantern at Clyde. It missed. He came at Clyde with the pickax in his hand. Clyde fired twice more. Web staggered, moaned, and fell. Then Jake lunged at Clyde with a dead tree limb, knocking Clyde over as it crashed down on his skull, snapping the limb in two. Clyde fired twice more at Jake, who then ran.

Bewildered, Clyde looked at the empty gun in his hand. He wasn't sure whether Jake had been hit with any of the bullets, but Web was apparently injured because he lay on the ground, moaning.

Reuben ran up to Clyde, yelling, "Don't let 'im get away!" He snatched the gun from Clyde's hand and headed into the brush behind Jake. Carrying the lantern and the shotgun his brother had handed him, Mark raced over to Clyde. Clyde got up and retrieved the lantern Web had thrown at him, and he and Mark rushed in the direction that Jake and Reuben had gone.

Jake, hit by a bullet, had fallen about one hundred yards away from the scene of the shooting. As Clyde and Mark approached the spot, they saw Reuben beating Jake's head and face with the barrel of the empty pistol. The sight of the bloody-faced Jake made Clyde vomit. When Jake ceased to make noise and thrash about, Reuben climbed off his chest.

"Let's get back to Web," said the breathless Reuben, holding the bloody pistol in his hand.

The trio made their way back through the brush to find Web, groaning in a pool of dirt and blood. Reuben took the shotgun from Mark and handed him the red-barreled pistol. "Beat the b——'s head in," Reuben ordered his little brother. "He insulted our sister."

Mark obeyed, stooping down over Web and crashing the gun barrel into his face four times with all his might. Web was then silent.

"Now we've all had a part in it," stated Reuben. "We can't tell on each other without all of us getting into trouble."

In an attempt to make the murders look like robbery, the boys searched the pockets of the O'Dells and found $3.62 between them. They went back to Web's cabin, stole a few things, and hid them.

Chapter
3

CLYDE AWAKENED SATURDAY MORNING with the usual sounds of roosters crowing in the distance and the smell of pancakes cooking on his stepmother's griddle downstairs. Still half-asleep, he started to plan his day. Suddenly he bolted upright in bed, his eyes wide open as memories of the previous night shot into his mind. "Was it a dream? Please, God, let it be a dream!"

But, no, it wasn't a dream. It had really happened. Two men lay dead in the woods.

"If only I hadn't pulled the gun. But I did, and now they're dead. Dead!" Clyde buried his face in the pillow, trying to muffle his sobbing so it couldn't be heard by anyone else in the family.

Clyde's crying did little to relieve him of the haunting thoughts of the previous night. It was as if someone had taken a branding iron and burned the memory into the forefront of his consciousness. There were the sounds of the scuffle interrupted suddenly by the booming of the .45. There was the smell of the discharged gunpowder combined with the sight of Web's falling and the surprised, anguished, and fearful look on Jake's face after seeing his brother fall. There was the bloody-faced Jake putting up his arms, trying in vain to prevent Reuben's clubbing him with the pistol. And there were the sickening thuds of the gun barrel crashing against Web's head, quieting him once and for all.

One of the items Clyde, Reuben, and Mark had stolen from Web's cabin was a shotgun. It was a good shotgun, and Clyde had hidden it at home. He wondered if he should throw it away or hide it somewhere. Then there was the murder weapon—the .45 caliber six-shooter that belonged to Mr. Welsey. Upon returning to the Welsey home, they had hidden the gun in the barn. The gun had blood all over it; it had been bent and broken as it was smashed into the skulls of the O'Dells. Mr. Welsey was bound to miss it.

And what about the O'Dells lying dead in the woods? It had been hot, and the bodies would decay. Should he go back and bury them? Clyde wasn't sure. Surely they would be missed. Someone would look for them, and then what?

Clyde lived with despair but had thoughts of survival. He didn't want to get caught. Men were being electrocuted in Texas for such crimes. In some states, they were still being hanged. Clyde didn't want to die; yet at the same time he felt as if dying might be better. It was as if there were two Clydes. One Clyde continued to go about his business. The second was a heavy-hearted observer of the first. "This will blow over, and everything will be back to normal. They probably won't find the bodies, but even if they do, they could never blame it on me. Yeah, this will pass. Time heals all wounds," Clyde Number One would say. But Clyde Number Two would be quick to interject, "Except for the wounds of the O'Dell boys."

For the next few days Clyde walked through the motions of life, doing his chores and saying little to anybody.

Web and Jake O'Dell had a married sister who lived in Cisco. Web had told her they would come into town after he got his paycheck on Saturday. When her brothers didn't show on Saturday, the sister presumed that they were having a good time together and wasn't overly concerned. But she became genuinely worried when they didn't come into Cisco for church on Sunday.

First thing Monday the sister drove to the cabin to look for her brothers. She found a note on the kitchen table from one of Web's fellow oil company workers. The note asked Web to check on one of the oil wells in the area. Web's two hounds were near the cabin, and they appeared to be hungry. The O'Dells' sister returned home and notified the sheriff. A hunt for the men began late Monday. The bodies were discovered early Tuesday morning by Lee Kelly, a man who lived near Web's cabin and had helped in the search. Word of the gruesome findings spread quickly.

The faces of the corpses had been beaten almost beyond recognition. The bodies had swollen and turned purple in the heat. Web's body had two bullet wounds in the head, possibly from buckshot, concluded one law officer. Jake had been shot once in the body. It also appeared that Jake had crawled and thrashed about for some time after the assault and that dogs had licked his wounds before he died. It looked as though the O'Dells had been ambushed. Since items were missing from the cabin, robbery was assumed to be the motive.

The sister told law officers that a few weeks before, Web had stumbled on a man making moonshine at a still in the woods. The moonshiner had ordered Web away at gunpoint. The officers searched the area for three or four miles in each direction, looking for the moonshiner as a suspect and for any other clues.

Word of the slayings reached Clyde's stepmother that morning. She told the rest of the family about it at lunch. "Justice always wins out," she said. "The murderer of those boys will be caught and punished."

Clyde winced, but no one saw him. His stepmother's announcement was the first he'd heard of the murders from someone other than the Welseys or his own throbbing mind. And he hadn't seen the Welseys since Friday night. Clyde had hoped that the fact of the two murders would somehow go away. He hadn't known that anyone was even searching for the bodies. But now the murders were public knowledge. And the sheriff would be looking for the killers. Clyde didn't want to be caught and punished, as his stepmother was so sure would be the end result.

Rees had contracted to do a roofing job on a house in Cisco, and Clyde went with his father on Tuesday afternoon to reseal the roof. The job consisted of carrying hot tar up a ladder and spreading it with long-handled, moplike devices. It was another hot day, and the job of spreading tar was not pleasant. Even more unpleasant to Clyde was the fact that the bodies had been found. *When will they be coming after me?* Clyde wondered.

Rees noticed that his son, normally a steady helper, was not quite himself. Clyde seemed to be unsure of what he was doing and to work halfheartedly. It just wasn't like him.

"Something the matter?" he finally asked.

Clyde's throat was parched from nerves and the hot sun. When his father spoke, he tightened his grip on the handle. "What d'ya mean?" Clyde answered, with a note of defensiveness in his voice.

"Well, what d'ya say?" Rees tried once again.

"Nothin', Dad," mumbled Clyde. "Just too hot to talk."

His father smiled, wiping his forehead. "You're sure right about that."

The afternoon dragged on.

About 3:30 the sheriff's car pulled up. Clyde saw the car but kept spreading tar, his hands starting to tremble. *Maybe they're not here for me—maybe it's for another reason,* thought Clyde, his pulse starting to race. Rees also noticed the sheriff's car and watched with curiosity as a pair of deputies walked straight for the ladder. Clyde could feel tears coming into his eyes as the deputies began climbing up.

"Howdy," said Rees in a friendly manner as the first deputy reached the roof, his gun drawn.

"Howdy," the deputy replied.

The deputy looked at Clyde as the second deputy joined them on the roof.

"You Clyde Thompson?" asked the first deputy.

At first the lump in Clyde's throat seemed so big that he couldn't answer, and he just stood there feeling his legs shaking. Finally, he mustered, "Y—y—yes, sir."

"Put your hands in the air, Mr. Thompson," said the deputy calmly. Clyde obeyed instantly. Rees was confused. He wasn't sure if he was supposed to raise his hands or if Clyde was.

"What's this about, officers? What's the matter?" Rees asked.

"You kin to this boy?" inquired the deputy.

"Yes, sir, I'm his father."

"We're arrestin' him for the murders of Web and Jake O'Dell." At that the lawmen approached Clyde, who still had his hands raised over his head. While one deputy had his gun aimed at Clyde, the other searched him and found nothing but a well-used pocketknife.

Rees watched the proceedings in amazement and incomprehension. It hadn't fully registered that his son was being arrested for the murders they'd talked about at lunch. "What?" Rees blurted out, louder than he had intended.

Then catching himself, Rees directed his questions to Clyde. "What's this about, son? This is a mistake, isn't it?"

The deputy had completed his search, but Clyde still stood in the same spot with two shaking hands pointed skyward. The two lawmen looked at Clyde curiously, anxious to hear how he would answer his father's question.

"N—no, Daddy. It ain't no mistake. I shot 'em. I killed the O'Dell boys."

Clyde was taken to the jail at Eastland, where a number of law officers from surrounding areas had gathered. When he was guided through the front door with hands cuffed behind him, Clyde had all eyes focused on him. He didn't like the way they looked at him. Some of them glared, as though they hated him. Clyde didn't want anyone to hate him.

He found that Mr. Welsey had been arrested that morning, along with Reuben and Mark. Mr. Welsey had been released, but both of the Welsey boys were upstairs in a jail cell. They had spent the latter part of the morning with law officers in the wooded area of the murder scene and had been locked up for just a few hours.

Bill McDonald, deputy district clerk, produced a long, written statement of confession that had been prepared. McDonald told Clyde that the statement could, and probably would be used against him if he signed it. Clyde couldn't read very well, and he didn't feel like reading the papers because he felt so badly about what had happened—to him, to his friends the Welseys, and to the O'Dells. Clyde stared blankly at the statement, his eyes not seeing the words. How could he try to read at a time like this?

Clyde looked up. It was deadly quiet in the office area of the jail, and nine or ten lawmen were there. All of them were looking at him, as if they wanted him to sign his name. He put the confession flat on the desk, took the pen, and scrawled his name at the bottom. He was then led upstairs to the second floor of the jail to a cell across from the one holding Reuben and Mark Welsey.

The confession that Clyde signed contained information given that morning by the Welsey brothers. It said that Clyde had gone to Web's cabin on the previous Wednesday night, found no one at home, and stole a shotgun and a banjo. The confession stated that on Friday night Clyde stole a six-shooter from Mr. Welsey before returning to Web's cabin with Reuben and Mark. Clyde told the Welseys to wait for him in the brush while he went up to the cabin. He expected the cabin to be unoccupied, but both Web and Jake were there. Web came to the door and accused Clyde of stealing his shotgun. Both the O'Dells said they wanted to go home with Clyde to talk to his father about the theft of the shotgun. Clyde assented, and the three of them left, walking in the creek bed with the Welseys following behind, out of sight. Neither Web nor Jake knew that Clyde had the .45 tucked in his pants, beneath his shirt.

As they were walking, the confession continued, Clyde drew the gun from his belt with the idea of shooting the O'Dells in the back, but he changed his mind. Shortly thereafter, an argument broke out when the O'Dells renewed the charge that Clyde had stolen Web's shotgun. Web started to run at Clyde with a hunting horn in his hand. Clyde pulled the revolver from his belt and shot Jake. Web threw the hunting horn at Clyde, and Clyde shot at him. Then Clyde shot Jake again, and Jake ran away. Web then came at Clyde with a lantern, and Clyde shot him again and hit him with the gun. Web picked up a stick, and Clyde shot him again.

The confession further stated that Clyde ran after Jake, attempting to take the empty shells out of the gun as he ran. Jake fell in a ditch, and Clyde began to hit him with the gun. Every time Clyde tried to hit him, Jake would grab his hand. Finally, Clyde managed to hit Jake with the gun until his victim was unconscious.

Clyde then got off Jake and found the Welsey boys. Clyde told them to wait while he went into the cabin to get some things. They tried to talk him out of it, but he went anyway.

After that, according to the confession, Clyde went to Web's body and stole thirteen dollars out of the pocket. Then he went to Jake and hit him two or three times to make sure he was dead. Finally, Clyde took the money and placed it in the banjo box, which was hidden in the weeds about three hundred yards from the house.

"I guess we're in trouble this time," said Clyde remorsefully to his friends, Reuben and Mark, sitting in the cell across from him. Mark had been lying face down on the cot, crying.

"Yeah, we sure are," replied Reuben. "But Daddy says he's gonna do everything possible to help us."

Word spread quickly throughout the county that Clyde had confessed to the slayings. There also was a rumor that he had confessed to the mass murder of eight members of a family near Cisco a year earlier. Within two hours of his incarceration, men began gathering outside the jail. Although no one had been lynched in Eastland County since the 1890s, the sheriff was concerned. Clyde was secretly taken forty-six miles northeast to Palo Pinto and placed in the jail under an assumed name. Other prisoners were told that he had been locked up for stealing a car.

Palo Pinto jail was a small, two-story structure built in the last century, before the advent of indoor plumbing. Makeshift flush toilets and a shower had since been installed. Temperatures on the outside exceeded 90 degrees daily, which meant that it was oppressively hot inside the cramped jail. Prisoners would lie sweating on their bunks throughout the day, cursing the heat and anxiously awaiting the cooler night temperatures.

Once inside the cell area, Clyde winced at the smell of sweating bodies and human excretion. A dozen roaches scurried to crevices as Clyde was led to a cell. He lay down on the bunk and watched a roach crawling across the floor and up the wall. He wished he was dead. *If only . . . but, no, it happened. And here I am waiting for my murder trial.*

Chapter

4

CLYDE HAD GREATLY ADMIRED his father's father. But the rugged spirit extended further than that in his family. Clyde's great-grandfather was the only one of seven brothers from Georgia who had returned from the Civil War. And he didn't come back whole. One of his legs was missing. After the war he farmed in Alabama.

One of his sons—Clyde's grandfather—put his bride in a covered wagon and headed for Texas.

W. Rees Thompson, Clyde's father, was born in 1887. Rees's mother later gave birth to twin boys. She became ill and died at the age of thirty-one. Rees grew up farming and taking care of chores around the homestead, while his father was absent for two or three months at a time on horse-trading trips. Rees enjoyed people and church. He would travel for miles to attend a tent meeting and would often stay late into the night to discuss biblical issues with the preacher. There were few chances for formal education, but Rees finished the third grade at the local school. With his formal education over, he would read at night by the light of a candle so that he could continue learning.

At the age of eighteen Rees worked as a Bible salesman,

traveling throughout Texas and Oklahoma. This job enabled him to visit with people in many places and also drew him closer to his study of the Bible. While Rees attended church in Comanche County, Texas, a young lady caught his eye. She was fourteen, and he was nineteen. They were married in 1906.

With his gift of gab and his increasing knowledge of the Bible, Rees was occasionally called upon to take the pulpit on Sunday morning at the church that he and his wife, Burlie (called Dolly), attended. He was a good preacher and soon was asked to preach regularly. He held revival meetings throughout central and west Texas. A son, William, was born to Rees's fifteen-year-old wife. Next was a son who died as an infant.

In 1910 Rees felt compelled to carry the word of God to what had been Indian territory just three years before. He moved with his wife and three-year-old son to the Oklahoma panhandle. The Thompsons settled in Guymon, and Rees became the only white preacher in the area. Clyde Vernon Thompson (his first and middle names coming from the names of Texas towns) was born in Guymon on October 5, 1910. Six months after his birth, the Thompsons returned to Texas.

Churches were small in rural Texas, and most of the members were poor. As a result, ministers were paid little, if at all. In order to support his growing family and to continue his preaching, Rees sharecropped. He seemed unable to stay in one place for very long at a time. He farmed in central Texas throughout the spring and summer, preaching on Sundays in various rural churches. Then he and the family would move to west Texas to help harvest the cotton crop in the fall—his wife picked cotton by his side as did his sons, when they were old enough. The Thompsons had two more sons, one of whom died in infancy. Clyde's surviving younger brother was named Bentley. Clyde also had two younger sisters, Dorthula (called Darry) and Abigail.

Rees preached and farmed in the Texas towns of Goree, Rule, and Munday, located some 90 to 110 miles northwest of Cisco, after returning from Guymon. In 1918 the family moved to Erick, Oklahoma, just a few miles east of the Texas panhandle. With the war against the German kaiser in progress, Rees was told that he would be drafted, in spite of the fact that he was a minister and the father of five children. The entire family rejoiced when the war ended two weeks before Rees was to report for active duty. In Erick, Clyde enrolled in school for the first time.

In 1921 Rees put his family in a mule-drawn covered wagon and headed for Texas. On good days they would make twenty-five miles. Clyde and William would hunt or fish to supply rabbits, squirrels, quail, or fish for the family's evening meal. In the wagon about three feet behind the spring seat were a bed and mattress. Rees, Dolly, and the two girls would sleep on the bed. The three boys would sleep on a pallet in the bottom of the wagon or, if the night wasn't too cool, Dolly would make up a bed for the three of them beneath the wagon.

The family settled in Oil City, Texas, a makeshift boom town on the Brazos River some sixty miles west of Fort Worth. It had skyrocketed to a population of two thousand since the recent discovery of oil there. There was big money to be made, either working on the rigs or supplying some type of service to the men who were. With the free-flowing money came prostitutes, gambling, and fighting.

Upon arrival in the boom town, Rees traded the wagon and mules for a large army tent in which the family lived and operated Oil City's first and only hand-laundry. Since there was no school in this new town, Clyde's formal education had to wait. Instead, he helped with the family's laundry business and did assorted other jobs. He and Bentley delivered laundry to his parents' customers. And although there was no charge for delivery, the boys usually received tips of a quarter, fifty cents, and occasionally a dollar, which went a long way with a boy in 1921.

Clyde also shined shoes and hawked newspapers, *The Dallas Morning News* and *The Fort Worth Star Telegram*, on the street. Just about everyone in Oil City knew Clyde from his laundry deliveries, so he didn't have any trouble finding shoeshine customers or selling all the newspapers he carried. Money from newspaper sales was split fifty-fifty with the druggist, who supplied the papers to Clyde.

It was in Oil City where an ex-con "walked around" the deputy sheriff with a knife. The deputy had fallen dead in front of Clyde. The ex-con made a hasty exit from town, never to be seen again.

The slain deputy was replaced by another, but this new deputy was shot in the stomach during a saloon brawl. Rees and another man put the injured deputy in a Model T Ford and rushed him to the doctor in Graham, fifteen miles away. The deputy lived but did not return to his job.

After this shooting, the Young County sheriff asked Rees to be a deputy, a job which he accepted in addition to his duties at the hand-laundry. He walked the streets with a .45 caliber Colt pistol on his hip and a sawed-off shotgun in his hand. Although he made many arrests, he was not injured nor did he kill anyone during his tenure as deputy.

This new job was cut short by a flu epidemic. Half the town came down with it. All seven members of the Thompson family got sick, and some of them might have died except for John Crain, a young oil field worker. Crain left his new job for two weeks to care for the Thompsons in their tent. Miraculously, he never came down with the flu himself. Six members of the family recovered, but William still lay sick in bed. His flu turned into pneumonia, and then typhoid set in. William lingered between life and death for weeks. His weight dropped from 140 to 70 pounds.

With William still fighting for his life on a cot in the tent, Oil

City caught on fire. It didn't take long for the wooden buildings and sidewalks to go up in smoke. The Thompsons threw bucketsful of water on the tent to keep it from igniting as the town burned down around them. William recovered; Oil City didn't. It was one of several boom towns in the area that thrived during oil exploration but quickly faded into oblivion once production was established. The fire hastened Oil City's demise.

Divorce was rare then and nearly unheard of for a minister. But Clyde's parents had been having problems ever since they had been married. There had been an earlier six-month separation. But now the marriage was over. Clyde's mother took the two girls and moved to Oklahoma, where her parents had relocated. Rees kept the three boys, and they moved in with Alma Fox, who was introduced to them as a widowed aunt. She had two boys. Marshall Hervie Fox was usually called by his middle name and was just slightly older than Clyde. The other boy was a toddler who was accidentally hit and killed by a car shortly after the two families came together.

After the move from Erick, Rees had quit preaching. With his new living arrangement, he no longer took the family to church. Previously Rees would gather the family around a lantern and read to them from the Bible and pray with them; now he just read western stories. Clyde missed the days when he would fall asleep in church while his father was holding a tent meeting at night and wake up the next morning in bed at home. He missed his mother and sisters, too.

Rees moved his new family to Jacksboro, Texas, sixty-two miles northwest of Fort Worth, and then to Arkansas. In each location Clyde only briefly attended school. Then it was back to Texas, this time to Graham.

While Rees worked as a farmer and salesman, the boys worked at odd jobs and had some time for boyhood pursuits. On Saturdays the boys would go into the picture show in Graham, but Clyde had a hard time reading the captions. He especially enjoyed Tarzan and cowboy Tom Mix. The Thompson boys trapped possums and raccoons, and with the money from the pelts, they bought their school supplies and came up with the nickels it took to get into the movie house.

Not starting school until he was eight and the constant moving had put Clyde behind in school. Although not large for his age, Clyde was the biggest kid in the fourth grade. He was fourteen and still not a good reader. The age difference between Clyde and most of his classmates was a source of embarrassment for him, and his awkward adolescence made him feel self-conscious. Clyde could hardly stand to make eye contact with the gawky-looking face that stared back at him from the mirror. Because of his fair complexion, his nose constantly peeled from exposure to the sun. His lips would chap, and Clyde thought they stuck out too far. He didn't like the hazel green color of his eyes either. Then there was a certain amount of clumsiness, especially in front of others. To top it all off, his voice sometimes cracked when he talked, jumping up an octave or two.

But there was a bright spot for Clyde. She was a black-eyed, black-haired eleven-year-old with skin that was fairer than Clyde's. She sat in front of him in school. He often walked her home, carrying her books and hanging around her front porch for as long as he could. He dreamed that someday they would get married, and he would support her and their children by working for the border patrol.

The Thompsons moved west near Lubbock for the cotton harvest in the fall of 1925. Clyde never returned to school after that. Nor did he ever again see the beautiful girl who had won his heart. Clyde cried when they left. His family told him it was just puppy love. As he was pulling cotton bolls in the hot sun, he thought almost continually of her.

When the season's cotton harvest was completed in January, 1926, the family moved to Ranger. On the way they stopped in the courthouse at Breckenridge, some thirty miles north of

Cisco, so that Rees and Mrs. Fox could officially get married. The boys resented the fact that they had at first been told she was their aunt. But any resentment was outweighed by the kindness she had shown to all the boys. They at first called her "Auntie" but later knew her as "Mama."

After six months in Ranger, Rees moved his family to Leeray. Clyde chopped wood for four dollars a cord, a chore that took him all day. He also did other jobs he could find. In the harvest of 1926, Clyde and Bill left the remainder of the family and followed the grain thresher up through the Texas panhandle. They returned home when the grain harvest was over. Clyde then started making money from trapping and hunting. Possums, raccoons, skunks, and bobcats brought a minimum of one dollar per pelt and sometimes as high as three dollars. In the summer Clyde again chopped wood and worked as a farmhand.

Chapter
5

WHILE CLYDE WAITED for his trial in Palo Pinto, public sentiment ran high against the accused murderers of the O'Dell boys. The crime was being called "one of the most brutal murders in the history of Eastland County." The prosecuting attorney announced the day after the arrests that he would seek the death penalty for both Clyde Thompson and Reuben Welsey, although he was uncertain whether he would seek death for the younger Mark Welsey. A total of eighteen charges had been filed against the three. Besides two counts of murder, each was charged with robbery with firearms, felony theft, petty theft, and burglary.

On Friday—three days after the arrests—Clyde, Reuben, and Mark were formally indicted for murder by an Eastland County grand jury, which had convened especially for the purpose of investigating the murders. Before the grand jury was dismissed, it was announced that there was sufficient evidence to bring later indictments on the other charges, if necessary.

The following day, September 15, 1928, Mark was released on $2,500 bond, while Reuben and Clyde remained in jail with no bond figure set. His release indicated that the prosecutor might go easier on him because he was just thirteen years old.

When the grand jury reconvened in early October, Clyde's trial was set for Monday, October 15, and Reuben's would commence immediately thereafter. Both would be tried for the murder of Web O'Dell. Seventy-five prospective jurors, all men, were called up for each of the cases. Although each jury would consist of twelve members, many extras were summoned because many would be disqualified for prejudice in the case. The jurors would all be from Eastland County. And if a person lived in the county, it would be difficult for him not to have some prior knowledge of the murders, if not predispositions concerning the guilt and punishment that should be assessed the accused. The trial would be held in the auditorium of Eastland High School because "Ol' Red," the courthouse built in 1897, had recently been torn down and a new one was under construction.

On Sunday, the day before his trial was to start in the eighty-eighth District Court at Eastland, Clyde was transported from the jail at Palo Pinto to the Eastland jail. He was happy to leave the hot, roach-infested Palo Pinto lockup, but he found the two-story Eastland jail, built in 1897, to be equally hot, though cleaner. Under normal circumstances, he would have felt edgy about being in front of so many people, important people, too. But the fact that he would be the subject of all the proceedings intensified his anxiety. He also despaired from the guilt of shooting the O'Dells.

J. R. Stubblefield, who had been practicing law in Eastland since 1894 and was known locally for never having lost a client to the electric chair, was hired by Rees as Clyde's lawyer. His counterpart at the trial would be Eastland County Prosecutor J. Frank Sparks. Stubblefield was wary of the confession Clyde had already signed; he knew that its contents all but condemned his client before the proceedings began. A second strike against Clyde was that the prosecutor had dropped all charges against Mark Welsey in return for his testimony as a witness for the state. It seemed likely that Mark's testimony would favor his brother and condemn Clyde.

To make matters even worse, Eastland County juries had been in a hanging mood of late. Marshall Ratliff and Henry Helms, two men convicted of taking part in what became known as the "Santa Claus" bank robbery in Cisco, had been sentenced to die in the chair. Another man, E. V. Allen, was given the chair for a bank robbery in nearby Carbon in which no shots had been fired and no one was hurt. Prior to those cases, the death penalty had been assessed only twice in the history of Eastland County.

Stubblefield lined up some character witnesses to testify in Clyde's favor. These people included Clyde's father, the Thompsons' landlord, and others who knew the family. Stubblefield could also use the defendant to testify in his own behalf. A few days before the trial started, Stubblefield asked Clyde about testifying. In his remorse, Clyde stared vacantly at the floor of his cell and refused. Five weeks in jail had not alleviated his overwhelming feeling of guilt. He thought about the murder victims he could never bring back. Then there were the times he had spent the night with his friends, the Welseys. Now they were in trouble because of him. There was also his love for their sister. "After all, I shot 'em," Clyde said dejectedly to Stubblefield. "And I guess I'll take what's comin' to me." Death could easily be the verdict, Clyde knew. He really didn't want to die, but he still wasn't so sure he wanted to go on living.

"But what about the confession you signed?" probed Stubblefield in frustration. "Is that all true?"

Clyde closed his eyes and shook his head affirmatively, tears streaming down his cheeks.

Jury selection for Clyde's trial started as scheduled on Monday morning, October 15. By 2:00 P.M. eight of the twelve had been selected, but many people had been disqualified. Judge Elzo Been (pronounced "Bean" and said to be somehow related to the late Judge Roy Bean) told the sheriff to summon twenty-five more potential jurors. The remaining four were selected that afternoon, and the trial was set to commence at 7:00 P.M.

A steady stream of spectators filed into the auditorium, and latecomers had to stand along the back wall. Judge Been was situated on stage. The jurors sat at the side of the stage, facing toward the judge, while the attorneys had tables set up on the other side. Front row seats were reserved for witnesses. The manacled Clyde winced when he drew a few scattered jeers as he was led to the empty chair beside Stubblefield.

After opening formalities, Prosecutor Sparks introduced the confession Clyde had signed. Stubblefield objected to the reading of the confession but was overruled. Sparks read the entire statement aloud, bringing gasps and looks of horror from the packed gallery in the makeshift courtroom. Sparks knew that these audience reactions did not go unnoticed by the jury. Clyde watched a moth flutter around near the judge and then circle a light on the ceiling. How he wished that he could somehow be like that moth and fly away from it all. He leaned back in his chair, closed his eyes, and tried in vain to remove himself from the proceedings. Some of the spectators viewed Clyde's actions as complacency. Someone dubbed him "the sleepy slayer." But Clyde listened to what Sparks read. He wished the words didn't pertain to him.

Clyde realized that the way the confession read was not the way he remembered it. He hadn't earlier visited Web O'Dell's cabin on a mission of theft. The Welsey boys hadn't followed along behind out of sight, as the confession said. He wasn't the one who hit the O'Dells across the face and over the head with Mr. Welsey's .45. But these discrepancies made little difference to him. It was true he had shot the O'Dells, and nothing that was said in court would bring them back. Clyde didn't think the difference between the confession and the way he remembered it was important enough to tell his lawyer or even his father.

After the confession was read, Deputy Clerk Bill McDonald took the stand to tell that before signing it, Clyde had been advised that the confession could be used against him. McDonald told the court that Clyde had not been forced to sign, nor had he been promised any special treatment for signing the confession.

Deputy sheriffs Lee Reid and M. Newman took the stand to relate the condition of the bodies when they were found. Their descriptions brought more gasps from the audience.

Reid also had discovered the broken .45 caliber Remington pistol in the Welsey garage after the bodies had been found. Reid later arrested Clyde on the roof of the house in Cisco. He testified that Clyde had come peacefully.

Others who testified that night included undertaker A. C. Green and Ero Bowles, a farmer who lived near the cabin of Web O'Dell. Both men provided further details of the condition of the bodies when they were found.

With the confession and evidence that supported it, Sparks was building a strong case against Clyde. Despite probing cross-examination of the prosecution witnesses, Stubblefield scored few points. It seemed there was little he could do to refute the truth.

It was 11:00 P.M. when Bowles stepped down from the witness stand, and court was adjourned until Tuesday morning. Clyde spent a restless night in his cell. When the lights were turned off, he started seeing what he thought were ghosts or spooks. "I'm seein' some boogers in here," Clyde yelled down to the jailer. "Could you please turn on the light?" The jailer complied with Clyde's wishes.

Rees Thompson took the stand the next morning. He lied when he testified that Clyde was born October 5, 1911, in Guymon, Oklahoma. But Rees's testimony about Clyde's birthdate was refuted by Sparks, who produced a second confession that Clyde had signed while he was at the Palo Pinto jail. The confession stated that he had been born on October 5, 1910, his true date of birth. The one year difference in birthdates would have made Clyde sixteen at the time of the murders. According to Texas law, sixteen-year-olds were tried as juveniles and could not be given the death penalty. Stubblefield was unaware of the second confession until it was read in court. The defense attorney objected vehemently against allowing the second confession as admissible evidence since, as Clyde's lawyer, he wasn't present when Clyde gave the confession. Sparks countered that he didn't know Stubblefield was representing Clyde at the time he obtained the second confession. Stubblefield's objection was overruled.

In his state of rejection and remorse, Clyde hadn't told anyone of Sparks's visit to the Palo Pinto jail nor of the second piece of paper that he'd signed during that visit.

The most condemning evidence against Clyde came at midmorning Tuesday when Mark Welsey took the stand. He had been given immunity from prosecution in exchange for his testimony. Mark quoted Clyde as saying, "It would be a good time to kill O'Dell." Also, "This will be the last sunset that O'Dell will ever see."

After Web O'Dell had been shot, he was lying on the ground, pleading, "Please don't," but Clyde then hit him over the head with the pistol, Mark said. There were "blood and brains" all over the pistol and Clyde's shirt, according to Mark's account.

From their hiding place in the bushes, Mark testified that he told his older brother that they had both better run away. But Reuben had replied that if they did, Clyde would kill them, too.

Later that night, Clyde was reported to have said, "Well, I got 'em, didn't I?"

To this, Reuben was supposed to have said, "You got 'em, but before long they will get you."

To which, according to Mark's testimony, Clyde retorted, "I don't care, let 'em!"

Mark also testified that Clyde said he now had two notches on his gun and by the time he was twenty-one, he would have twenty-one notches. Clyde threatened to kill both the Welseys if they told on him, Mark told the courtroom.

Clyde was genuinely puzzled at Mark's testimony; he did not fully comprehend what was happening to him. But his bewilderment was so far outweighed by his remorse that he had no desire to tell the court any differently.

The audience of spectators was about evenly divided between men and women with a few children sprinkled throughout. Most parents had no doubt taken the attitude that they didn't want their children's ears exposed to the grisly tale that would unfold in the court. Their notions were correct. A gruesome tale about a sadistic killer had been told.

Among those present were several members of the O'Dell family, understandably shaken by the double loss. Besides Jake and Web, there were four other sons and two daughters in the family. Earlier that year Mr. O'Dell, head of the clan, had died in Stephenville, Texas. His widow and children still mourned his loss.

Jake had been the family prodigy. He had played violin in the Cisco High School Orchestra, and he hoped to attend college, the first member of his family ever to do so. The family was poor and hardly in a position to send a boy to college, but they vowed to pool their resources so that Jake could receive the college education that he desired. The parents and younger children moved from Eastland County where they had farmed for many years to Stephenville, home of John Tarleton College. A younger brother dropped out of high school to earn money for Jake. Web had contributed much of the money he earned working for the oil company. All chipped in the best they could. When Mr. O'Dell died, it had been tough. But the family rallied and kept Jake in school. Now, with the sudden and senseless deaths of both Jake and Web, it was as if the bottom had dropped out for the entire family. Why Jake and Web? The two sisters of the murdered boys flanked their mother at the trial. They wept openly during Mark's testimony.

Concluding statements to the jury were made by Sparks and Stubblefield late Tuesday morning. For Stubblefield it had been a steep uphill battle. It was quite obvious that Clyde was the murderer. His only hope for Clyde was that the jury might somehow believe that he was only sixteen at the time of the murders. And perhaps for this reason they might spare him from the ultimate penalty. In his closing statements, Stubblefield continually referred to Clyde as a boy and "an inexperienced country boy" who was so remorseful over the killings that he hadn't even testified on his own behalf.

As expected, Sparks concluded a well-prepared case with strongly worded remarks against the defendant. It was his job to show that Clyde not only was old enough to face the chair, but because of the dastardly nature of the crime, he deserved it.

Judge Been charged the jury, and Clyde was returned to his cell at the jail. The uncertainty of what to expect from the jury scared Clyde, but he tried not to show his fear. Stubblefield told Clyde that the longer the jury deliberated, the better his chances would be.

Clyde was tired from the tension of the trial and his own continual pacing in the hours since. He was beginning to think of trying to sleep when a deputy came to get him from his cell. It was 11:00 P.M. The jury had reached a verdict. He was handcuffed and returned to the school, where the jury, judge, and some of the spectators awaited him. Clyde was asked to remain standing in front of the judge as the verdict was read aloud.

Clyde could suddenly feel his heart thudding in his chest, head, and hands, and he tried in vain to steady his shaking legs. He knew that the jury would not only determine guilt or innocence but also would recommend a penalty if he was found guilty. Usually judges followed the recommendation of the jury. Clyde heard every word the foreman of the jury said, but the two words that seemed to strike out at him were *guilty* and *death*. Clyde trembled and felt as though he might fall down because of his wobbling knees; a deputy steadied him and guided him back toward the door. As he was led past the spectators, Clyde could see his father and stepmother weeping.

Back in his cell, Clyde paced as the two words volleyed back and forth in his mind. Then there was his weeping father. *It's almost as if someone took a picture of Daddy crying and stuck it into my head,* he thought.

Chapter

6

BEFORE RECEIVING an actual death date, Clyde would go through the appeal process. Stubblefield assured Rees Thompson that there were several possible reasons why the conviction might be overturned. He felt, for example, that Sparks had overstepped his bounds when he told the jury that Clyde's failure to testify in his own behalf was a sure sign of guilt.

The trial of Reuben Welsey got underway with jury selection on Wednesday morning. Reuben's lawyer, James Grisham, sought to have bond posted so that his client could be free until the outcome of the trial. Although this request was denied, there were some indications that Sparks might not seek the death penalty for Reuben. After all, Clyde had done the actual killing and had been convicted to lose his life for it. Reuben's crime was simply being present when the deeds were done—at least according to the facts as they had been presented. As was Clyde, Reuben would be tried for the murder of Web O'Dell. That way if a hitch developed for the prosecutor in the first trial or the defendant won his case in appeal, there was always the possibility of trying the defendants for the murder of Jake O'Dell.

Reuben's trial dragged through the week. First there was trouble finding twelve men to serve on the jury who were not disqualified. Then there was laborious testimony. Rees Thompson testified as a character witness for Reuben. Mark repeated the story that he had told in Clyde's murder trial.

On Sunday afternoon the jury reached its verdict. By this time interest had waned so that only about twenty-five spectators, including Mr. Welsey and Ruth, remained. The foreman of the jury handed the verdict to the sheriff. In a moment the jury was sent back because the wording on the verdict was declared improper by the judge. Reuben openly wept during the five-minute delay. When the jury returned the second time, Judge Been took the slip of paper and solemnly read the verdict aloud: "We find the defendant guilty and assess his punishment as death." Reuben held his head in his hands and cried. His muffled sobs were the only sound that could be heard in the auditorium. Reuben leaned heavily on the sheriff and deputy who led him to the sheriff's car. He was returned to the Eastland jail, where Clyde also remained incarcerated.

The attorneys for Clyde and Reuben were given ninety days to file appeals for their clients. In the meantime, both boys stayed in the Eastland jail. The cells at the jail were upstairs from the office area, and there were two separate cell areas. The maximum security area consisted of individual cells for prisoners whom lawmen didn't want mingling with the others. The "tank" was a large holding area for many prisoners. Clyde and Reuben were in the tank and met many "short-timers," men arrested for fighting or being drunk.

The jail also contained living quarters for the jailer and his family. Their apartment could be reached through a steel door that opened from the office area of the jail.

Despite the condemning testimony from Mark, Clyde and Reuben were still friends. Clyde held little animosity toward Mark, who was now staying with an aunt in Houston. Clyde felt sorry that Reuben had also been given the chair. He blamed himself for their mutual plight.

After Clyde and Reuben had been in the tank for two months, a short-timer who was allowed to get the food tray that was brought in, hit the jailer over the head with it, and attempted to get his keys. He failed in his efforts, but since he and Clyde had earlier argued over a piece of cornbread, he said that Clyde had instigated the maneuver. Clyde was put in one of the single cells in the maximum security area. Clyde was lonely and bored in his new cell. The days dragged by slowly. The initial remorse that he felt at the time of the murders subsided, and his thoughts turned more toward survival.

Clyde's only relief from boredom was his father's frequent visits. Rees had gone into debt to pay Clyde's lawyer. "Money doesn't matter all that much when it comes to something like this," Rees had told Stubblefield. "You do the best job you can to save my boy, and I'll take on extra jobs or even get loans from the bank to pay you."

Mark Welsey had said that Clyde made the statement that he wanted to shoot Web O'Dell "just to see him kick." Clyde hadn't said that, but Mark's statement earned Clyde the title of "kick-killer" and "thrill-killer." The nicknames later were used in newspaper headlines. Because of this and a rumor that someone was going to try to "spring" him, the key to Clyde's cell was locked up in the safe of Eastland's new courthouse.

There were some delays in Clyde's appeal because his attorney, the sixty-two-year-old Stubblefield, was severely injured in an automobile collision. But when the case was heard by the court of criminal appeals in mid-1929, a new trial was ordered for Clyde on the same charge—the murder of Web O'Dell. The higher court overthrew the ruling of the district court on the basis that prejudicial statements had been made to the jury by Sparks. In particular, the appeals court took exception, as Stubblefield had predicted, to Sparks's statement that Clyde's not testifying was a certain sign of guilt. A new trial was set for October 28, 1929. In the meantime, Reuben was waiting in jail while his lawyers filed petitions for an appeal trial.

Because Judge Been became ill, Clyde's trial was postponed a week and got underway with the arduous selection of a jury on the morning of November 4—nearly fourteen months after the double murder had been committed. Sparks, acting again as prosecutor, quickly dismissed any juror who had moral objections to capital punishment, while Stubblefield dismissed prospective jurors who had strong preconceived notions about the case. With Clyde's designation as thrill-killer turning up in newspaper headlines, many men were firmly convinced that Clyde deserved to die.

Jury selection took three days; then the testimony began. Though there was still keen public interest, many spectators at the first trial were now content to follow the second trial through daily newspaper accounts or word of mouth. It was noted that Clyde seemed to take a keen interest in the proceedings the first day of jury selection, but by the third day he was looking at a magazine. Clyde had dreaded the prospects of the trial, but at the same time he was anxious to get on with it. He had the naive hope that somehow the trial would settle the matter once and for all, enabling him to return to a normal life. But the trial also reopened a dark door in Clyde's mind. Somewhere beyond that door loomed the ominous device known as the electric chair. And Clyde knew that at the trial he could be condemned to walk through that door to what lay beyond. Clyde's older brother sat beside him. Also present were his stepmother, father, and uncle.

Stubblefield had no doubt that Clyde shot the O'Dells. About the only hope of saving Clyde from the chair lay in his earlier attempt to show that Clyde was sixteen at the time of the crime. And if that didn't work, he had hopes of planting in the minds of jurors that Clyde was not mentally responsible. Much recent publicity had been given an old Texas statute that said an insane man could not be executed. Lawyers for many already condemned to death row were trying to save their clients via use of the law, and the condemned were acting the parts.

Lengthy debate took place when Stubblefield introduced a deposition from Clyde's real mother, who had remarried and moved to South Dakota. It stated that Clyde was born October 5, 1911. Sparks managed to have Dolly's deposition thrown out of court. The prosecutor then introduced a document that was purported to be Clyde's birth certificate, showing Clyde's true birthdate, October 5, 1910. Stubblefield managed to have this thrown out, too. Then Sparks presented Clyde's school records from Graham that showed Clyde was born in 1910. Although Stubblefield proved the alleged birth certificate and school records were taken from the same source, the court admitted the school records. This admission established Clyde's age as seventeen at the time of the murders and meant that he was now a nineteen-year-old standing trial for his life for the second time.

"Clyde has suffered all of his life with various ailments, and I haven't ever considered him too strong either physically or mentally," Rees testified. He told of occasions when Clyde had simply disappeared and later showed up, not telling where he had been.

"I would not say that Clyde is crazy," stated Rees. "But I think he has the mind of a child and one that has not developed with his body."

Rees also testified that he had never heard Clyde mention the names of the O'Dell brothers. He said Clyde told him that the only reason he had confessed to the slayings was to save Mr. Welsey, but he didn't elaborate on how Clyde was supposedly saving Mr. Welsey.

Mr. Welsey took the stand to say that he also thought Clyde was of an unsound mind. He recalled an instance when Clyde stood up at a gospel meeting and sat down without explanation.

A neighbor of the Welseys told the court that Clyde had banged on his door one night and breathlessly muttered something about Mrs. Welsey's needing to be taken to the hospital. Then, without further explanation, Clyde had run off into the night.

The neighbor drove his car to the Welseys' to find Clyde lying on the ground, delirious, and speaking nonsense.

As the man continued to speak, Clyde was reminded of happier times and of how his romance with Ruth Welsey had really started.

There had been several gospel meetings around Cisco during the summer of 1928. These tent meetings drew large audiences, and Clyde had attended some of the meetings with the Welsey family. On one occasion they went to a meeting held in a one-room schoolhouse not far from Leeray. The meeting was being conducted by "holy rollers." Clyde watched in amazement as the preacher jumped, clapped, and cajoled, and repenters went tearfully forward to sit on a bench in the front row. In their fervor, they would sometimes roll off the bench and onto the floor. Rees Thompson also was at the meeting. Much to the embarrassment of Mrs. Welsey, Rees stood up and took issue with the minister right in the middle of the sermon.

That night Mrs. Welsey couldn't seem to catch her breath. Clyde and the Welsey family all feared she would simply run out of breath and die. Mr. Welsey's automobile sat helplessly beside the house. It hadn't cranked in two days. Clyde ran out the door and made a beeline across the pasture for the nearest neighbor with a car. It was a mile-and-a-half run. Once he breathlessly alerted the neighbor, Clyde didn't wait for the man to start his car. He ran all the way back to the Welsey home.

Clyde collapsed and became delirious when he completed the sprint back to the Welseys'. About the same time the neighbor arrived in his car. The Welsey boys put Clyde to bed, and Mrs. Welsey was taken to the doctor.

After ten or fifteen minutes, Ruth entered the room where Clyde lay. She kissed him on the forehead. Clyde pretended to be asleep, but he smiled when she left the room. It was the first time any girl other than a sister had kissed him. Clyde knew it must be love.

Clyde's case went to the jury at 3:00 P.M. November 7. At 10:00 A.M. the next day the jury announced that it had reached a verdict. The jury foreman read, "We the jury find the defendant guilty of murder in the first count of the indictment and assess his punishment at death."

Clyde laughed hysterically when the verdict was read; he had laughed inappropriately throughout the latter parts of his trial. Spectators felt he was feigning insanity in order to miss his date with the chair. Clyde wasn't sure he was crazy, but he figured it wouldn't hurt to act the part. He was aware of the statute prohibiting the execution of an insane man.

Immediately following the trial, Clyde was returned to his cell. Stubblefield said he would seek a new hearing, again because of prejudicial statements made by the prosecution. Clyde had been called "the darkest and blackest murderer of all ages." If the motion for a new hearing in the local court was turned down, there was always the possibility of some positive action from the criminal court of appeals. And if that didn't work, they might be granted a sanity hearing. In the meantime, Clyde waited in the Eastland jail, bored, and hoping that Stubblefield's legal maneuverings would somehow return his life to normal.

49

Chapter
7

DURING CLYDE'S SECOND TRIAL, a new prisoner was placed in a cell directly opposite Clyde's in the maximum security section of the Eastland jail. The lives of Clyde and this fellow prisoner had brushed nearly two years earlier under much different circumstances. At the time neither was a prisoner. *Could this be the same man?* wondered Clyde, as he had expected to see an outlaw-hero like his grandfather's friend Jesse James.

It had been two days before Christmas of 1927. Clyde and his father and brothers were driving into Cisco from Leeray for Christmas shopping.

Clyde had more money in his pocket than he had ever had before. He was looking forward to buying some nice presents. He had earned the money mostly through trapping and hunting. Clyde figured his dog, Jack—one-half hound, a quarter Airedale, and a quarter bulldog—was the best hunting dog in those parts. And he wasn't alone in this opinion, especially after Jack helped Clyde get thirty dollars' worth of hides his first time out.

Clyde was still pondering what to buy his father when Rees

drove onto the brick-paved Main Street. A shotgun boomed, and its noise echoed off the buildings in the downtown area. The echoing of the shotgun blast was followed by the repeated crackings of pistol and rifle fire.

The boys craned their necks to see that a dark blue Buick pulling away from the First National Bank was the target of the gunfire. Armed townspeople pursued the fleeing car on foot, shooting as they ran, while other armed men ran for their cars.

"It looks like a bank holdup," said Rees almost calmly as the Buick went out of sight in the opposite direction.

"Let's chase 'em, Daddy. Maybe we can catch 'em!" shouted Clyde with enthusiasm. Pursuing these bank robbers would be good practice for the day when he hoped to chase criminals as part of the United States Border Patrol.

"Yeah, let's go git 'em, Daddy!" urged Bill. "Maybe we can git the five-thousand-dollar reward money." Just a few months earlier there had been a reward posted by the Texas State Bankers Association for anyone who killed a bank robber in the act. Banks in the small, isolated towns of rural Texas were being hit at an alarming rate, and the bankers hoped that the reward would serve as a deterrent.

With the mention of the reward, Clyde, Bentley, and Hervie all pleaded with Rees to join in the chase. "It looks to me like they've got enough people chasin' 'em," replied Rees. "How about if we just get out and see what's happened here?"

This suggestion seemed the second-best alternative, and the boys reluctantly agreed as Rees pulled into a parking spot near the bank.

There were confusion and crying as the Thompsons approached the one-story brick First National Bank building. Several people were gathered around a big man who lay bleeding on the ground beside the bank. It was Police Chief G. E. Bedford, known to everyone as "Bit." A woman screamed that her daughter and another girl had been taken as hostages. The girls had been used as shields so that the robbers could escape

51

from the bank to their getaway car that was parked in the alley beside the bank. The kidnapped hostages were ten-year-old Emma May Robinson and twelve-year-old Laverne Comer.

Local law enforcement officers and townspeople had been tipped off that there was a bank robbery in progress by a hysterical woman who fled from the bank to the nearby police station. Police and armed citizens had then surrounded the bank and opened fire. The robbers returned the shots and took the hostages. It was believed that at least one of the robbers had been hit.

As Rees talked to a man he knew, Clyde and Bill walked into the alley. There, lying in a pool of blood, was Police Officer George Carmichael; he had been shot in the head. Several people were trying to help him. Others had been shot: a bank employee in the jaw, a college student in the body, and a heavyset man in the foot, to name a few.

After the wounded were taken away, the remaining people were eager to tell their versions of what had occurred. "I was standing right over there when Bit went down," a man related. "He dropped his shotgun when he was hit, then pulled out his revolver, and fell to the ground. Then someone else picked up his gun."

Someone pointed to a hole in the side of the bank building that hadn't been there before. The owner of a nearby restaurant had walked up to the driver of the getaway car and held a shotgun to his head. The shotgun either didn't work or jammed. Finally, in his attempt to get the gun to work, the man had shot the side of the bank as the robbers pulled away. There were several places where bullets had hit near the side door of the bank from which the robbers had come with their hostages.

It was believed that four robbers had jumped into the getaway car. One of them wore a Santa Claus suit.

The robbery had started shortly after Santa Claus walked down Main Street and entered the bank. Since it was two days before Christmas, both children and adults had greeted Santa enthusiastically. But inside the bank, he suddenly pulled out a gun and announced a holdup. At least three men inside the bank turned out to be his accomplices, and they, too, brandished pistols.

Within a short time, some members of the posse returned with the stolen money—about twelve thousand dollars—and one of the holdup men. The robber had been shot in the throat, and he was not expected to live. His name was Louis Davis. He lived in Wichita Falls and had no prior criminal record. It was later learned that Davis was a relative of one of the other robbers and he had been substituted at the last minute for another would-be robber who had come down with the flu.

The men who returned with Davis and the recovered money said that one of the tires on the getaway car had been shot as the car left the bank. On their way out of town, the robbers stopped a car coming toward them. The occupants of the car were a fourteen-year-old boy, his parents, and his grandmother. They fled after being stopped at gunpoint. The robbers carried the money and the wounded Davis as they herded their two young female hostages to the new getaway car, an Oldsmobile. But then they discovered that the fourteen-year-old boy had turned off the car engine and fled into the woods with the key.

By this time armed townspeople in their cars caught up with the robbers and shot at them. The robbers quickly returned to the Buick, leaving Davis in the Olds. Also inadvertently left behind was the satchel of money. The armed thieves had continued to use their hostages as shields, but in spite of this, one of the men had been hit in the arm by a bullet as he was reentering the Buick. With a flat tire, the three headed down a country lane just ahead of their pursuers.

The police chief had sustained five gunshot wounds and died later that day. Dead, too, was the police officer who had been shot in the head. Others who had been hit by bullets at the scene were not seriously injured. In fact, the bank employee who was shot in the jaw was back that afternoon to help count the recovered loot. The girls who were taken hostage were found unharmed in the battered and bullet-ridden car that had been abandoned in the woods when it had finally bogged down. A bloodstained Santa Claus suit was found nearby.

The first-time felon Davis died on Christmas without disclosing the identities of his accomplices. In the meantime, the three remaining bank robbers were chased through the thickets on foot. They returned to Cisco, stole another car, and wrecked it. Then they went up to a farmhouse, stole yet another car, and took the farmer's son as hostage. As they attempted to make their escape, the farmer fired at them with a shotgun, hitting his teen-aged son in the arm. The boy was later released, and the bandits stole another car.

Lawmen pursued the trio, causing them to abandon their most recently stolen car. As they were ducking into the brush, a bullet downed one of the men while the other two managed to outrun pursuers. The fallen bandit was Marshal Ratliff, a native of Cisco who had recently been granted a parole from Huntsville prison for a bank holdup he had pulled in Valera, Texas, with his brother Lee. The Ratliff boys had continually been in trouble as they grew up in Cisco, while their three sisters were model citizens. Their mother, the twice-widowed Rilla Carter, was a religious woman who was highly regarded in Cisco. Ironically, Mrs. Carter had recently sold the Manhattan Cafe that she operated in town to the mother of Laverne Comer, the twelve-year-old girl taken hostage.

The captured Ratliff had seven bullets in his body. He wasn't expected to live. The other two robbers continued to elude lawmen. Roadblocks were set up, and airplanes were used to spot the men. It was the biggest manhunt in Texas history. The two, Henry Helms and Robert Hill, were finally captured in Graham more than a week after the robbery. Helms carried five bullets in his body and was on the verge of death. His chances for living were practically nil. Hill was expected to lose his arm from a rifle bullet wound.

After being an eyewitness to the getaway, Clyde listened for all the news of the robbery in the ensuing days. Little did he dream that he would later be in close personal contact with some of the same criminals—as a criminal himself, not as the border patrolman of his dreams.

Although Ratliff had been expected to die, he recovered fully, as had his accomplices Hill and Helms.

Ratliff was tried for the murder of both law officers during the shooting at the bank. In the first trial, he was convicted and given a ninety-nine-year prison term. The Eastland County prosecutor then pursued the second murder charge. Found guilty for the second murder, Ratliff was sentenced to die in the electric chair. The twice-convicted murderer was sent to death row at the state prison in Huntsville to await execution. It was said that in his cell Ratliff had a hand-cranked phonograph given to him by his mother; supposedly he played a death march as fellow inmates were led toward the chair.

Henry Helms also had been sentenced to die in the chair for his participation in the same crime. It was then that the lawyer for convicted murderer Harry Leahy resurrected the little known statute forbidding the state from executing a person who was insane. Leahy's lawyer said that his client had become insane as a result of his incarceration. In spite of the way he acted, Leahy was found by a court to be of sound mind. He kept his date with the chair on September 2, 1929. But Helms and others on death row had new hope with the legal maneuverings of Leahy's lawyer. Shortly after Leahy began acting crazy, Helms and others on death row followed suit.

Throughout the day and night Helms would chant, "It ain't gonna rain no more . . . hey, captain." This had won him a sanity hearing. Helms was taken from death row for the hearing but he, too, was found to be sane by a jury. He was then returned to Huntsville. Despite a special plea to the governor from Helms's wife and six children, guards carried a violently struggling Helms to the electric chair just four days after Leahy had made the same trip. Ratliff was on death row at the time but didn't play the death march for his partner in crime.

Shortly after that, Ratliff started acting oddly. Over and over he would say, "The Lord have mercy on my soul." He seemed to develop a type of paralysis, so that he lost control of his hands and feet and his motions were disjointed. He no longer would or could feed himself. Guards tried to put food in his mouth, but he often would spit it out and let the food run down his chin, chest, and stomach. He became emaciated. Rilla Carter filed a petition for a sanity hearing for her son in Walker County, the county in which the state prison was located.

This action upset the people of Eastland County. Two of their good law enforcement officers had died at the hands of Ratliff and his cronies. And two banks had been robbed. Ratliff's insanity and the petition for a sanity hearing in Walker County were viewed as a means of circumventing the justice Ratliff deserved.

In an apparent attempt to prevent the hearing, Judge George L. Davenport of the Eastland district court issued a bench warrant for Ratliff on the charge of armed robbery. This charge stemmed from the attempt of the robbers to steal the Oldsmobile as they made their quick exit from Cisco the day of the robbery. Before his sanity could be determined in Walker County, Ratliff was whisked back to Eastland to wait during the legal battle that had erupted between Eastland and Walker counties.

Clyde looked at the cell across from his to see a twenty-seven-year-old Ratliff who appeared to be near forty. He was obviously insane. His face was gaunt, and his eyes at the back of hollowed-out sockets appeared to focus on nothing. The man murmured nonsense and apparently couldn't hold himself up.

Ratliff was fed by a special jailer who was hired specifically to care for him.

Clyde had heard the jailer speculate that Ratliff was faking it. But Clyde was thoroughly convinced of Ratliff's insanity when he watched the man defecate on the cot in his cell, then turn around and eat his own feces.

Chapter
8

TOM JONES, known as "Uncle Tom," was appointed to assist jailer Pack Kilborn with the care of Ratliff and with other duties. The father of eight, the fifty-five-year-old Jones had served for years as an Eastland deputy.

After Ratliff had been at the Eastland jail about three weeks, both Jones and Kilborn were convinced of his insanity. Ratliff couldn't perform the most simple tasks for himself.

Clyde watched when Mrs. Carter came to see Ratliff, who gave no recognition of her presence. Clyde turned away when the woman broke down in tears as she tried to talk to her son. Clyde knew the pain she had been through as a result of her son's crimes, just as the Thompsons and the Welseys had suffered from their sons' crimes.

On the night of November 18, 1929, Clyde watched as Jones and Kilborn tucked Ratliff into bed. Intending to return momentarily, they left Ratliff's cell door open. The two then went to the tank holding Reuben Welsey, E. V. Allen, and some short-timers. As soon as the two were out of sight, Clyde was amazed to watch Ratliff suddenly spring from his cot, take the house shoes that his mother had brought for him, and walk quietly out of his cell. Ratliff slipped on the house shoes and looked around to see if Clyde was going to yell. As far as Clyde was concerned, it was none of his business. He had been in jail long enough to know that you don't rat on another prisoner. There were no words exchanged, but Clyde's expression was apparently enough to let Ratliff know that Clyde wasn't going to say anything. Ratliff crept down the stairs.

Since the jailers did not wear guns while making their rounds, Ratliff knew he could find a weapon in the now-unoccupied office of the jail. He found Jones's .38 in the desk drawer. He opened the gun to see if it was loaded. It was. But one of the bullets rolled out onto the floor. Ratliff didn't bother to pick it up but quickly headed for the front door. It was locked. There was a second door that led to the living quarters for Kilborn. He tried it, but it, too, was locked.

For Ratliff to gain his freedom, he had to get the keys to the outside. He knew that they were in Kilborn's pocket. Ratliff went back up the stairs and waited. Jones entered the maximum security area from the other side with the idea of locking Ratliff's cell for the night. At the same time, Kilborn came around the corner where Ratliff waited. "Throw me those keys!" demanded Ratliff. Kilborn ducked back around the wall.

Clyde watched as Jones entered. The special jailer saw the empty cell at the same time he heard Ratliff's demand to Kilborn. Sensing that it was his fault that the door had been left open in the first place, Jones rushed in the direction from which the voice had just come. He rounded the corner, running toward Ratliff. Ratliff squeezed off three quick shots, hitting Jones in the stomach, left shoulder, and right leg. Jones tumbled down the stairs.

Kilborn then rushed Ratliff. Ratliff fired and missed as Kilborn grabbed him. The two struggled and tumbled down the steel stairs together; Ratliff fired the .38 harmlessly into the ceiling as they fell. Locked in combat, the two landed at the base of the stairs on top of the wounded Jones and broke his leg. Kilborn had little trouble in overpowering the weakened Ratliff. He wrestled the gun from Ratliff's hand, held it to Ratliff's head, and squeezed the trigger. The hammer snapped on an empty chamber. The sixth bullet lay on the floor a few feet away.

Kilborn's married daughter was visiting her mother in the living quarters of the jail. When they heard shots, they called the sheriff. The daughter then grabbed her father's gun and attempted to enter the jail. Finding the door locked, she ran outside and looked in through the window to see her father struggling with Ratliff. She fired the gun into the air and called for help, bringing a crowd to the outside of the jail.

After finding that Jones's .38 caliber revolver had no more bullets, Kilborn beat Ratliff across the head with it. Ratliff begged for his life as he tried to fend off the blows with his hands. Kilborn finally got off the subdued Ratliff and unlocked the door to let in the law enforcement officers who had arrived.

Jones was taken to the hospital, and the doctor felt his prognosis for recovery was good. A doctor bandaged Ratliff's head before the escapee was stripped and returned to his cell, which had been stripped, too.

Clyde felt some responsibility that Jones had been shot. Clyde had assumed that Ratliff was going to run out the front door, never to be seen again. The shooting had surprised Clyde. But the fact that Clyde didn't yell out a warning put him on the same side as Ratliff. *After all*, thought Clyde, *both Ratliff and I are looking at the bars from the inside out*. At the same time Clyde hoped that Uncle Tom would recover. The man had been kind to him.

From his cell, Clyde could look out onto the street below. He could see that a crowd was milling around in front of the jail. He was startled when a voice came from the cell across from his. "Anything happenin' down there?"

Clyde did a double take to make sure who was speaking. It

was Ratliff. "Yeah," Clyde finally got around to saying. "Quite a few people gatherin' outside the jail . . . I thought you were crazy."

Ratliff didn't answer right away. He seemed to be in pain. "When you're facin' the chair, you'll do anything," said Ratliff, grimacing as he shifted positions in his cell. "I shot the jailer tonight an' would of shot ten more just like him to get outta here. I was gonna wait to see if I could make a break for it during my sanity hearing but saw my chance tonight and decided to take it."

"But you ate your own . . . ," Clyde trailed off.

"I didn't know whose side you were on," answered Ratliff. "I didn't even let on to my own mother that I wasn't crazy. I'm tellin' ya, when it comes down to you or them, you'd better make it them."

Clyde reported several times on the status of the crowd until people started going home around 1:00 A.M.

The next day the sheriff took bank robber E. V. Allen to death row, and a deputy took another prisoner to the state asylum. Kilborn was left alone with the prisoners. Jones had taken a turn for the worse during the night, and the doctor was concerned that he might not live.

The Ku Klux Klan was strongly organized in Eastland and the surrounding area. Many of the county's most prominent citizens were members. The Klan had previously taken law and order into its own hands, but not necessarily against the Negro population. On one occasion it had become known that a white man was beating his wife frequently. Hooded men showed up at his door one night, dragged him out of his house, and beat him up. On another occasion an Eastland police officer was believed to be crooked. He received a letter from the Klan telling him to leave Eastland immediately. He did.

On the afternoon of November 19, 1929, some Klansmen were busy on the telephones in Eastland and Cisco. They felt that the law had been too liberal with Ratliff and that he should already have been executed. Instead, he was back in Eastland, and the much-thought-of Jones might die. Enough was enough, according to the Klan. The word was that Ratliff would receive some Old-West-style justice that very night.

A small crowd of people milled around in front of the jail all day long. The group was mostly men, but there were also many women and children. By the time the sun went down, more than a thousand people had gathered.

A group of men, who stood impatiently at the door of the jail, were met by Kilborn at 9:00 P.M. "Let us have 'im, Pack!" one of the men demanded.

Kilborn knew some of the people and could have called them by name. But there were many strangers, too. He told the gathering that Ratliff's death sentence would be upheld, and he asked them to go home. Some men argued that they didn't want another innocent man being shot while the legal process dragged on. More and more people crowded around the door of the jail.

Someone shouted, "We want action!" With that, a curious, almost eerie laughter broke out among the throng.

Another voice yelled, "Get him over there!" Then some one hundred men rushed Kilborn, carried him to the lawn in front of the jail, and held him there. Someone reached into his pocket and extracted the keys. Kilborn's son went to his father's aid but was quickly subdued.

Men rushed through the door of the jail and headed upstairs to Ratliff's cell. Kilborn broke loose from the men holding him and made his way into the jail. He climbed past men on the stairway and got in front of the first one, who by now stood in front of Ratliff's cell. Holding out both arms, Kilborn managed to herd the group back down the stairs and out the front door. He did not, however, retrieve his keys. No sooner was the last intruder pushed out the door than an even-more-determined crowd rushed the jail. This time they would not be held back. Kilborn was taken to the floor by half a dozen men who sat on him. Others rushed up the stairs, and one of them produced the keys from his pocket. Still naked, Ratliff cowered in the back of his cell and appeared to be trying to cling to the wall. They found the key to Ratliff's cell, and unlocked the door.

Ratliff struggled as several men rushed him. He was hoisted into the air and carried out of his cell, facing upward; he wore only the bandage on his head.

Pointing to Clyde, one of the men said, "Let's get this cold-blooded killer, too!" Others agreed. A half-dozen men in the mob stayed behind, trying the keys one by one on Clyde's cell door. Clyde paced back and forth, hands sweating, heart pounding.

By this time, Ratliff was carried out the front door of the jail. When the crowd saw the naked man being held aloft, the eerie laughter of men, women, and children could be heard upstairs at the jail. Clyde shuddered at the sound. It was an unearthly, hellish sound, like a noise that belonged in another world. Horns honked in the confusing din below.

"Come on, come on, which one is it?" said the man, impatiently trying the different keys to Clyde's door.

Clyde kept pacing, fearing to make eye contact with the men. He knew that the key to his cell was locked up in the new courthouse safe a few blocks away. Every time his father visited, the jailer had to make a special trip to get it. But Clyde feared that one of the other keys might accidentally fit.

None of the keys worked. The man started going through them a second time but was interrupted by one of his companions. "Let's go," he urged. "We're gonna miss it."

"Yeah, I guess," replied the man with the keys. Then he added, directing his gaze toward Clyde, "Don't worry, Thompson, you ain't gonna git outta this. We'll be back tomorrow night with a blowtorch!"

"I'll be waitin'," said Clyde, trying to keep his voice from quivering.

The man with the keys said nothing more but stared at

Clyde for a moment and then joined the others walking down the stairs. Clyde let out a sigh. He was safe—at least for the moment. He walked over to the window to see what was happening below.

Ratliff was being carried down the street on the shoulders of several men, while a horde of men, women, and children pushed close. Someone yelled, "Let's drag him behind a car!" There were a few yells of agreement. But the men holding Ratliff continued down the street.

In the alley about a block from the jail, someone produced a rope that had a hangman's noose already tied in it. The rope was thrown over a cable stretched between two utility poles. The noose dangled about six feet off the ground. As the group approached, someone grabbed the noose and slipped it over Ratliff's head. It was tightened, and several men holding the end of the rope suddenly hoisted Ratliff into the air. There was a cheer that stopped abruptly when the rope broke. Ratliff fell to the ground.

The code of the Old West called for Ratliff to be released, but that code was ignored. Several men ran to get a new rope. Someone tied a burlap bag around Ratliff's loins, apparently for the sake of modesty. Then the men returned, carrying a new rope with a hangman's noose tied in it. It was thrown over the powerline and cinched tightly around Ratliff's neck.

A group of people now held the opposite end of the rope, while others hoisted Ratliff onto their shoulders.

"You got any last words?" someone yelled to Ratliff.

"Let me down, I'll talk," he replied. He was then lowered to the ground. Much of what he said was unintelligible, but he did ask for forgiveness and mercy. "Forgive me, God," Ratliff muttered. Then, "Forgive me, boys."

With that, the group holding the end of the rope all heaved, as if at a tug-of-war. Ratliff went into the air. When a person is hanged, he usually falls through a gallows, and his neck breaks. He dies instantly. Being hoisted into the air, however, did not break Ratliff's neck. Instead, he strangled to death, after kicking and struggling for several minutes. Car headlights illuminated the event. If any people in the crowd were sickened by the sight, their sensitivities were lost in the mob. When Ratliff stopped moving, some people grabbed his feet, which dangled limply at the level of their heads. They turned the body around so that it could be viewed from different directions. Some jeered the corpse.

These activities went on for about twenty minutes until County Judge C. L. Garrett appeared on the scene. He asked that someone take down the body, since he felt it was the county's duty to assume responsibility for the corpse.

"Let it hang there," came a voice from the crowd.

"No," replied Garrett quickly, showing that he meant business. The justice of the peace was then ordered to remove the body. The remains were taken to a funeral home, where Garrett ordered the body embalmed.

Chapter

9

THE SHERIFF RETURNED to Eastland at midnight. Knowing that the crowd might keep their promise and return the next night to lynch Clyde, the sheriff took him 120 miles to the Dallas County Jail for safekeeping. Clyde had gained enough notoriety so that it was no longer possible for him to be kept anonymously in the jail at Palo Pinto or another neighboring commmunity.

Jones, who lay dying of the bullet wounds inflicted by Ratliff, was told of the lynching. He died the next morning.

There was talk of a special investigation into the lynching of Ratliff, but nothing ever came of it due to a lack of evidence. It was said for a long time afterward that there was one night in Eastland when everyone could recall where they were. That was the night Ratliff was lynched. And everyone could recall they were somewhere else.

The lynching of Ratliff and his own near-miss had a startling effect on Clyde. Except for some jeers at his first trial, there had been little evidence that people on the outside hated him. His jailers had been polite, and his father had always given him the impression that at least some people were on his side. Ratliff's lynching changed this view. Clyde now grouped people in the outside world together with Prosecutor Sparks, the man who seemed so intent on sending him to the electric chair. Clyde felt alienated from the outside and more at home on the inside, even though he hated being locked up. "It's like they're all out to get me," he reasoned. "Even if I got out and went home, someone would probably try to kill me." Clyde knew that his life would never be what it was before the O'Dell killings.

The Dallas County Jail contained the grim reminder of the means of executing men in Texas only a few years before. A gallows had been erected inside the jail and still stood there. The electric chair was first used in Texas on February 8, 1924. Before dawn that day, five men, all blacks convicted of murder, were electrocuted in the new chair at Huntsville. Prior to that time, persons convicted of crimes carrying the death penalty were hung by their own counties. Clyde wondered what the difference was between being hanged and being electrocuted. He wished his choice was neither. At the Dallas jail Clyde became friends with other men facing the chair, including "Dagger" Bill Pruitt, convicted of the brutal slaying of a teen-aged boy, convicted murderer Dewey Hunt, and a pair of rapists not much older than Clyde.

About the time that Clyde was sent to Dallas, Reuben Welsey was transferred to the jail at Breckenridge until the outcome of his appeal trial. On April 1, 1930, the court of criminal appeals in Austin ordered a new district court trial for Reuben. In its ruling the appeals court wrote, "The issue of appellant's subnormal mentality was overwhelmingly raised, if not established. . . . Under such a statement of facts death is an extremely harsh penalty against a boy of only 17 [actually 18 at the time of the murders] charged with his first offense." Reuben was returned to Eastland, where his attorneys were attempting to have him freed on bond. The local court refused bond. The case was taken to a higher court and overturned. In May, 1930, Reuben was released on ten thousand dollars bond. He was free for the first time since he and Clyde were arrested some twenty months earlier.

In the meantime, Ruth Welsey had run away from home. She felt Clyde had been framed and was taking more of the blame for the murders than he deserved. This news of Ruth gave Clyde a glimmer of optimism. At least there was one person outside his family who supported him. However, the small measure of optimism was outweighed by the influence exerted on Clyde by his fellow prisoners.

There was more of a prison atmosphere in the big Dallas County Jail. For the first time Clyde was exposed to men who had made a career of crime. He found that prisoners who had committed the most dastardly crimes were held in the highest esteem by their fellow inmates. As a double-murderer already convicted to die in the chair, Clyde was treated as a genuine tough guy by his fellow inmates. Clyde enjoyed it when other prisoners spoke to him as if he was somebody important. It was respect he'd never been given in the outside world.

When there was talk of staging a riot in May, 1930, Clyde was one of the first to support the idea. It was his first open defiance of authority. At an appointed time, inmates threw food on the walls, scattered mattresses and papers on the floor, and screamed protests at the top of their lungs. As an instigator, Clyde was sent to solitary confinement and lived in a dark cell that had previously been reserved for those waiting to die on the gallows. In solitary, Clyde's clothes were taken away; he was not allowed to bathe or shave, and he was given just one meal a day, which he refused. He wanted to show everyone that he was as tough as a double-murderer is supposed to be. To be anything but tough would be to fall short of his image with other prisoners. But after five days, Clyde was weak and listless. He wondered if he was going to starve.

On the fifth night, he lay in his dark cell, half-awake. It was two in the morning. A protesting prisoner could be heard cursing guards in another part of the jail.

"Thompson, you awake?" came a quiet voice from outside his cell.

"Uhhh, yeah," answered Clyde.

"Come here,"

Clyde got up, walked to the door, and peeked out through the hole through which food was poked in to him. The small hole was the only opening in the solid steel door. A guard stood on the outside.

"Here," he said, placing a steak sandwich and some candy into the hole for Clyde. "These are from Hunt."

Clyde smiled and eagerly took the food. Hunt had bribed one of the midnight guards. Clyde wolfed down the sandwich, then took his time eating the candy. He couldn't remember when anything tasted that good. Clyde knew then that being tough had paid off for him. The clandestine late-night meals came regularly. Jail officials wondered how Thompson went day-in and day-out without eating.

Even though Reuben Welsey was free on bond, the state was asking for the death penalty in his new trial for the murder of Web O'Dell. This trial was set for June 23, 1930.

Mr. Welsey was the first to take the stand on behalf of his son. The elder Welsey testified that he didn't think Reuben knew right from wrong. His son had been subject to seizures as a child, and Mr. Welsey had always considered him to be mentally subnormal.

Mark Welsey returned from his aunt's in Houston to testify on behalf of his brother. Mark's testimony was about the same as it had been in the first trials of Reuben and Clyde—the crime was premeditated by Clyde, who had shot the O'Dells "just to see them kick." Mark repeated his charge that Clyde had threatened the lives of him and his brother if they told anyone about the murders. In cross-examination, the prosecutor pointed out some discrepancies between the story

Mark now told and the one he had related shortly after the arrest.

After starting on a Monday, the case went to the jury on Wednesday. Early Thursday the jury announced its verdict—Reuben was guilty of murder. But instead of the earlier death sentence, Reuben was given a five-year suspended sentence. He walked away from the courthouse a free man—at least temporarily. He was arrested again a week later. This time he was charged with one count of robbery with firearms, one count of assault with intent to rob, and two counts of burglary. These charges all stemmed from the O'Dell murders, and by pressing them it appeared that the prosecutor was not willing to let Reuben off with a suspended sentence.

In Dallas, several newspapermen requested permission to photograph Clyde. The head jailer agreed, and Clyde assented to the request with the stipulation that he be given copies of the photos. The journalists promised to supply prints to Clyde, but he didn't trust their word. He hated journalists, feeling they had turned public sentiment against him by labeling him thrill-killer and kick-killer. Clyde was taken naked from his cell, without having had a bath, shave, or haircut in several weeks. It didn't matter to the photographers that Clyde was naked, because they planned to take photos of his face only. Just as they were about to snap their pictures, however, Clyde turned around quickly to expose his bare buttocks to the cameras.

The journalists were angry. And so was the head jailer. Clyde struggled to run but was quickly subdued by two large black trustees. They held Clyde while his picture was taken. The picture that appeared in newspapers the next day made Clyde appear to be the madman that many already thought he was. Under the photos were stories saying that Clyde's case was soon to be heard for the second time before the court of criminal appeals. After delays, on October 15, 1930, the higher court officially affirmed the lower court's ruling of death in the electric chair for Clyde Thompson.

Clyde's attorneys petitioned the appeals court in Austin for another rehearing. This petition was denied on December 3. Any chance of a change of verdict based on an appeal was almost exhausted.

A week later the attorneys filed an affidavit with the court on behalf of Rees Thompson, stating that Clyde had become insane in the two years since he was first sentenced to die. A sanity hearing was set for December 29, 1930, before Judge Been in the Eastland district court. After Christmas, Clyde was returned to Eastland from the Dallas jail, where he had spent more than a year.

The first day, a Monday, was taken up by jury selection. One hundred men were called to jury duty for the sanity hearing, but only forty-five showed up in court. Eastland County residents were seemingly more intent on celebrating the holidays.

Clyde entered the courtroom smiling. Interest in the case had waned in the more than two years since the murders, and there were just a few spectators besides Rees and the rest of the Thompson family. Clyde was escorted to a seat and soon started jabbering, sometimes laughing loudly. Having seen the insanity acts of both Ratliff and Helms, an Eastland County jury would not be taken in easily by another murderer playing the part of crazyman.

It took until 3:00 P.M. Tuesday before the twelve-man jury was selected.

The defense witnesses were the first to testify. They were neighbors of the Thompsons, and all said Clyde was probably not right mentally to begin with and had gone completely insane since being convicted of murder.

On Wednesday, New Year's Eve, there was a surprise witness for the defense. Ruth Welsey said she wanted to testify on Clyde's behalf. Ruth's sudden appearance in court after having been missing for several months was a complete surprise to everyone, including the Welseys. Ruth testified that she and Clyde had been together the night the O'Dells were murdered. They met early that evening and walked to the top of a mountain nearby, Ruth said. They didn't return home until 11:00 P.M.

It had been a long time since Clyde had seen Ruth, but he had thought of her a lot. The fact that she was going against her own family to testify on his behalf brought tears to his eyes. He wished that he could somehow get loose and they could run away from the whole mess together. Maybe they could get married and settle in some distant place like Utah.

As soon as she stepped down from the witness stand, Ruth was placed under arrest and taken by Eastland police to the jail. After she had run away, her father had sworn out a warrant for her arrest on a charge of juvenile delinquency.

After Ruth's testimony, the state introduced several witnesses in an effort to prove Clyde's sanity. Eastland County Sheriff Virgil Foster took the stand to say that based on his observations, Clyde wasn't insane or even of a low mentality.

Clyde had a pleasant surprise when he was returned to the second floor of the jail. Ruth was in the cell across from his. Thus, in a way, they could spend New Year's Eve together. "I'll do everything I can for you, Clyde," she promised. "Even if it takes goin' to the governor."

"I sure appreciate ya stickin' by me like this, Ruth," he said. "I still love ya, and I wanted ya to know that I've thought about ya every day that I've been locked up."

Ruth told Clyde that her father had done everything possible to keep her quiet. He had hidden her clothing and shoes so that she couldn't leave the house. Finally, though, she had sneaked away and had stayed with friends until Clyde's trial came up.

Following a one-day break for New Year's, the trial continued with summations by both sides on January 2, 1931. The jury took little time to reach its finding: Clyde was sane and therefore mentally fit to be executed in the electric chair.

While Clyde was awaiting further legal steps, Ruth was taken from the jail. They vowed love to each other, and Clyde watched sorrowfully as she was led away. He didn't know he would never see her again.

Clyde's attorneys filed a motion for another rehearing in the appeals court. This motion was denied on January 22, 1931. Next, his lawyers petitioned Judge Been for another sanity hearing in Eastland. The judge denied the petition on February 24 and at the same time set May 8 as the date when Clyde's sentence would be carried out. Thus, Clyde had a little more than two months before his turn to ride Ol' Sparky, the Texas electric chair. Clyde had reached the end of his rope, legally. Only the governor could save Clyde by an act of executive clemency.

Robert Hill, the only surviving member of the Santa Claus bank robbery gang, had been given a ninety-nine-year sentence. He had twice escaped from the Wynne Prison Farm but had been recaptured each time. After his second escape, he had ended up with Clyde in the maximum security section of the Eastland jail. In early March, 1931, Sheriff Foster joined the two men with leg irons and marched them to his car. They were driven to the main prison facility at Huntsville, located 172 miles southeast of Dallas.

From fellow inmates in jail, Clyde had heard of "The Walls." When they arrived in Huntsville that night, Clyde could understand how the prison got its name. It was surrounded by a high red brick wall with guard towers, which had been constructed in the 1880s. As Clyde was led in, he looked up at the moon. He figured it would be the last time he would ever see it.

Chapter
10

THE ONE-STORY CONCRETE BUILDING known as death row looked small, almost squatty, in comparison to the nearby three-story cellblocks. But it was a building with a well-earned reputation that inmates looked upon with a special deference. As had been true in the Dallas jail, the toughest cons had the most respect, but death row was tougher than any con. The toughest men walked in, but they were carried out.

The guard escorting Clyde knocked on an outside door. There was a rattle of keys on the other side, and the door opened. Clyde's eyes darted around nervously as both guards escorted him inside. There were eight cells, all facing the same way. They were separated by steel walls painted green. In front of the cells was a narrow walkway, where a table stood. On the table was a radio that emitted the strains of a country western song and occasional static. It was the only radio in the entire prison, a luxury afforded men who were about to die. There were two doors in death row. Clyde had just entered through one of them. Immediately to his right was another door, painted green. Adjacent to the cell closest to the green door was an alcove that contained a bathtub.

The condemned men pressed their faces against the bars,

watching as Clyde was led to the cell closest to the green door. "They're bringin' in a baby today," Clyde heard one voice say.

"It looks like the chair's robbin' the cradle now," said another.

If executed on schedule, Clyde would have the distinction of being the youngest man ever to ride Ol' Sparky.

Clyde's cell contained a bunk, sink, and toilet. It did not differ much from jail cells where he had sat and stared at the ceilings for some two and a half years. But, in the sense that there was a real feeling of finality here, his death row cell was different. *Maybe it would have been better to have been lynched with Ratliff,* thought Clyde. His thought was interrupted by the guard.

"We don't cause no problems for the inmates here, as long as they keep in line and don't cause no problems. You'll get pretty good meals, and you get to listen to the radio. It's the only one in the whole joint. Okay?"

Clyde nodded his head. The guard locked the door and walked back toward the table. With unconsciously tightened jaws and pursed lips, Clyde fought the tears and turned toward the green steel wall at the back of his cell. *Sixty days to live, and I guess this is what I've got comin' to me,* he thought. He didn't like the idea but tried to resign himself to it. Maybe the chair was better than hanging. Maybe it was quick, and he wouldn't feel anything but one sharp jolt.

"Hey, Thompson. That's your name, isn't it?" The voice seemed to be coming from the next cell. Clyde turned to the wall separating his cell from the next but could see only green steel. Prisoners on death row recognized each other by voice. Only infrequently did they see the faces of their fellow sufferers.

"I said, hey, Thompson," the voice persisted.

"Wh—what?" answered Clyde.

"Your name Thompson?"

"Y—yeah, it's Thompson," Clyde replied nervously, still trying to adjust to his new quarters.

"What'd you do?"

"What?" asked Clyde, irritated by the probing.

The voice insisted. "What'd you do? You know, why are you here?"

"Killed two men," Clyde stated.

"They got me for killin' a man at a gas station," replied the voice. "But I ain't gonna die. My lawyer's gonna get me outta here. I got a new trial comin' up, and if that don't work, my lawyer's gonna talk to the governor. You know, the governor just commuted a man's sentence from here to life in prison a coupla months ago. And I'll bet he'd do that for me."

"We're all better off dyin' and 'scapin' from this worl' of sin," said another, older voice.

"That's nonsense. That old nigger don't know what he's talkin' about," angrily retorted the voice in the next cell.

Clyde was curious about the door to the left. "What's behind that green door? Is that . . . ?"

"Yep, that's Ol' Sparky in there," the voice said, seeming happy to affirm Clyde's suspicion. Then he added, "That green door's probably the last one you'll ever walk through."

Clyde grimaced.

"Now there's no sense in scarin' the boy," said the older voice.

"Naw, I ain't tryin' to scare 'im, just tell 'im what's there. Say, Thompson, how much time you got?"

"What?"

"I said, how much time you got? You know, when you supposed to walk through the green door?"

"Oh, uh, sixty days."

"What's your number?"

"What do you mean?"

"I mean your execution number. Everyone here's got one. I'm execution number eighty-two, which means I'm supposed to be the eighty-second guy to fry in the chair since they started usin' it. Since you came in right after me, you must be execution number eighty-three. Right?"

The guard was sitting on the table beside the radio. He nodded, verifying that Clyde had been assigned execution number eighty-three.

About this time a voice came from a cell at the opposite end of death row. "You've got a big mouth, McKee! Why don't you shut up?"

"Shut up yourself, Shield!" he yelled back, but then spoke in a loud whisper to Clyde.

"Oh, Thompson, my name is Ira McKee. What's your first name?"

"Clyde."

The clock in the tower of the prison administration building sounded ten gongs. There had been some talking at the other end of death row, but everyone had stopped talking when the clock made its first sound. No one said anything while the clock gonged.

"What's that?" whispered Clyde.

"We call it the 'hell clock' around here," McKee answered. "Every time it gongs, each man knows he's got one less hour to live."

After a mostly sleepless first night, Clyde found out more about death row and the men there. Clyde was in the cell closest to the green door, which indicated he would be the last man there to go through it. The man in the first cell at the opposite end, Ofilio Herrera, was next in line to be executed. When Herrera vacated his cell, each man would move down one cell farther away from the green door, and each man would be one step closer to making the final trip down the walkway, through the green door, and into the death chamber. Normally, the cell closest to the green door was left unoccupied. A few hours before his scheduled time for execution, the man was put in the cell to which Clyde was now assigned. In that

77

cell a condemned man spent the last few hours of his life. Clyde had been put there because all the others were occupied. In less than a week, Herrera had his date with the chair, and then Clyde would be moved.

Herrera was in his early thirties. He was nearly six feet tall and weighed close to 250 pounds. Despite his fast-approaching death date, he was nearly always in a good humor. The rest of the men called him "Big Mex." He had been convicted of killing Sheriff A. T. Murray of Mason County.

In the second cell was Joe Shield, who bragged about killing his wife, mother-in-law, and father-in-law from a distance of two hundred yards with a 30-30 rifle. The murders occurred in the town of Brookesmith less than a year earlier. He claimed that his in-laws had encouraged his wife to take their children and leave him. Shield hoped that the governor would commute his sentence for the children's sake.

Two more Mexicans, Nicando Munoz and Victor Rodriguez, shared the third cell. Neither spoke English. They were both convicted of killing a law officer in Weslaco, a south Texas city near the Mexican border. They were scheduled to die the same night as Herrera.

Monuose Twitty, convicted of raping a three-year-old girl in a small town in the Texas panhandle, was in the fourth cell. Twitty was known to be insane, so insane that he hadn't tried to get out of his death sentence through the insanity route. He hadn't uttered a word to anyone since his arrival at death row.

Joshua Riles, a thirty-year-old Negro convicted of raping a white woman in Galveston, was in the fifth cell. He claimed that he hadn't done it. He was scheduled to die on his thirty-first birthday.

Will Jenkins was in cell number six. He, too, was convicted of rape. Jenkins, forty-six, had spent most of his adult life on a prison workfarm in Texas. After finally being released, he had married a woman in Houston. His wife had a twelve-year-old daughter who subsequently accused Jenkins of raping her.

Jenkins said he was innocent, that his wife and daughter had trumped up the charge to get rid of him. He said repeatedly that there is no justice in this world, and he had high hopes of getting a better deal in the next one. Jenkins was the first man to be facing the chair under the state's habitual criminal statute. Under that law, a person convicted of a third felony would automatically be sentenced to life in prison or could face the chair.

Finally, next to Clyde was Ira McKee, a Palo Pinto County farmer convicted of murder. Although McKee and Shield in cell number two had both been convicted of murder, their respective cases were both in appeal and no definite death date had been set for either of them. McKee liked to talk, and Shield thought McKee talked too much. McKee thought Shield was arrogant. And even though there were four cells between them, the two often argued loudly. If it got out of hand, the guard had to quiet them. The personality clash between the two sometimes seemed amusing and sometimes irritating to the other immates, depending on their moods.

The cells measured five feet by ten feet, and there was little to do except pace back and forth or lie on the bunk. Clyde found that three steps would take him from the front to the back of his cell. Then he would pivot and walk back in the opposite direction. Clyde wondered how many miles had been walked in these cells, three steps at a time. How many miles would he walk before it was his turn to "walk the last mile"? The expression "walk the last mile" was used to describe a man walking toward the green door. The saying had been popularized first by a novel and then by a Broadway play. A Hollywood movie, *The Last Mile*, was in the making. It was based on the life of former Texas death row inmate Bill Smith, who had continually moaned "Oh, Jones!" during his stay in the death house.

Herrera had been on death row when Smith was there. He had written an eighty-three-stanza poem about Smith, which he was glad to recite to the other inmates. Herrera had seen Smith and twenty-two others walk through the green door. In October of the previous year, Herrera was present when Joyce Shepard, a man convicted of murdering both the sheriff and a deputy in Fisher County, gouged out both his eyes with a nail loosened from a ventilator two weeks prior to his execution. The reason, according to Shepard, had been the Bible verse, "If thine eye offend thee, pluck it out. . . ." Shepard had also confided in prison officials that he wanted to show them that he had no intentions of escaping.

With four days to go, Herrera came down for a bath. On death row, the inmates bathed weekly and received a shave every few days. Though Clyde could not see the bathtub from his cell, it gave him the opportunity to talk with Herrera.

"Yeah, go ahead and call me Big Mex, that don't bother me one bit," said Herrera to Clyde with a slight accent.

"What did you do before . . . uh . . . before you got in trouble?" asked Clyde.

Herrera laughed. "Oh, a little bit of everything, you know. Anything to make a buck. For a while I worked as a hoer."

"A whore?" asked Clyde innocently.

The way Clyde said it made Big Mex laugh. He leaned back in the bathtub, laughing, creating a wave that could be heard sloshing onto the floor. Clyde started laughing, too. So did McKee. But Clyde wasn't sure what he was laughing about. The only whores he knew about were women who plied a quiet trade in run-down houses near some of the towns his family had lived in. Clyde had never visited one, but he had heard about what went on inside. He had never heard of a man being a whore.

"No," Herrera finally managed. "A hoer, you know with a hoe where you chop down weeds on the farm."

"Oh," replied Clyde. "Sure, I know what you mean."

"You ever do any of that?" asked Herrera.

"Sure," answered Clyde. "When I was little, my daddy was

a preacher and farmer. I've hoed in Texas, Oklahoma, and Arkansas."

"Oh," injected McKee. "So your father's a preacher-man."

Clyde paused. "Well, he was," said Clyde in a lowered voice.

"Good," said Herrera. "I'm Catholic. And when I get outta here, I'm gonna go to mass every Sunday."

Clyde was puzzled. "But I thought you only have a few days 'til . . . ."

In spite of the grim reminder that his turn was next, Herrera still sounded jovial. "Yeah, but that's what they think. You'll see. Something will come up. The governor will save me."

"Sure," interrupted McKee. "That's what they all say."

There was a brief silence from the bathtub, and Herrera at first sounded cross but then returned to his usual, more pleasant mood. "No, McKee, they ain't gonna fry me, you'll see. When I get out, the first thing I'm gonna do is go to mass. Then I'm gonna get a great big bottle of tequila and celebrate with a señorita." With that, Herrera laughed heartily. "You expect to be getting out of here, too, Clyde?"

"No," he answered. "I expect to go to the chair on May 8."

That seemed to irritate the Mexican, reminding him of the inevitability of his own fast-approaching execution. "You must be crazy, boy," he said pointedly to Clyde.

With that Jenkins spoke. "He ain't crazy. He's smart. Soon we'll all be dead and 'scape from this worl' of sin. We'll all be better off for it, too."

As Jenkins talked, the hell clock started chiming. They all listened and didn't hear what Jenkins said. When he quit talking, he too looked up. Herrera was the first to interrupt the silence after the last gong. "You must be crazy," he said, starting to stand up in the bathtub. "And we ain't better off, neither. I'm gonna get outta here. You'll see. Something will come up. Right, Clyde?" With that, Herrera laughed again. Clyde didn't laugh with him. He wondered why just about everyone except Jenkins didn't think it was going to happen to him.

Three days later the radio was quiet. McKee told Clyde that it wasn't played on the day before a man was executed. It was Thursday, and Herrera was due to be executed on Friday. The executions took place immediately after midnight, so it meant that this was the Big Mex's last day on earth. That afternoon, a prison official walked onto death row, stood in front of the first cell, and briefly read from a document. It said that since he, Ofilio Herrera, had been prescribed the death sentence in a court of law, it was the state's duty to execute him the next day.

The bell gonged four times. Big Mex had eight hours to live. The sound of the hell clock seemed even more foreboding on this day as there were very few sounds of talking or anything else on death row. There was a crunching sound, however, coming from the next room. It startled Clyde. McKee explained that the electric chair was being tested.

The guards brought in Herrera's last meal. According to tradition, the condemned man could order whatever he wanted for his last meal. It was said that Henry Helms, execution number fifty-four, had ordered sausage and cabbage. Herrera ordered and received fried chicken and ice cream. He didn't feel like eating it himself, which was typical of condemned men, so instead had it sent to the two non-English-speaking Mexicans who were to have followed Herrera to the chair but had been given a temporary stay by the governor.

At 6:00 P.M. Herrera was taken from his cell and led to the bathtub. Clyde was placed in the first cell on death row, the one just vacated by Big Mex. By pressing his face against the bars, Clyde could still make out what was happening on the other end. After his bath, Herrera was given a new suit to wear, albeit a cheaply made suit that didn't fit his large frame very well. It was the suit he would be buried in. He was then seated in a chair, and with his razor a prisoner-barber cut upward along the seam of the left pant leg and rolled the pant leg up around Herrera's knee. He applied lather to the left calf and ankle and shaved the hair off Herrera's leg from the knee down.

Big Mex twisted nervously when the barber applied lather to the crown of his head. Clyde watched curiously as the ritual proceeded. The barber shaved the hair from the top of Herrera's head. Clyde quietly asked Joe Shield why they had shaved Herrera. Shield informed Clyde that electrodes from Ol' Sparky were placed in those places. The electricity went in through the top of the head and brain, proceeded through the heart, and exited out the left leg. The shaving allowed for better electrical contact. Clyde winced at the thought.

Herrera then was taken to Clyde's old cell, and a priest entered. Clyde could hear them talking, but he couldn't hear the words. The priest stayed as the hell clock tolled away the last hours for Big Mex. At 11:30 some noises came from the death chamber. The law stated that there had to be witnesses to the execution. They had apparently arrived. Sometimes they were members of the press. None of the witnesses were seen by the inmates on death row. The witnesses entered through a door from the prison grounds. It was the same door through which Herrera's remains would be taken following the execution.

A small concrete building that served as a morgue was located near death row. The body would be placed in a coffin and kept in the morgue until claimed by relatives. Many times bodies would go unclaimed, either because the dead men had no known relatives or because they had been completely disassociated from the families. These bodies were buried in a place near The Walls known to prisoners as "Peckerwood Hill." Simple markers containing names, death dates, and in some cases, execution numbers, were scattered in the cemetery.

The warden of the prison and some other officials showed up on death row shortly before the hell clock tolled midnight.

Herrera asked anxiously, "The governor, did you talk to the governor?"

"Yes," replied the warden. "I talked with him this afternoon. He said there is nothing he can do for you."

The priest put a comforting hand on the condemned man's shoulder as a guard opened the door to the cell. Herrera was then allowed to say good-by to each of the other inmates. With the priest in front and guards on either side, Herrera approached Clyde's cell. He looked at Clyde and smiled. It was a sincere smile. Shaking Clyde's hand through the bars, he said, "Good-by, my friend. I hope they let you live."

Clyde tried to return the smile but couldn't. He felt tears welling up in his eyes.

Herrera said a word of encouragement to each man. After bidding farewell to McKee, Herrera was led through the green door. There was silence on death row for the two minutes that followed. The sound of the warden's voice could be heard, then Big Mex's. The warden had asked him if he had any last words, and he said, "Antonio Chavez is an innocent man." Chavez had been indicted along with Herrera for the death of the sheriff, but his case had still not been disposed of. After that, Big Mex was strapped to the chair, and a hood was put over his head.

There was silence from the death chamber. Then there was the sudden crunch of the generator. The tension on death row continued to mount, and McKee suddenly screamed obscenities. The guard went over to his cell and asked him to be quiet. Then it was over. There was the sound of talking and the shuffling of feet on the other side of the green door after Herrera was pronounced dead by the doctor in attendance.

Clyde sobbed quietly in his cell. He was still crying when the horrible odor of burning hair and human flesh permeated death row. He didn't have to be told what it was. He vomited into the toilet bowl.

Chapter
11

WITH ABOUT FIFTY DAYS before his own date with the chair, Clyde started thinking about religion. He had gone to church regularly until he was ten years old. He believed in God and that Jesus had walked the earth some nineteen hundred years before. But Clyde hadn't gone to church on a regular basis since his parents divorced. Further, Clyde had never been baptized. In the Churches of Christ where his father preached, people waited until they made up their own minds about baptism. For some, this was at ten or eleven years of age, while others were teen-agers. Sometimes adults were baptized. As a boy, Clyde had seen his father baptize many people in lakes and rivers.

Baptism meant that the person's sins were being washed away. Because of the murders, Clyde felt a need for forgiveness. He also was worried about what would happen to his soul after he died.

When Rees first visited his son on death row, Clyde mentioned his thinking about baptism. Rees brought Clyde a copy of the New Testament and Psalms on a return visit. Reading had never been one of Clyde's strong suits. His eyes would look at the words, but he would skip many that he did not know. His reading was slow and laborious. Clyde tried to devote some time each day to religious matters by looking at the Bible and then praying. Inmates on death row couldn't go to church on Sundays, but the guard would tune the radio to church programs.

Normally, the men were kept in the cells in the order in which they were to be executed. But with the crowded conditions and the fact that both Shield and McKee were under death sentences but still had upcoming appeals court dates, the order had been temporarily mixed up. After the execution of Herrera, Riles was put in the first cell, then came Jenkins, the two Mexicans, and Twitty. Clyde was in the fifth cell, followed by Shield and McKee in six and seven, respectively.

Riles was next to walk the last mile. Four days later it was Jenkins. On his way to the green door, Jenkins stopped at Clyde's cell and said, "Behold, son, ya see the end of a convict's life. Ya oughta be glad to be here 'fore ya get a lyin' wife and 'fore ya give your life as a slave to the state that murders ya." Clyde wept as Jenkins walked slowly for the door, his body bent forward from the years of manning a hoe on prison workfarms.

Twitty went down without saying a word to anyone.

New inmates took the places of the recently departed. Among them was Will Fritz, a convicted murderer from Kent County in west Texas. Another was thirty-nine-year-old Chief Red Wing, a Cherokee Indian from Oklahoma who was found guilty of attacking and murdering a two-year-old girl in New Braunfels, Texas. Red Wing was the first Indian to get the chair in Texas. Another was Dave Goodwin, a hog raiser from Texarkana who had been dubbed "The Bard of the Sulphur River." Goodwin was convicted of shooting a man in a fight over a hog. After shooting the man, Goodwin was said to have bound his body and thrown it into the Sulphur River, where it was found three days later.

With cells right next to each other, McKee and Shield argued and swore at each other throughout the day and sometimes into the night. Each seemed to have a growing hatred for the other. But on Saturday nights when the Grand Ole Opry came over the radio from Nashville, there was an unspoken truce between them. On one Saturday they decided to write a letter to the Opry to request songs. Shield helped dictate what to say in the letter, while McKee wrote. Shield requested that they play "Eighth of January," while McKee wanted them to play "Black Bottom." Later, when the two resumed their fighting, McKee said he had requested "Black Bottom" because he knew Shield's bottom would be burned black in the electric chair. Shield countered that his request, "Eighth of January," had been made because that's when McKee would die in the chair. Neither had a definite death date.

The next Saturday both men were delighted when the announcer at the Opry said he had requests from "two unfortunate men on death row at Huntsville State Prison in Texas." Both requested songs were then aired.

Clyde continued to move up as he watched his fellow inmates die in the chair. Time passed quickly. Munoz and Rodriguez had been given another temporary stay of execution by the governor. With a death date of May 8, Clyde sat in the number one cell with five days to go. He had wondered how it would feel in this cell. He had been temporarily moved there the night Big Mex walked through the green door. But now he was in the first cell for real. Clyde's father and lawyer had been making efforts on his behalf but to no apparent avail. It appeared that Clyde was going to the chair as scheduled.

What bothered Clyde was the uncertainty of what was behind the green door. He would see the chair one time, and a few minutes after that, he would be gone. *What would it feel like to be electrocuted? Then where would he be?* His family would no doubt feel sorrow and shame. Probably for the rest of his life, Rees Thompson would be known as the man whose son died in the electric chair. This knowledge bothered Clyde.

In some respects he didn't feel much different in the first cell from the way he had in the eighth. It seemed as though the whole thing really wasn't happening. It was like a dream. Clyde had been on death row for fifty-five days. *And this time next week it will be as if I was never here,* he thought. Clyde wondered about his purpose in life. *Why was he even born? Why hadn't he died as an infant? Why hadn't he been lynched with Marshall Ratliff?* These thoughts plagued Clyde as he walked the three steps up and down in his cell.

Scheduled to die on Friday, Clyde listened to the religious programs on Sunday morning. He had been reading his Bible the best he could and praying. He paid particular attention to the sermon on the radio that morning from Perry Wilmeth, minister of the Church of Christ in Huntsville. At the conclusion of the sermon, Clyde made up his mind that he wanted to be baptized. The guard on duty was getting off at noon, and Clyde asked him if he would call Wilmeth. The guard agreed.

That afternoon Wilmeth came to death row. Clyde was surprised when he saw Wilmeth for the first time, because the minister appeared to be not much older than Clyde. The young minister carried a Bible in his hand, and at his request he was locked into the cell with Clyde. The two sat on the bunk as Wilmeth opened his Bible.

"I understand that you want to be baptized, Clyde," said Wilmeth, at first nervous about being locked up but overcoming his anxieties with the mission of the trip.

"Yes," answered Clyde. "I've been studyin' on it and feel like it's somethin' I need to do. I jus' never got around to it before."

Wilmeth opened his Bible and the two talked about passages relating to baptism.

"I want to be forgiven for killing those two men and for all the trouble I've caused," Clyde told him.

"Through the grace of Jesus you can be forgiven for any-thing," Wilmeth replied.

Clyde felt good about this. He smiled, and Wilmeth returned his smile.

After a few minutes, Wilmeth was released from the cell to make arrangements for Clyde's baptism. This was a problem because Wilmeth needed some kind of tank where Clyde could be totally immersed in the water. A Methodist chaplain was on duty, and though the Methodists sprinkled for baptism, the chaplain was sympathetic to Wilmeth's dilemma. There was a baptistry in the old chapel that hadn't been used in many years, and the chaplain helped Wilmeth prepare it for Clyde's baptism.

Condemned men never left death row, however. This rule created another problem—getting permission for Clyde to go to the old chapel. Prison officials were wary of condemned prisoners, because those who were about to die had nothing to lose and could try anything. But permission for Clyde to visit the old chapel with Wilmeth was granted.

Wilmeth returned to Clyde's cell with three armed guards who would escort them back and forth to the chapel. With two guards in front and one in back, they walked out of death row and to the chapel. Clyde was already barefooted. When they arrived at the baptistry, Wilmeth took off his shoes and removed his wallet. Both men walked down the three steps of the baptistry into the waist-deep water.

Wilmeth asked, "Do you believe that Jesus Christ is the Son of God?"

"Yes," said Clyde.

Wilmeth was situated so that Clyde stood in front of him. "Upon this confession," said Wilmeth, "I baptize you in the name of the Father, the Son, and the Holy Spirit." With that, Wilmeth helped Clyde lean back into the water. As Clyde came up out of the water, Wilmeth said, "Amen." He put his arm around Clyde's shoulder as they walked up the steps of the baptistry together. Accompanied by the three guards, they returned to the number one cell on death row.

Clyde felt relieved. He still wasn't happy about facing death, but he felt better prepared for meeting his Maker. He liked the idea of having his sins forgiven. He had seen many people baptized when he was younger and had always thought he would someday do it himself. *But,* thought Clyde, *I never would have imagined I would be on death row when I was baptized.* He planned for the rest of the week to be devoted to praying and looking at the Bible.

Clyde followed his plan as the hell clock tolled away the hours. As the day approached, Clyde noticed that his fellow prisoners and the guards seemed to talk to him a little differently. He wasn't sure how it was different; he just knew that it was.

When Clyde awoke on Wednesday, he thought, *Tomorrow will be my last day here.* There would be no radio, and he would be given his last bath and last meal, then be led to the chair shortly after midnight. Clyde wondered about the funeral. At least his body wasn't going to end up on Peckerwood Hill. His father would see to that. Petitions bearing the names of several thousand Eastland County residents had been given to the governor on Clyde's behalf. There also was a petition that had been signed by twenty-three of the twenty-four men who had served on the juries that sentenced Clyde to death in both trials. These petitions asked that Clyde's death sentence be commuted. The only juror not signing the petition was dead.

As Clyde ate his evening meal on Wednesday, the warden approached his cell. "Son, I've got good news for you. Governor Sterling has granted you a ninety-day stay of execution. He wants to see how Reuben Welsey's next trial comes out." The warden smiled at Clyde after bringing him the good news. The men in the next cells yelled words of congratulations to Clyde. Clyde smiled and thanked the warden. But inwardly he had mixed feelings. He had prepared himself to die. What was the use of sitting on death row for ninety more days? He would undoubtedly be executed anyway. At the same time, he had the instinct to live, and he felt relieved.

Clyde's new execution date was August 6, 1931. He was moved from cell number one to cell six. McKee and Shield were still in cells seven and eight. They continued to fight and had again successfully requested that the same songs be played on the Grand Ole Opry.

Clyde was visited by his father and his brother Bill. Both still held hopes that Clyde's sentence would be commuted. If Reuben Welsey were given a light sentence, they thought it would be a great help for Clyde. Reuben's long-awaited trial was held thirty-six miles northwest of Cisco in Albany, Texas, on a change of venue. This time Reuben was given a ten-year sentence for the robbery charges from the O'Dell case. Clyde was immediately informed of the decision. But the hell clock tolled away another month, and Clyde was still sentenced to die on August 6. There didn't seem to be anything to prevent Clyde's getting the chair this time.

Meanwhile, Shield left death row for a new trial. When he returned, it appeared that his legal recourses were about exhausted. His date with the chair was to be on August 14, just eight days after Clyde's. His death row adversary, McKee, still had a chance of avoiding the chair with a new trial that was upcoming. It appeared that McKee would indeed be present to see Shield get a black bottom.

Clyde clung to his religion. He prayed several times daily. He spent time trying to read the Bible. He tried to live the way he thought God wanted him to live. But the pressure of nearly three years behind bars and four months on death row was taking its toll. He was restless. He had been ready for the final determination in his case some two months earlier. He had been ready to die. Why had he been spared from the chair in May just to wait ninety more days for the same conclusion?

Clyde did not understand the desperate gnawing inside him—the gnawing for staying alive, for being free, and for running loose in the woods with his hunting dog Jack. Clyde knew he would never see Jack again. The dog had disappeared shortly after Clyde was jailed for murder. Clyde had long ago accepted the dog's loss. Jack wasn't the first dog Clyde had lost, but now he yearned to get loose to find his dog. *Maybe Jack is dead,* Clyde thought, *and waiting for me, tail wagging, in heaven.* But then again, maybe someone had stolen Jack and was keeping him cooped up. If Jack wasn't already dead, Clyde wanted to help him.

Clyde's mind would sometimes escape to the days when he and Jack roamed free, hunted, and made good money from the pelts. There was that bobcat that had practically torn off Jack's ear. He had yelped loudly but kept on fighting. He wasn't a coward. But Clyde would be brought back to death row by the tolling of the hell clock, which seemed to be growing louder and harsher.

With these thoughts, Clyde began to lapse into unreality. *I'm not really crazy,* he said to himself. *But maybe if I can convince them I am, I'll be able to get out of here.* A more rational Clyde would have thought of Helms and Leahy and the more recent example of Twitty, taken to the chair seemingly unaware of his surroundings.

Clyde's insanity was deceptive, especially to him. Inwardly he felt that everything was all right in his mind. His insanity was just an act for him. But in reality, Clyde suffered from the pressures that had been a part of his life since the murders. There was the Clyde who felt guilty for killing two men and felt the need to be punished. Then there was the Clyde who wanted his freedom, who wished that none of the events had ever happened. This Clyde wanted to marry Ruth and work for the United States Border Patrol. A part of him also mourned for Ruth. She had followed through on her promise to go to the governor. But since then, Clyde heard that she had a new boy friend. In a way, he couldn't blame her. But he hated the thought of not having her on his side anymore. At odds with his own psyche was the Clyde who had grown mean, taken part in the riot in the Dallas County Jail, and shown his bare buttocks to the journalists' cameras. There was also the paranoid Clyde, who felt that a world he never understood was against him. The religious Clyde, who had been baptized two months before, still prayed silently to God as he feigned insanity.

Clyde refused a bath or shave. He sat naked in his cell and talked to himself. Sometimes he screamed for his mama. The only time he was dressed was when the guards put clothes on him before a visitor came onto death row. Clyde would eat only if fed by a guard. If someone talked to him, he wouldn't respond.

Having seen so many go the insanity route, the guards took Clyde's actions matter-of-factly. The other prisoners watched and listened with interest, however. If Clyde somehow dodged the chair through insanity, it would open an avenue that they might follow.

A doctor who came to examine Clyde poked around and asked him a few questions to which he didn't respond. "He's as loony as a bedbug," Clyde heard the doctor tell a guard as he was leaving. Clyde smiled inwardly at this remark.

Clyde remained the same during a visit by his father, which left Rees perplexed. Clyde really wanted to talk to his father but remembered that Marshall Ratliff didn't let his own mother know that he was faking it. The hell clock gonged away the hours and days, but Clyde's apparent insanity didn't seem to have any effect on his pending execution. With two days to go, Clyde felt that all was lost. He contemplated giving up his act but thought better of it, deciding to go to the chair as a crazy man. *If I showed them now that I'm only faking this,*

Clyde reasoned, *it could hurt the chances of someone who really is crazy.* Not on a conscious level was the fact that at this point, insanity was more comfortable for Clyde than sanity.

Things were not so much different on what was scheduled to be Clyde's last day on earth, except for the silence. Repeating the usual procedure, an official stood in front of the condemned man's cell and read the death warrant. In the middle of the afternoon, Clyde was taken from his cell and given his last bath. The guards dressed him in a suit and returned him to his cell. Soon the barber would come to shave his left leg and the top of his head. Dave Goodwin, the hog raiser, had followed him to the bathtub. He, too, was scheduled to be executed that night.

Throughout this, Clyde continued to pretend he was insane. Inwardly, he felt afraid on one level but fairly detached from the situation on another. In the number one cell Clyde waited for the barber. The clock gonged four times, giving Clyde and Goodwin eight hours to live. For the last six hours Clyde knew that he would be taken to his original cell on death row.

Just as the hell clock was telling Clyde that he had seven hours to live, a crowd of men walked onto death row. Among them were the warden and Lee Simmons, general manager of the Texas Department of Corrections. The rest appeared to be newspapermen, some of them with cameras.

The group gathered around Clyde's cell. Breathlessly, Simmons announced, "Governor Sterling has commuted your sentence to life in prison! You're off death row!"

The rest of the prisoners on death row cheered. So did the guards. At the same time Governor Sterling was telling members of the press in Austin that he had overruled the final judgment of the appeals board because "while I am not convinced that Thompson is insane, I regard him as having the mentality of a child. In view of these facts and in view of the inequality of the sentences imposed against Clyde Thompson and Reuben

Welsey, I feel that I cannot permit Clyde Thompson to go to his death in this case.

"Many people acquainted with the parties involved in this case have talked to me," the governor continued. "And it is the unanimous opinion of every one so far as I know that Clyde Thompson is of a very low mentality and without education. A telegram signed by numerous citizens of Eastland County, among whom are Chief of Police W. M. Miller, J. E. Spencer, secretary of the Cisco Chamber of Commerce, W. H. Laroque, manager of the *Cisco Daily News*, Guy Dabney, president of the Cisco Banking Company, and many others, ask that this sentence be commuted to life imprisonment. The trial officers also have recommended commutation."

The flashes of newsmen's cameras illuminated death row for brief instances. "How does it feel?" one of the newsmen asked Clyde.

"Yeah, kid," shot another. "How does it feel to have your life saved within hours of the chair?"

All of them talked at once.

Clyde looked at them uncomprehendingly and said nothing. The newspapermen were disappointed. They had hoped for a joyous reaction to describe to their readers. Instead, they got nothing. Simmons shook his head. Clyde felt he could have given them the reaction they wanted, but he reasoned that this was a trick to prove he really wasn't insane after all. It was a trick he wasn't about to fall for. As soon as they found that he really wasn't crazy, they would fry him in the chair, as they had done with Big Mex, Riles, Jenkins, Twitty, and so many others.

Simmons walked to the next cell, the one holding Goodwin. "You're off death row, too!" he announced.

Goodwin gave the press a more joyous reaction. Goodwin had maintained all along that the governor would commute his sentence. "I knew he wouldn't let me down!" exclaimed Goodwin, smiling as the flashes went off.

The captain of the guard later came to take Clyde off death row. When he and a guard opened the door to the cell, Clyde fought with them and said he didn't want to go. Clyde screamed for them to leave him there. If there were any previous doubts about Clyde's sanity, they were quickly erased.

Clyde fought for his life. Now that the newspapermen were gone, the guards were planning to take him to the chair through the door that opened to the death chamber from the prison grounds, Clyde reasoned. Telling him that he was to be taken elsewhere was just part of their trick.

Gaining reinforcements, the guards wrestled Clyde from his cell and took him to the unit of the prison known as "crazy row."

Chapter
12

CLYDE'S STAY on crazy row lasted two months. During that time he gradually became aware that his removal from death row wasn't a trick. His sentence had been commuted to life in prison, and he no longer had to think about dying in the electric chair. But he carried within him a deep-seated resentment from the experience.

After his release from the mental ward, Clyde was assigned to a cellblock at The Walls and given a job of picking up paper in the yard of the prison with "Ol' Dutch," a lifer in his sixties. Clyde's cell partner was Charles Lockhart, two years older than Clyde and nearly five inches taller, a lanky, blue-eyed brunet with a gap between his two front teeth. He had been sentenced to thirty-five years for an armed robbery in Houston.

Their cell was one of thirty-five or forty that stood side by side on the second tier of the three-tiered cellblock. It measured five feet by ten feet, the same size as the cells on death row. It contained two wooden slats bolted into the wall with mattresses placed on them for bunk beds, a sink, and a toilet. There were concrete walls on three sides and bars on the fourth. On the wall opposite the bunks a single light bulb stuck out sideways with a pull-chain dangling from it. In front of the cells on each side was a concrete wall that had long windows going all the way up to the third tier. Each of the windows was made up of small, square panes separated by steel. For their size, the windows didn't allow much light into the cellblock. Even on a sunny day, the light was always a kind of grayish, drab color.

The cellblock was mopped and cleaned daily. An ever-present antiseptic smell combined with the odor of cigarette smoke, sweat, and excrement.

With so many men in so little space, the cellblock was never completely quiet. Doors clanged constantly, and there was a continual buzzing of conversation. At night loud snores echoed off the walls, prisoners moaned in their sleep, and occasionally someone having a nightmare screamed.

Clyde and Lockhart got along with a surface friendliness for the first few weeks but then became friends and finally formed a partnership.

"Well, I jus' didn't know about ya, gettin' off crazy row and havin' that Bible in here," Lockhart said one night.

"It was just an act," replied Clyde. "I figured it was the only way of gettin' out of there alive. 'Sides, bein' in that place for five months would drive anyone nuts."

"Yeah, I guess," said Lockhart, trailing off into silence so that the only sounds were those coming from the adjoining cells.

"Say," he spoke up again. "What year were you born?"

"Nineteen and ten," Clyde answered. "Why?"

"Oh, I was jus' figurin' somethin'. Ever think how old ya might be when ya get out of here?"

"No, guess not," answered Clyde.

"Well, if they letcha out in twenty years," said Lockhart, "it'd be 1951, and you'd be forty-one years old."

Both laughed.

"Whew," said Clyde, "I can't even 'magine bein' that old.

But ya know, when it comes right down to it, it really ain't so funny."

"You're right," Lockhart responded. "It ain't. I figure I'd be at least that old, too."

"That's gettin' up there for sure," Clyde said.

Lockhart motioned for Clyde to come closer to him and whispered, "I don't know how you feel, but I don't feel like rottin' in here 'til 1951."

"I guess I don't either," Clyde whispered back.

The two crawled into their bunks and soon were asleep. But the next day as he went about his job in the prison yard, Clyde thought more about growing old in a cell. He looked at Dutch, who had spent most of his adult life in prison and now had thin, white hair. *I could be like him by the time I get out of here. Or maybe they'll never let me out.* Already ingrained in Clyde's thought process was "us versus them." "Us" in Clyde's case was the fraternity of cons, with its own special rules. "Them" included anyone who was not locked behind bars, but particularly the guards and wardens.

Back in the cell that night, Clyde and Lockhart talked about incidents from their childhood. Growing up in the city, Lockhart's background was much different from Clyde's. But Clyde suddenly changed the subject. "You know, Charles, 1951 is a long time away."

"Sure is," agreed Lockhart.

"If there's any way of gettin' out of it, I 'd sure do it," Clyde said.

Lockhart lowered his voice to a whisper. "You mean escape?"

"Well, yeah, I guess that's what I mean," answered Clyde quietly.

"What about that Bible you've been totin' 'round?" Lockhart inquired. "Didn't you tell me your daddy was a preacher?"

"Yeah, used to be," said Clyde. "He brought me this Bible

on death row. I ain't been tryin' to read it much lately. But it's okay, I guess."

"There ain't too many Bible thumpers who talk about escapin'," said Lockhart.

"I ain't no Bible thumper, and even if I was, it wouldn't mean I'd wanna spen' the rest of my life rottin' in a cell," Clyde replied, trying not to raise his voice over a whisper.

"So you really do want to escape?" probed Lockhart.

"Yeah, don't you?" asked Clyde.

"Yeah . . . but you got any idea how?"

"No. You?"

"No," replied Lockhart. "But I guess we could keep our eyes open. Pardners?" he said, extending his hand toward Clyde.

"Yep, pardners," answered Clyde with resolve, shaking Lockhart's hand.

While picking up papers and cigarette butts in the prison a few days later, Clyde noticed a manhole cover near the exercise yard. A building obscured it from a guard tower on the wall. He looked around and saw no one watching, so he pried up the cover. Beneath was a dark tunnel with a steel ladder leading down into it. It was big enough for a man to stand in. A few days later when most of the prisoners were in the yard, Clyde and Lockhart slipped away to the place where the manhole cover was located. Lockhart had obtained candles from another prisoner so that they could explore the tunnel. It had concrete sides and stopped after about thirty feet.

The purpose of the tunnel was unknown to them, but they thought it might serve as a means of escape. They made a plan to secure some tools, knock a hole in the concrete, and dig their own tunnel from there. Since Clyde had free roam of the prison grounds as a part of his job, he would have no problem stealing a pick and shovel. They would have to dig at least twenty-five yards to reach the prison wall. And beyond that was a street to go under. Since they both had until 1951, they figured they could work a little at a time, whenever they could. They vowed to keep their discovery a secret from the other prisoners.

Walking by himself a few days later in an area near the hospital unit, Clyde was confronted by another inmate. He walked on crutches and had a bandage covering one foot. When Clyde walked in front of him, the prisoner stuck out one of the crutches as if to trip Clyde. He was not much taller than Clyde and was a slightly built man. He appeared to be in his early twenties.

As he walked over the extended crutch, Clyde tripped slightly, quickly righted himself, and squared off in front of the man with his fists clenched. "What are you tryin' to do?" asked Clyde brusquely.

"Take it easy," replied the other prisoner with a slight grin on his face, unruffled by Clyde's anger.

"You want trouble?" asked Clyde between clinched teeth.

"Naw," said the inmate. "Jus' wanted to say howdy."

"Howdy," replied Clyde. "That all?"

"Come on," said the prisoner with crutches, attempting to reconcile. "I'm jus' tryin' to be friendly."

Clyde warmed up a bit. "Well, all right," he returned.

"Heard you killed two men," the other prisoner stated.

Clyde grew defensive again. "Where'd you hear that?"

"You know everyone knows everyone else's business 'round here."

Clyde knew that to be true because of the prison grapevine. "Yeah, I guess you're right," he said with resignation in his voice. "That's why I'm here all right, for killin' two men. But say, where'd you come from? Ain't never seen you before."

"Eastham farm just a few days ago. Now I'm on the hospital wing here."

"What for?" Clyde asked.

The inmate laughed and pointed to his bandaged foot.

"Oh, yeah," said Clyde, nodding his head at the obvious.

"It's the only way of gettin' off the workfarm. Ya gotta cut off a foot, hand, or somethin'. I meant to cut off the whole foot but missed and just' got the first two toes instead."

Clyde was revolted and then amazed. "You mean guys cut off their feet jus' to get off the workfarm?"

"Yeah," said the convict. "That place is hell on earth, boy. Hope you never have to go to one of them places. Oh, by the way, my name is Clyde Barrow." He extended his hand.

Clyde accepted the outstretched hand and told his name.

"Now I find out that the governor might give me a pardon," said Barrow. "But if it wasn't for that, they'd probably send me back to the farm with two toes missin'."

"Think so?" asked Clyde.

"I know so," replied Barrow quickly. "There ain't no way of getting off them farms except—whhtttt." With that he made a cutting off motion across his neck. "I sure hope the parole comes through. I sure as h—— don't wanna go back."

"Well," Clyde related, "the governor saved me from the chair with seven hours to go. Now he's left me in here to rot for the rest of my life."

"That was a pretty close call with the chair," observed Barrow.

"Yep," Clyde answered.

"When I get outta here, I got big plans," stated Barrow. "I'm gonna make 'em pay many times over for those two toes I had to cut off."

"How you gonna do that?" inquired Clyde.

"Don't know for sure. Maybe rob a bank. Jus' hafta wait 'n see."

"Hmmm," Clyde responded, still trying to figure out Barrow's motives for even striking up a conversation with him in the first place.

"I could use a guy who's not afraid to pull the trigger ever' once in a while. I sure would like to have someone like that with me," said Barrow.

As Barrow talked, Ol' Dutch approached. "Come on, Clyde," he said, motioning with his arm. "We've got some stuff to clean up over here. Ain't got time to jaw all day long."

Clyde intended to tell Barrow that he didn't want to shoot anyone else, but he never saw him again.

Within a week, Clyde secured a pick and shovel and hid them in the tunnel. He and Lockhart pounded their way through the concrete and started their own tunnel, working a half hour or forty-five minutes whenever they could.

As a part of his job, Clyde picked up papers near death row. He also kept up on the status of Ira McKee, still on death row. As it turned out, McKee wasn't there when Shield's bottom was "burned black" on August 14, 1931. McKee left for his appeal trial just before Shield was executed. McKee was returned to death row a few days after his own execution was upheld by the appeals court. When he returned, his swearing, screaming, and ranting could be heard throughout the prison yard. He had gone crazy. And when the Grand Ole Opry came over the death row radio on the Saturday night after he returned and the song "Eighth of January" was played, McKee threw things and literally beat his head against the bars of his cell. He had been sentenced to die in the chair on January 8, 1932. From his grave, with his bottom already black, Shield got the last laugh. He had correctly predicted McKee's death date.

Clyde and Lockhart made good progress on their tunnel. Both were working in it a few days after McKee was executed. Clyde was in the dirt tunnel that now extended back about ten feet. He filled a bucket with dirt, then Lockhart emptied the dirt onto the floor of the concrete tunnel. There was already quite a pile of dirt on the floor. They wondered what to do with it.

103

Suddenly there was a noise that sounded like someone was removing the manhole cover. Lockhart quickly blew out the candle. A beam of sunlight pierced the darkness. There was a voice from above. "Okay, you two. We know you're down there, so come on out."

Clyde and Lockhart remained quiet.

The same voice returned. "I said get up here. Now!"

A second voice quickly added, "You boys not outta there in ten seconds, I'll give ya a dose of tear gas you'll never forget."

"What you think?" Lockhart whispered to Clyde.

"Ever have tear gas before?" Clyde whispered back.

"No, but I hear it's awful. Makes it so you can't see, burns your nose."

"I guess we'd better climb on up," whispered Clyde.

Loudly, Lockhart yelled, "Don't shoot it! We're comin'. We're comin'."

The two ascended, squinting in the bright sunlight. There were two guards and a guard sergeant standing at the top of the manhole. Clyde and Lockhart were locked in their cell.

"Think someone stooled us off?" asked Lockhart, lying on his back, staring at the bunk above.

Clyde also lay on his bunk, staring vacantly upward. "Don't know," he answered with disappointment in his voice. "Maybe someone looked in there and saw the pile of dirt."

"Yeah, maybe," answered Lockhart.

"What ya reckon they're gonna do with us, throw us in solitary?" Clyde asked, not really expecting Lockhart to have the answer.

"Don't know," Lockhart answered.

Three days later Clyde was taken from the cell, while Lockhart remained. Clyde was put on a chain with several other prisoners and marched to "black Annie," the truck that transported prisoners from one location to another. Two benches in the back of the truck faced each other. Prisoners were connected with a long chain that was looped around their necks. A padlock secured the chain around each prisoner's neck, placed about where the knot in a necktie would be. The back door of the truck was padlocked.

"Uncle Bud" was in charge of moving the prisoners and was known for never having lost one. The truck headed for the Retrieve State Farm, in Brazoria County forty miles south of Houston, known to hold some of the toughest men in the Texas Department of Corrections.

Clyde later heard that Lockhart was sent to one of the other prison farms.

Chapter
13

ONE OF THE GOALS of the Texas Department of Corrections (TDC) was to be self-supporting. It would fall short of its goal by operating at a deficit of $1.5 million during 1932. This meant it cost the state $.76 to maintain a prisoner for one day.

Livestock and crops raised at the several state-operated prison farms were either fed to prisoners or sold for a profit, with the proceeds used to purchase items that couldn't be raised or manufactured in the prison system.

On a given day in 1932, there were slightly more than five thousand prisoners in the TDC, about 50 percent of them white, 40 percent black, and 10 percent Mexicans. They were convicted of crimes ranging from murder and rape to mule stealing and bigamy. Only about one hundred of the Texas prisoners were women, all incarcerated at the Goree unit.

Men were generally grouped together according to race at the other twelve TDC units. The three hundred prisoners at the Retrieve farm, Clyde's destination, were all white. Only blacks were sent to the Clemens farm, located in the same county as Retrieve. The Blue Ridge farm consisted of all Mexicans, but there were both blacks and Mexicans at the Ramsey farm. Invalids served their time at the Wynne unit, while insane prisoners were incarcerated at Rusk.

Cotton was the principal cash crop for the TDC, but corn was the main crop at Retrieve. Some three thousand acres of the farm were in cultivation, while the remaining four thousand acres were still covered by trees and brush. Thus, prisoners would plant, cultivate, and harvest from spring through early fall. And during late fall and winter they would clear land for future planting.

Twice in the twentieth century there had been investigations into the TDC that had focused on cruelty and inhumane conditions under which prisoners were forced to work. Prisoners had subsisted on skimpy diets; many had been beaten or worked to death. The cause of death for those who died at the hand of an overzealous guard was usually listed as a natural cause, such as heart failure.

In 1902 five state legislators investigated all state agencies, including the prison system. No guarantees of anonymity were offered to prisoners who testified, so many chose to keep quiet. Those who opened their mouths felt the wrath of retaliation after the investigation was over. Under the system, prisoners were "leased out" to farmers for a specified amount of money. As a part of the agreement, the state would provide the guards. It was up to the farmer to feed and house the inmates. Of course, some greedy farmers got the most for their money at the expense of the prisoners. Inmates sometimes worked eighteen or twenty hours a day in the fields, ate slop, and slept on the floors of shacks. It was a type of legalized slavery. Prison officials received kickbacks from the farmers to drive the men harder. These kickbacks were legally abolished as a result of the 1902 investigation, but prisoner leasing continued.

Seven years later a prison reform movement that was sweeping the nation also caught hold in Texas. A thorough investigation led to a complete reorganization of Texas prisons, and the leasing of prisoners was abolished. The prisoners continued to work on farms, but the farms were either leased or owned by the state—not private landowners.

In some ways Texas had been innovative in its reform. Education programs for prisoners had been initiated in the 1880s. But during harvest time, educational programs usually gave way to the economic reality of getting the crops in on time.

Prison reform in Texas was usually centered at the main prison unit in Huntsville—The Walls. Some one thousand prisoners were incarcerated there, and they would be the ones most likely to feel the effects of reform. Thus, according to the prison grapevine, The Walls was the best place to be if you had to be locked up in Texas. At outlying units in rural areas such as Retrieve, though the prison leasing system was gone, cruelty to prisoners was not unusual. Inmates worked long hours in the fields, and the food was generally substandard. Guards were sometimes arbitrary in their treatment of prisoners and often sadistic and cruel.

The reform movement of the early part of the century was somewhat forgotten during World War I. By the time Clyde arrived during the depression, the greatest consideration was the economics of having a good cash crop to make the prisons self-supporting.

The men at Retrieve slept in a building that resembled an army barracks, except for the bars on the windows. There were two wings, and each housed about 150 prisoners. The wings were separated by a fenced-in area, known as a picket, where guards stayed. From the picket, guards could observe the actions of men in either wing. There was a separate building that served as a dining hall for the prisoners, plus stables, barns, and many smaller buildings.

A couple of the administrators at Retrieve had said that any man who tried to escape would be killed. This statement had been documented by the corpses of would-be escapees.

For the most part, the prisoners had little formal education, but they claimed that the guards had even less. It was said that some of the guards had never learned to count. To keep track of the men in their squads, they would put a pebble in their pocket for each man. Then, periodically throughout the day, they would "count" the prisoners by transferring the pebbles from one pocket to the other. If a pebble was left over, someone was missing.

For the prisoners, the farm was a type of jungle. In order to survive, one had to learn the rules by which the guards (called bosses) and building tenders (inmates assigned to run things for the guards) operated the farm and live in accordance with them. Just as important was the prisoner code. To break the rules or the code meant that one wouldn't survive.

The prison code said that the most hated man in prison was a building tender. By siding with prison officials, he was a man who had turned against his own kind. Building tenders often abused their power. If a building tender was suddenly demoted to the regular prison ranks, chances were good he would soon be found dead.

The next most detestable man was a stool pigeon. In accordance with the unwritten code, prisoners never went to prison officials—no matter what happened. If there was a disagreement between prisoners, it was settled between themselves. A stoolie's life wasn't worth two cents.

The next most hated prisoner was a man who had been sent up for rape or another sex offense. Sex offenders usually fabricated stories about crimes they had committed, but if the truth ever leaked out, the other inmates would have nothing to do with them. And if a rapist or child molester ever crossed another inmate, there was a great likelihood that he wouldn't live to do it again.

Inmates also hated anyone who stole something from another prisoner. The prison code said that a thief caught with the goods in his possession could be beaten half to death by his accuser while guards and building tenders turned their backs to it.

Prisoners did little contemplating or thinking. They relied more on instinct and feeling. A man's instincts kept him alive

109

by helping him to avoid situations that would threaten his survival. His instincts dictated that he get as much food as he possibly could, because food meant survival. His feelings forced him to react rather than act, to base his actions on emotion rather than reason; these reactions built up a frustration in the inmates that caused them to hate practically everything around them and to envy anyone who had anything better.

For the prisoners it was not a matter of which iron to use for the approach to the green at the country club; it was not a matter of which tie would go best with a particular suit or even whether to vote Democratic or Republican in the upcoming election. It was simply a matter of surviving through the day. Then maybe there would be a next day. The only hope for the future was release or escape.

"Think you could give me two padlocks? One might not hold me."

The guard ignored the remarks from the con next to Clyde and finished securing the chain around the neck of the sixth and final prisoner who would be making the trip to Retrieve.

The talkative inmate turned to Clyde. "Guess he ain't gonna give me another lock. Reckon this one will hold me?"

Getting in the spirit, Clyde pretended to tug hard at the lock that dangled at his neck. "Yeah," he said. "I think one'll hold ya."

"Well, if my teeth were strong enough, I could bite right through this chain," he said, holding it in his hands and showing his teeth like a mad dog.

Clyde laughed.

"You two ain't gonna be funnin' once we get to Retrieve," spoke the man sitting across from them. He had deep lines running from his eyes and a leathery skin, as if he had spent a lot of time in the sun. He appeared to be somewhere in his forties. "I already spent seven years down there, and it'll break a coupla punks like you."

"Yes, sir," shot back the inmate sitting next to Clyde in a type of mock humility. "We're sorry for funnin'."

Clyde could hardly keep from laughing at his antics. Clyde had immediately liked him. The wisecracking con was named Barney Allen. He was brown-haired and brown-eyed, slightly taller, and about two and a half years older than Clyde. Barney was a native of Tennessee. After his father died, he had enlisted in the army as a teen-ager, but he was discharged when he was found to be underage. Later, he served twenty-nine months in Indiana for burglary, and he escaped once from the penitentiary there. He now had a twenty-five-year sentence for robbery in Texas.

Uncle Bud delivered his prisoners to the farm late on a Monday afternoon. Each man was issued a pair of work boots, one pair of underwear, white work pants, a white work shirt, and a hat. There were also striped uniforms, but none of the new men were given stripes. These uniforms were reserved for the "bad actors"—prisoners who were constantly in trouble with the authorities. Prisoners were given a change of clothes once a week. Someone asked about socks and was told he had to supply his own.

The barracks were quiet when Clyde, Barney, and the others arrived. The beds were stacked three-high, and the only empty bunks they could find were the top ones.

Just after dark, the other prisoners returned from the fields. There was little talking among prisoners as they marched through the door. Some looked as though they might fall down from exhaustion. The men had five minutes to wash up before lining up for the chow hall.

Clyde remembered what both Clyde Barrow and the older prisoner had said about the farms. He watched as men covered with sweat and mud dragged into the barracks that night. Some of them fell right into their bunks after they walked through the door, not even bothering to get the dirt off their clothes or themselves. Some were in bed without taking off their mud-caked boots.

Clyde and Barney were assigned to the same squad and fell in at the end of the line going to the chow hall. The men marched to chow with their right arms on the shoulder of the man in front of them. The meal consisted of cornbread and turnip greens that were scooped out of large kettles onto their metal trays by inmates who served as cooks. After that, they returned to the barracks and went to bed.

A bell sounded at four o'clock the next morning, signaling the time to get up. There were two toilets for the 150 men on Clyde's wing, and they were given five minutes to get ready for breakfast. After breakfast, they returned to the barracks and stood in squads. At the first crack of dawn, the man known as the "little captain" (equivalent to an assistant warden) called out the squads. Each squad had its own guard who rode on horseback. Rain was pouring down outside, but that wouldn't prevent the prisoners' working.

In squads the inmates jogged about a mile to a tool crib, where each man was issued a shovel, pick, and hoe. Still in squads, they then jogged through the heavy, black mud carrying their tools about three miles to the place where they would be working. The guards rode either alongside or behind their squads. Each guard carried a double-barreled shotgun loaded with buckshot and a blackjack. If any man lagged behind, the guard would chastise him with threats of punishment that night.

Since it was winter, the prisoners usually cleared land. On Clyde's first morning they dug ditches.

Having grown up picking cotton and doing farm work, Clyde knew how to handle a shovel, pick, and hoe. But during the more than three years behind bars, his muscles had grown soft, and the callouses on his hands had long since disappeared. His legs ached from trudging through the miles of mud; he was winded and already had blisters on his feet from the new boots when his squad finally stopped at the place where they would work that day.

The inmates were lined up about ten feet apart. Each man was given a strip to dig measuring about ten feet long, four feet wide, and five feet deep. One inmate in the squad was designated as the lead row man, and it was his duty to set the pace on the job. Usually, the man who worked hardest and knew how to handle his tools was made the lead row man. Any man who hadn't completed his part within five minutes after the lead row man was finished received punishment that night.

Punishment for slow workers was standing on wooden barrels or soft drink cases that were turned on end. The punishment started as soon as the inmates returned to the barracks at night, before chow. They would stand on these all night, miss breakfast the next morning, and then fall in with their squads running out to the fields. Already tired from working and running all day, inmates found that their legs would soon cramp as they tried to keep their balance. After a few hours, it became torture. The only rest that punished men would get was during the half hour lunch break in the field the next day.

Ordered by the guards, the punishments were carried out by building tenders, who had hunting knives and clubs to protect themselves from the other prisoners. If a man fell off the barrel or soft drink case on which he was standing, he was beaten by the building tender until he could climb back up and regain his balance.

Clyde almost felt good having farm tools in his hands again. For the first hour he dug enthusiastically. But then his muscles started aching, and his soft hands became sore. A blister formed on his right hand and popped open.

The men weren't allowed to talk as they worked, but Clyde found that he could get away with saying a few things to Barney working next to him when the guard was at the opposite end of the ditch. The rain hadn't let up, and the latter part of the morning had dragged by. Now, in midafternoon

Clyde couldn't see how he could make it until the end of the day.

"How you doin' over there?" he asked in Barney's direction.

"Terrible. Think I'll just crawl into this hole and let you bury me here," Barney replied as he threw out a shovelful of soggy, black dirt.

"My hands sure are sore," complained Clyde.

"Mine turned into one big blister that popped about an hour ago," replied Barney. "Think we could get the guard to hold an umbrella over us while we dig?"

Clyde smiled and shook his head, amazed that Barney could still wisecrack even though he was exhausted.

The guard heard their talking and cantered his horse down the row. "You two had better keep your mouths shut and dig a little harder," he ordered.

"Sorry, Boss," Barney replied. "I was just wonderin' if you could get us some umbrellas?"

The guard glared at Barney with a cold stare of disbelief. "Crawl on out of there, boy, and come over here," he said with mock kindness.

Barney put down his shovel and stepped up beside the mounted guard.

"So you're a funny man, huh?" the guard stated more than asked.

Barney just shrugged his shoulders. Suddenly the guard rammed Barney's forehead with the butt of his shotgun. Barney fell backward into the hole he had just dug, holding his head, rolling in the mud, and moaning.

The guard pointed the barrel of the shotgun at Barney's chest and cocked one of the hammers. "Now get to your feet, start digging, and keep your d—— mouth shut," he growled.

Barney obeyed.

At the end of the day they sloshed back to the tool shed and then to the barracks. Barney was none the worse for his run-in with the guard except for a big bump in the middle of his forehead. Both he and Clyde were sore, tired, and wet. As other men lined up for the chow hall, Barney and Clyde crawled up to their bunks and fell into bed without removing their wet clothes or mud-caked boots. Before dozing off, Clyde looked with pity at the fifty or so men who had fallen behind in their work that day. The building tenders were lining these men up against the walls of the barracks to undergo their punishment. Clyde was glad he wasn't one of them.

Chapter
14

CLYDE AND BARNEY were still sore when Saturday dragged around. At Retrieve it was no different from any other work day; the inmates worked from sunup to sunset.

An inmate in his early twenties from Dallas had been sent to Retrieve on the same chain as Clyde and Barney. He didn't say one word from The Walls to Retrieve. And at the farm he wasn't catching on well because he had never done farm labor. Although Clyde and Barney had blisters that had broken open on their hands and feet, they managed to keep up with the lead row man in their week of ditch digging. James Craig Williams, the city boy, hadn't kept up. As a result, he stood on a barrel both Thursday and Friday nights. Having eaten just the noon meal in the fields the two previous days and getting no sleep for two nights, he could barely walk.

Williams was dragging his feet and staggering from exhaustion as the squad jogged to the tool crib on Saturday morning. Clyde and Barney jogged beside him, trying to encourage him.

"Once we get out there, get between us," Clyde told him. "We'll try to help you keep up today."

It was against the rules to help another man with his job, but

Clyde found that he could get away with helping the man right beside him; he had helped Barney with his section of the ditch on more than one occasion. The morning of digging went okay. Clyde and Barney hustled to finish their section of ditch and then pitched in to help Williams. But the week of digging and the extra work that morning had them exhausted midway through the afternoon. Clyde, Barney, and Williams finished their sections more than five minutes after the lead row man.

That night the three of them ended up standing on the same barrel together. After two hours on the barrel, it was torture. In addition, Clyde and Barney had to hold up Williams who was sleeping on his feet. Clyde wanted to scream because of the pain in his legs. When the building tender stepped away, he whispered to Barney, "I wonder if I really was executed in the electric chair and ended up in hell."

"Maybe" was all that Barney could muster for an answer.

When the next morning finally came, the building tender told Williams that he could step down from the barrel. As he was getting down, he gave Clyde and Barney a look of appreciation that almost made bearing his weight throughout the night worth it. They wondered when they would be permitted to get off the barrel but found that those who went up on Saturday night had to stay up there all day Sunday, too. The building tender had made an exception for Williams since it was his third night in a row. Inmates not being punished had Sunday off from digging ditches and loafed in the barracks. Some received visitors.

During Clyde's second week at Retrieve, a member of the board of pardons and paroles came to talk with him. His name was Stanhope Henry, known to the prisoners as "No-Hope" Henry. The three-member board made recommendations on whether men should be paroled from prison, and they had other authority. Clyde already knew about the board because his case had gone before them while he was on death row. The board had recommended that Clyde's execution be upheld. If the governor hadn't overruled the board's decision, Clyde knew he would have been long gone.

"I'm glad to see that you're making good progress here at the farm," Henry told Clyde.

"Yes, sir," Clyde replied aloud while he inwardly thought, *If it were up to you, No-Hope, I'd already be dead.*

Henry continued, "If you keep a clean record for nineteen more years, there's a strong possibility that we'll consider you for parole."

Clyde wanted to laugh in the old man's face but just nodded his head. First, it appeared that ol' No-Hope was already on his last legs. How on earth did he figure he would be alive in nineteen more years to consider Clyde's case? He looked as though he might drop dead before he reached the door to leave. Second, Clyde had no intentions of staying on the prison farm for nineteen more years. A week and a half had been bad enough. Clyde planned to escape at the first opportunity.

Portions of meat were served an average of twice a week in the Retrieve chow hall, and it was usually of poor quality. The men could supplement their meat rations by killing wild game that they came across while working in the fields. Rabbits and squirrels were skinned and sent to the cook. The man who killed the animal was the one who got to eat it that night.

It paid to stay on the good side of the bosses, because they were the ones who determined if the inmates would be allowed to pursue wild game. Clyde had short legs and had never been a fast runner. He knew that he was at a distinct disadvantage if it came to running down a rabbit. While watching others chasing the rabbits, however, he observed that many times the rabbits would win the race. Sometimes the rabbits would lead their pursuers in a circle and would run right back to the area where they started. Rather than chasing rabbits, Clyde let the others chase them while he stood with a stick beside the likely trail the rabbit would take on its return. When the rabbit came by, Clyde would whack it over the head. If a rabbit ran into a brush pile, the men would circle it. But most of the time the rabbit would run out between their legs. When the rabbits ran into these piles, Clyde would stand back thirty or forty feet beside what appeared to be the most likely rabbit trail. Then he would ambush the animal if it came his way. Clyde also found the right strategy to use for squirrels. He attributed his extra meat rations mainly to the fact that he had learned a lot about the habits of animals as he grew up.

Clyde had never eaten a possum, but he killed one in the field, skinned it, and sent it to the cook. One bite and Clyde knew why it had never been served at his home. It tasted the way a skunk smells. The inmate sitting beside Clyde asked if he could try it. Clyde was glad to let him. The man sampled it, found it tasty, and ate the whole thing. This proved to Clyde how much the prisoners craved meat.

This desire for meat was demonstrated again shortly thereafter. The prisoners were served meat for supper. Clyde had taken one bite and decided it was tainted. He didn't eat any more but watched as most of the rest of the prisoners eagerly devoured it.

When a man had to go to the bathroom during the night, he would yell up to the guard on duty in the picket, "Alley, Boss." (The alley was the narrow walkway at the foot of the bunks.) By yelling "alley," the convict was asking permission to walk down the alley to the restroom at the end. The guard would usually say, "Okay, go 'head."

Shortly after they all went to bed that night after eating the bad meat, a man urgently piped up, "Alley, Boss!" The guard gave him the go-ahead. Then another inmate made the request with equal urgency. Soon there were twenty-five or thirty men lined up in front of the two toilets in the wing. Some men became too desperate to wait and relieved themselves beneath the three showers. Since the toilets and the showers were occupied, other men were forced to back up to windows to pass their excrement directly to the outside. This continued through the night and the next morning when all the men, sick or not, were forced to fall into their squads for work.

Williams, the Dallas city boy, still didn't seem to be catching onto farm work very well. He stood on the barrel every few nights for not being able to keep up.

As Clyde Barrow had done, men at Retrieve regularly cut off toes or fingers, hands or feet to get off the farm. Clyde once watched a young Indian sit down and put his leg on a railroad tie. He beat his leg with the dull side of an ax, and before he finished, he had hacked through the bone. It was a sickening sight. Lee Simmons, general manager of TDC, was told of the self-mutilation problem on the farms. "Give them more axes," he was quoted as saying.

"I just can't take this anymore, Clyde," complained Williams one morning as they were standing in their squad, waiting for daylight. They had been at the farm a month.

"Don't worry," Clyde assured him. "Keep at it. You'll catch on."

"No I won't," Williams replied desperately. "Half the nights I'm on the d—— barrels and that makes it twice as bad the next day. I never lifted a shovel in my life until I came here."

"You're gettin' pretty good at it," Clyde told him.

"No I ain't. It's gonna kill me."

Clyde looked closely at Williams. His face was gaunt, and even though they spent every day in the sun, the skin around his eyes and forehead was colorless. He looked as if he might faint at any moment.

"To tell ya the truth," Clyde said, "ya look like you're sick, like ya don't feel good."

Tears came to Williams's eyes. "I don't. I tell ya, this place is gonna kill me unless I do somethin' about it."

Clyde looked quizzically at him.

"I've been trying to get up nerve to cut off my foot, but I just can't make myself do it," Williams confided.

"That's pretty drastic," said Clyde.

"Yeah, I know," replied Williams.

Clyde thought for a moment. "Ya know, ya wouldn't have to cut off the whole foot. The big toe would do. That'd probably be enough to get you a soft job at The Walls."

"Anything to get outta here. Listen, Clyde, I've tried to do it and can't. You've been a good friend. Would you do it for me?"

Clyde pursed his lips together. "I don't know. Let me think about it a bit."

Clyde looked over at Williams as they were jogging to the field that morning. It appeared that Williams could barely put one foot in front of the other, and he had a fixed look of anguish and exhaustion on his face. "Okay, we'll do it when we get out there," Clyde said as they ran.

Williams smiled and nodded his head. It was the first time that Clyde could remember seeing him smile.

The squad was still digging ditches, Williams again working between Clyde and Barney. When Clyde was about thigh-deep in his section of the ditch, he called over to the mounted guard. "Boss, kin I get an ax? Ran into a big root."

The guard nodded his head. Clyde climbed up and walked over to the nearby water wagon that carried three axes for the purpose of chopping out roots or clearing small trees. He returned to the ditch and waited for the guard to walk his horse toward the other end of the ditch.

"You ready?" Clyde asked.

Williams nodded, then slowly stuck out his foot, and clenched his eyelids shut, wrinkling his entire face in anticipation of the pain.

Whapppp.

The ax came down quickly, cutting through Williams's boot. It appeared to have severed the big toe on the right foot.

"Ahhhhhhhh!" screamed Williams, instantly drawing the attention of every man in the squad.

"His foot got in the way!" yelled Clyde. "Are you all right? Are you all right?" Clyde asked to make it look like an accident.

"My toe! My toe!" moaned Williams through clenched teeth.

The guard slowly walked his horse over where the "accident" had occurred. Still on horseback, he simply nodded with his head in the direction of the water wagon. Clyde and Barney helped Williams out of the ditch and loaded him onto the water wagon. Another inmate drove the wagon to the infirmary, while Clyde and Barney returned to digging ditches.

Williams spent the afternoon in the infirmary, where the doctor discovered that the ax had cut through the top layer of flesh and the bone but not through the flesh at the bottom of the toe. He stitched the torn flesh and bandaged it. The next morning Williams was made to fall in with the squad as if nothing had happened. Clyde and Barney helped him hobble out to the fields and finish his work for many days after that.

Clyde vowed that he would never cut off a toe or finger. He wanted all his toes for running away from Retrieve and all his fingers for shooting while he escaped.

Six weeks later Clyde had his first visitor. His father made the long drive on a Saturday, spent the night in the nearby town of Angleton, and drove to the farm on Sunday. They sat in a special area where prisoners and visitors were separated by a heavy mesh screen. They each held a hand to the mesh so that their hands were touching.

Rees told Clyde what each member of the family was doing and asked about life at Retrieve. Clyde bitterly told him.

"It sounds tough," Rees said earnestly. "But I'm glad to see that you've still got your religion," he added, motioning to the Bible Clyde held in his hand.

"That's somethin' I wanted to talk to you about, Daddy,"

Clyde stated firmly. "I'm not readin' this Bible, and I ain't got no religion. The only reason I've got this Bible with me today is to give it back to you. As far as I'm concerned, the only thing this book is good for is to roll cigarettes with the paper."

"Now that's no way to talk about God's Word, Clyde."

"God's Word?" Clyde shot back quickly. "There ain't no God, and He ain't got no word. If there was a God, He wouldn't let me be rottin' in a hellhole like this!"

"Clyde, there is a God, and He's probably your only hope," Rees replied quietly with a sense of urgency in his voice.

"I don't see you doin' too much about it," Clyde retorted.

Rees didn't answer. He looked sadly at the floor.

Clyde hadn't intended to lash out at his father. He loved him. But he wanted his father to know how he felt about the religion business. In a moment Rees talked about how his business was going, and the subject of religion was not mentioned again. At the conclusion of the visit, Clyde handed the Bible to the guard in the visiting area and asked him to return it to his father.

Chapter
15

IT WAS SPRING, 1932, with its inevitable long, hot, muggy days. Clyde found that his clothing and sheets became filthy in a week's time, and his underwear would become unwearable. Clyde, along with most of the other inmates, chose to sleep naked. Then they were totally exposed to the mosquitoes that invaded the barracks every night during warm weather, and to the ever-present bedbugs.

A torrential downpour for three days and nights made spring planting impossible. So the men dug ditches in the rain. They were supplied only with hoes and were told to dig ditches eight feet deep. Clyde resented this order. He knew it was busy work, since these particular ditches weren't needed, and even if they were, there was no need to make them eight feet deep. Besides, it was twice as hard to dig a ditch with a hoe as it was with a shovel.

A big man standing taller than six feet and weighing more than two hundred pounds worked beside Clyde in the rain one day. Every time the guard turned his back, the big man would sing loudly. His song selection was limited to, "The music goes around and 'round ohhhhhh, and it comes out here."

After the other prisoner had broken into song a few times,

the guard approached him and Clyde. "If you men don't stop yellin', I'll put you in the hole," he said. They kept working, but as soon as the guard started to ride away, the man picked up the song again. The guard quickly reined his horse around. "I thought I told you two to shut up!"

"I wasn't yellin', Boss," replied Clyde.

"Are you calling me a liar?" countered the guard.

"That's what you are if you say I was making noise," Clyde yelled back.

"You stand right there and don't move," he ordered, pointing to Clyde. "And you," he said, pointing to the big man who had been singing, "get back to work." Both men obeyed, and the guard galloped away on his horse. He returned with the new field boss, whose job it was to oversee the work of several squads. The field boss had been on the job just a few days, and Clyde inwardly felt the man didn't have what it took to do his job.

The two halted their horses about twenty-five feet from where Clyde stood. "You think you're bad, don't ya?" the field boss taunted, shaking his shotgun at Clyde. "I oughtta blow your d—— head off!"

The men had quit digging in the ditch behind him and were watching. If Clyde backed down, he would be a coward. If he stood up to the new field boss, he would show his fellow prisoners how tough he really was. "Why don'tcha, yella belly!" Clyde taunted. "It takes guts to kill a man, and you ain't got 'em." Holding the hoe in his hand, Clyde reared back and threw it in the direction of the field boss. It sailed past the man's head and landed in the mud behind him. The field boss leveled the barrel of his shotgun at Clyde.

Clyde tore open the front of his shirt, popping buttons and exposing his bare chest. "Put it right here!" yelled Clyde. "You ain't got the guts, you cowardly b——!"

The field boss held his aim momentarily, then lowered the barrel of the shotgun, and backed his horse away. The field captain heard the commotion and rode over to investigate. Clyde's squad was now finished with that section of the ditch and ready to move down. "Fall in with your squad, Thompson," the field captain ordered. Clyde obeyed. The captain looked over at Clyde's hoe sticking in the mud. "If you want that hoe, you'd better get it."

Clyde walked over to the hoe and picked it up but had second thoughts. "But if I'm going to the hole tonight," he yelled to the captain, "I don't want it."

"You're d—— sure going into the hole," the captain said pointedly.

"Then to h—— with the hoe," said Clyde, flinging it to one side.

"I guess you want to fight me, too," stated the captain.

"No, captain," Clyde answered. "I know you got some guts and kin fight. But you take away that field boss's shotgun and put him down on the ground with me, and I'll show you what I do to a yella-bellied b—— that threatens to kill me."

"Jack," said the captain to the field boss, "give me your gun, get down there, and teach 'im a lesson."

"No, captain," he answered.

"I said get down there and fight him!" the captain insisted. The field boss again refused.

"Give me your gun, stop by the office, and draw your pay 'cause you're through here," the captain told him. The man handed his shotgun to the captain, trotted off on horseback, and was never again seen by the men at the farm.

Clyde retrieved the hoe and fell back in with his squad. "Boy, you really showed 'em," said Barney, patting Clyde on the back.

"You really put him down, kid," added an older prisoner. "I've never seen a field boss fired like that before."

"He was a gutless worm," answered Clyde, who felt that he had won the battle and enhanced his fellow prisoners at the same time.

That night Clyde found that he had lost the war. The captain pulled Clyde out of line as they were marching to chow and took him over to the small wooden building known as "the solitary shack." It contained wooden cubicles that measured three feet high, three feet wide, and five feet long. Clyde was stripped, and his hands were secured behind his back with handcuffs. A large chain was wrapped around both his feet and then looped over the chain that connected the handcuffs. The chain was drawn so tightly that his feet went into the air, and a padlock was put on the chain to hold him in that position. Clyde was carried to one of the cubicles and shoved in; then the door was locked, leaving him in complete darkness.

The pressure of his legs pulling against his hands caused the handcuffs to cut into his wrists. Mosquitoes feasted freely on his face and body, but there was nothing he could do about it. He would lie in one position for two or three minutes until the wooden floor felt like a rock jutting into his body. Then he would change positions, creating more pressure on his hands and feet as he moved. His hands began to swell.

If I could have taken on that field boss with my fists, Clyde thought, filled with anger and nagging pain, *I'd have ripped the b—— to pieces!* Clyde pictured the way the fight would have gone. He would have landed solid punches to the field boss's face until the man was wallowing in the mud, begging for mercy.

I'm smaller than most, Clyde thought, *but I'm tougher.*

Clyde's mind went back to his boyhood days when the family lived in Oklahoma. He'd never had a haircut, and the long, blond locks flowed down past his shoulders. Rees knew a man who claimed to know Buffalo Bill, and this man had promised to help the Thompsons get Clyde into the wild west show.

The thought of show business and fame appealed to the eight-year-old Clyde, but having to put up with the hair flowing down over his shoulders didn't. Not only was it a nuisance,

127

he had also been mistaken for a girl on many occasions and gotten into plenty of fights.

Finally tired of waiting for Buffalo Bill, Clyde one day walked quietly into the living room of the small, wooden house his family rented. His mother was there sewing; a baby daughter slept on a blanket beside her. His father was out of town conducting a revival meeting. Clyde snitched a pair of scissors and went into the kitchen. Not too carefully, he whacked away and watched his golden curls fall onto the wooden floor. Then he walked back into the living room.

"Hello," said Clyde, attempting to attract attention to himself without sounding guilty.

"Not now, Clyde," replied his mother, concentrating on her sewing but sneaking a quick glance at the baby.

"Mommy," Clyde insisted.

"What is it?" said Dolly impatiently at the same time she looked up. When she saw Clyde, she knew. Aghast, because any chance of Clyde's getting on with Buffalo Bill was now gone, her mouth dropped. "What have you done?"

Reacting to her look of horror, all Clyde could do was point vaguely to the place where his hair had fallen over his shoulders just a few minutes earlier. His mother started to cry; the baby woke up and she, too, cried. Clyde tried to console his mother but was swatted several times. Then he cried.

That night his mother put a bowl over his head and finished cutting his hair.

The next week the family learned that Buffalo Bill had died two months earlier.

A building tender came in once a day with bread and water to feed Clyde. The cuffs were removed so he could eat, but his hands were so swollen that he couldn't hold anything. The building tender would hand-feed him and pour water into his mouth before securing the cuffs behind his back again.

The incident that got Clyde into his predicament occurred

on a Saturday afternoon. On Sunday he thought about Barney and the others taking it easy in the barracks. On Monday morning, he could hear them falling into squads outside the barracks, getting ready to run to the fields. Clyde wished he could join them. He had never thought he would be in a position to be happy for the labor in the fields. But now he longed for it.

Clyde's throat was parched, and his stomach hurt from hunger. His hands were numb, and they ached from a lack of circulation. It seemed as if there wasn't an inch of Clyde's body that didn't itch from mosquito bites. In the daytime it was hot and muggy outside. Inside Clyde's wooden cubicle it was smothering hot. During the nights Clyde was kept awake by his own shivering and the buzzing of what sounded like dozens of mosquitoes.

Clyde lived for the twenty-five or thirty minutes each day when the building tender would take off the cuffs and allow him to sit up. The water refreshed him, and though there wasn't much of it, the bread tasted good. Then the building tender would lock Clyde back into his painful position and shove him into the pitch black of the cubicle for another twenty-three hours and thirty minutes. Within moments of being returned to the hole, Clyde yearned for his brief respite the next day.

I'll pay back all the s—— of b—— for this pain, Clyde said to himself, in his mind machine-gunning a bunch of guards as they screamed for mercy. *But there'll be no mercy for those b——!* He longed for a knife to slowly slit the throat of the field boss who had been fired.

Clyde knew there was nothing he wouldn't do to escape. *I'll kill 'em all,* he pledged inwardly.

Clyde remembered how quickly time passed on death row. In contrast, time in the hole limped along painfully. When a week passed, Clyde had hopes of being released on Saturday morning. But nothing changed. Then Sunday morning came. Still nothing. Finally they got him on Monday morning while it was still dark, nine days after he'd been thrown in the hole. When the chains and handcuffs were removed, Clyde could barely move. A building tender helped him to put on his clothes. By the time he was dressed, the men were falling into their squads outside the barracks. Clyde was told to join them, and he painfully hobbled over to join his group.

Though Barney tried to help him, Clyde couldn't keep up as they trotted to the field that morning. Feeling sorry for Clyde, the guard pulled the squad out of line and had them go slower.

Clyde couldn't hold his own in the field for the first two days, and the guard seemed to take his swollen hands as evidence that he wasn't able to do any better. Clyde did the best he could, but inwardly he vowed more intensely to find a means of escape.

On August 13, 1932, a severe hurricane hit the Texas coast at Brazoria County, where Retrieve was located. The sky became black with hues of green and purple. The men were locked in the barracks. A strong wind blew for a while, and then it became deadly still. An eerie feeling pervaded, and not one prisoner spoke.

Occasionally a single engine airplane would fly over the farm. When it did, all the prisoners would look up to see it because airplanes were still a novelty. From their visitors, prisoners heard about Charles Lindbergh and Amelia Earhart, who were often in the newspaper headlines of 1932. After the dead still, there was a noise that sounded like a thousand airplanes approaching.

Clyde saw men down on their knees, praying to God that they would be spared. Clyde was surprised at some who prayed. They just didn't seem like the type. Clyde steadfastly refused, because he clung to the notion that if there was a God, which he seriously doubted, Clyde didn't want to have anything to do with Him.

The wind hit right after they heard the noise. The building rattled and groaned as though it might fly apart. Some men cried. Others prayed out loud. A few laughed nervously. Most thought they were about to die. The wind continued for about ten minutes before the roaring noise went off into the distance. Everyone was relieved. The building was still standing, but in one place, two walls had been separated. Clyde tried to crawl through, but he couldn't fit.

Euphoria over the passing of the storm was short-lived. The dead calm and eerie quietness returned within a few minutes after the winds had passed. The air was heavy, almost suffocating. Then came the noise again, followed by the winds. They subsided again, and the building was still intact. There was a third dead still, and the wind returned, even stronger than before. The entire building leaned but didn't fall. After fifteen more minutes, it passed.

The next morning the men fell in line only to find they would have no breakfast. The kitchen had been blown away, as had most of the smaller buildings in the immediate area. Huge poles holding power lines had been broken into pieces small enough to fit into a wood-burning stove. The men were in their squads at daybreak, cleaning up the area. A makeshift kitchen was put together to give them their noon meal.

Although no one at Retrieve was killed, the hurricane claimed the lives of forty persons in the surrounding area and injured two hundred more.

Chapter
16

ONE OF CLYDE'S preoccupations in the summer of 1928, just before he shot the O'Dell boys, was robbing bee trees. He would find a place where honey bees were, sometimes in patches of wildflowers, sometimes at a watering hole. Clyde would drop a pinch of flour on a bee and then watch it take off. The bee would always head directly to the hive so that Clyde would know in which direction the hive was located. To find out the distance of the hive, he would keep track of how long it took the marked bee to fly to the nest and return to the flower patch or watering hole. With this information, Clyde would know about how far to walk before looking for the bee tree. He didn't have beekeepers' paraphernalia, so it was a matter of getting the honey without being stung excessively. Except for being caught by a swarm on one occasion, the stings were minimal.

While resting in the woods as they hunted for a hive one day, Clyde and his brother Bill puzzled over a slight mound in the ground. The raised area had a different look from that of the surrounding soil. Rocks on the surface looked as if they might have come from deeper in the soil. The raised area measured about twenty feet long and ten feet wide. At one side there was a V-shaped stone sticking out of the ground about three feet. At each corner there were similar yet smaller stones protruding about one foot. "Reckon this is where the Spanish buried that gold?" questioned Clyde.

Bill laughed. And there was nothing more said about it as they continued to search for a nearby bee tree.

According to legend, sometimes repeated by old-timers in the area, centuries earlier the Spaniards had journeyed from Mexico into what later became Texas to establish a capital city, from which Spain could rule the new world, in the central part of North America. Carrying mule-loads of gold, the Spaniards were surrounded by Indians somewhere in the area of what became Cisco, Texas. It seemed inevitable that they were about to be attacked by the Indians, so the Spaniards dug a hole and buried the gold. They then piled wood on top of the turned-up earth to hide their cache. Only two of the men lived through the Indian attack, and one of them was severely wounded. He died within three days. The sole survivor managed to return to Mexico and tell his story, but he, too, died before he could form an expedition to recover the gold.

Adding credence to the legend was the fact that Clyde's uncle had found the skeletal remains of seven persons in a washed-out creek bed shortly after Clyde and his family had moved to Leeray. The skeletons were examined by doctors who concluded that the bones belonged to the Spaniards who had died in battle with the Indians. When this news became public, treasure hunters had come from as far away as New York. Some stayed with Clyde's uncle, who also caught "gold fever." They searched for four or five miles in every direction from where the skeletons had been found but only turned up occasional arrowheads. The treasure hunters had finally gone home, and the locals who had caught the fever, including Clyde's uncle, went back to farming.

The area where Clyde and Bill had rested was three or four miles from where most of the treasure hunting had gone on.

Maybe the Spaniards had buried the treasure and then got into a running battle with the Indians, accounting for the skeletons located several miles away, Clyde speculated.

Bill and Clyde found the bee tree nearby, took the honey, and returned home. Clyde always intended to return to the spot with a pick and shovel but never found the time to do it before he was arrested.

It was January, 1933, and Clyde had been at Retrieve for a year. While working in the fields, his thoughts frequently returned to the place that he and Bill had discovered in the woods. Clyde was sure the gold was located there, and that gold would be the answer to all his problems. It would allow him to move to a foreign country and live like a king. Or, he could assume a new identity and buy a mansion in New York or San Francisco. But first he would have to escape from the hellhole prison farm. He knew that would be no easy matter.

Clyde had seen several inmates try to escape, all unsuccessfully. An escape attempt usually cost a prisoner his life. A few months earlier one of the prisoners had surprised a guard, taken his shotgun and pistol, and made off into the woods on the guard's horse. The guards had gone after the escapee armed with rifles and a pack of bloodhounds. A guard was winged by a shot from the pistol before the inmate was shot and killed. After that, guards in the fields no longer carried pistols.

Barney and Clyde still worked together in the same squad and plotted methods of escaping, even though no one else had been successful. They thought maybe they were smart enough to come up with a plan that hadn't been thought of before. Working with them on escape plans were Neil Hobson and E. L. "Shotgun" Lester, both in their midtwenties. Lester had received his nickname for pulling a series of armed robberies with a shotgun. He was finally caught and sentenced to fifty years. Hobson had a thirty-five-year sentence for armed robbery.

Inmate Tommy Ries, who had a large red birthmark on his face, told all the prisoners that he wanted in on any escape plans. Ries claimed he had been given thirty-five years for robbery, but someone heard that he had actually been convicted of rape. He wasn't included in the plans.

The rumor that Ries was a rapist was wrong. He had, in fact, been given a thirty-five-year sentence for robbing a seventy-five-year-old Galveston woman of about seven thousand dollars in 1930. Ries was said to have slugged the woman before taking her money. But what happened after that would have put Ries even further down on the prison pecking order than a rapist. Ries was known as "The Squealer" by inmates incarcerated elsewhere in the TDC.

With the help of outsiders, Ries had escaped from the Galveston jail and drove an automobile across the Galveston causeway through a hail of police bullets. During the escape, a guard at the jail was shot and killed. Ries was later recaptured in Houston—the birthmark on his face leading to a quick identification. Apparently in an attempt to avoid the murder rap for the guard, Ries turned state's evidence and named the men, Roy Britton and Sam Rivette, who had helped spring him from the jail. Both Britton and Rivette got ten years for helping Ries escape. The Fort-Worth *Star-Telegram* reported that Ries pinned the murder on Britton, but authorities never found enough evidence to charge anyone.

Since it was winter, the men were chopping down trees and "grubbing" roots, clearing the land for future planting. Clyde, Barney, Hobson, and Lester thought the right opportunity for escape might come during this work. Hobson had been having trouble with one of the building tenders. He finally lost his temper and struck at the man. With that, two building tenders ganged up on Hobson and gave him a beating that sent him to the hospital for three weeks. As a result of his absence, Ries was reassigned to work more closely with Clyde, Barney, and Lester. Thus, despite their distrust of him, he had to be included in the escape plans, because he would be present during the most crucial planning.

The right day for escape came as Clyde's squad was working in woods about a mile from the rest of the prisoners. It was January 19, 1933. Clyde, Barney, Lester, and Ries were chopping down a huge oak tree. Another group from their squad was chopping down another oak about one hundred yards away. There was one guard between the two groups, and that morning he seemed to divide his time equally between them. Every time he got out of earshot, the four talked about escaping. It wouldn't be easy.

Where they worked was about seventy-five yards from a fence. Then there was a plowed field that was about two hundred yards wide. After that there was another fence. And beyond the second fence was about one hundred yards of ground that had been cleared of underbrush. In order to succeed, they would have to make it into the underbrush that lay beyond the cleared land. Since there was just one guard with a double-barreled shotgun, at least two of the four men would be able to make it to the underbrush. After that, whoever made it would have to run as fast as he could.

That morning neither of the two groups in the squad had been able to cut through the trunks of the big oaks. They rejoined at noon and jogged the two miles back to the chow hall for lunch. When they returned to chopping, the four cemented their plan. They noticed that the other group would soon chop through the trunk of their tree. It would fall and distract the guard temporarily. That was when they would make their run for it. From where Ries stood as he chopped, he could see the other group. He would give the others the signal at the right time.

Clyde's hands sweated in anticipation. It was his first chance at freedom in over four years. It would be tough. He might be shot. But he considered it well worth the chance. The gold and a new life were waiting for him.

"How they doin' over there, Tommy?" Clyde asked while taking a half-hearted whack at the oak with his ax.

"Looks like it might be a few more minutes," Ries told him.

"When it happens, we're jus' gonna have to run like h——," said Clyde to no one in particular. He knew he would be at a disadvantage because he had short legs and had never been a fast runner. The tall, slender Lester could really move and probably had the best chance of making it.

It was less than an hour after returning from the chow hall when someone from the other group yelled, "Timber!" as the huge oak crashed through the underbrush to the ground.

"Get ready!" said Ries anxiously. Clyde, Barney, Lester, and Ries still chopped but were poised for action. Ries watched as the guard galloped to where the other group was standing. The guard got off his horse.

"Okay, now!" exclaimed Ries.

With that, Lester, Barney, and Clyde dashed toward the first fence. As he ran, Clyde turned around to see that Ries was still standing by the tree. Ries was waving his hands and yelling, "Hey, Boss! Boss! Boss! They're runnin' for it!"

Oh, no, thought Clyde. *We should have known better than to trust a rapist.*

But it was too late to change the plan. Lester was in the lead, followed by Barney and then Clyde. When they came to the first fence, Lester hurdled it, and Barney vaulted over. Clyde didn't think he could get over, so he squirmed under the bottom wire that was some six inches off the ground. As he ran in the plowed field, the dirt gave way beneath his feet. It was like trying to run in a dream. But he knew it wasn't a dream and the guard would be shooting a load of buckshot at any moment.

The inevitable blast came, and Barney went face down into

the dirt. Then there was a second shot, and Lester tumbled. Clyde kept running. When he reached the place where Barney had fallen, Barney was trying to get back to his feet.

"Come on, we can still make it!" Clyde urged.

Barney staggered up with blood spurting from his right shoulder and started running again, soon catching up with Clyde. They were headed toward the second fence when, off to their left, they spotted a second guard cantering his horse toward them on the outside of the second fence. Clyde and Barney veered to the right, aiming for the fence at an angle. They reached the fence and ran down the fence line. The guard was on the other side just a short way behind them and didn't seem to be in any particular hurry. He knew they had to cross the fence to escape and he would have no trouble catching them.

"Can't outrun the horse," panted Barney. "Gotta cross the fence."

Barney jumped over the fence, and Clyde crawled under. The two then headed across the cleared land toward the underbrush with Barney in the lead. Clyde could hear the pounding hoof beats of the horse bearing down behind him. He looked around to see the mounted guard only twenty-five or thirty feet to the rear leveling the shotgun toward his head. Clyde instinctively ducked the moment the guard squeezed the trigger. Clyde's hat flew off, and he rolled to the ground in a heap.

The guard picked up his pace and had no trouble catching Barney. "Stop, or I'll kill you, too!" he ordered. Barney halted, the back of his shirt soaked with blood. Barney turned around to face the guard and to see Clyde lying motionless, face down on the ground. On the other side of the fence was Lester, who hadn't moved from where he had first fallen.

"Let's go," said the guard, directing him with the barrel of his shotgun to where Clyde lay. Barney walked slowly toward his fallen friend, the guard walking the horse behind him.

"Turn the s—— of a b—— over to see if he's dead," ordered

the guard. Barney bent over and started to touch Clyde's shoulder. But just before he did, Clyde rolled over and got up sheepishly. The buckshot had taken off his hat but hadn't touched his head. Clyde was playing possum, hoping the guard might leave him for dead. The guard turned white, as though he had seen a ghost. Then his wide-eyed expression turned to anger. "I ought to kill both you s—— of b—— right here!" snarled the guard with rage. But Barney and Clyde knew it would take two shots to kill them, and the guard had already discharged one of the barrels of his shotgun. He wasn't likely to shoot one of them, because the other could make a dash for the woods while he was reloading.

"Let's go," the guard said finally, pointing them in the direction from which they had run. They walked the long way along the outside of the fence and back to their squad. The shotgun fire had alerted everyone on Retrieve that there was some sort of trouble, and the captain had ridden over to find out what had happened. He arrived about the time Clyde and Barney were returning to their squad. Still on his horse, the captain at first went toward Barney but then reined away when he saw Barney's blood-soaked shirt.

He walked his horse toward Clyde. "You b—— had to wait 'til I was over on the other side of the farm to make a run for it. Well, it's a d—— good thing for ya that I didn't catch ya. I woulda left ya both out in the woods, dead!" Swinging his blackjack, the captain caught Clyde behind the left ear. Clyde fell to the ground, letting out an unconscious moan from the blow and feeling a kind of hollowness in his head. The captain turned his horse around and took one of his feet out of the stirrup. The 250-pound captain had a determined scowl on his face, and Clyde thought the captain was going to jump on him. Clyde tried to move but couldn't. He seemed to be paralyzed from the blow to the head. With all his might, Clyde tried to roll, move, do anything to get out of the way of the captain who was coming down on him, boots first.

Clyde yelled and felt sudden pain shoot through his entire body as he heard his ribs snapping like dry twigs. Muttering curses under his breath, the captain let loose with a series of kicks to Clyde's body and face. The frightened Clyde tried to cover himself, but his arms wouldn't work. He was still paralyzed. He grimaced in pain with the continual thuds of the captain's boots against his body. Suddenly Clyde regained the use of his arms and partially absorbed the captain's kicks with his hands and forearms.

The captain left Clyde, moaning and rolling on the ground in pain, and ordered Barney and three other inmates to carry Lester from where he lay in the field. Clyde finally struggled to his feet as they carried Lester to the water wagon. Lester had been hit in the back and went into convulsions as they hoisted him onto the wagon. Bent over with pain, Clyde walked to the wagon. He and Barney were told to hold Lester as they rode back to the infirmary. The convulsions continued as they rode.

About halfway to the infirmary, Lester regained consciousness. He was blue around the lips and gasped for air, seemingly unable to catch his breath. Clyde was holding Lester's head in his lap. "Hold on, Shotgun," Clyde told him. "We'll have ya to the doctor in a little bit."

"Tommy Ries is the cause of all this," Lester managed to say between gasps. "Promise me you'll kill 'im for it."

"If you don't live to do it, I will," Clyde promised.

"I'm dyin'," gasped Lester. "Tell my sister I love her."

"Where does she live?" Clyde asked.

"Fort Worth," whispered Lester. He sighed, his head turned to one side, and his eyes remained open. He was dead. Clyde later tried to find out the sister's name, but he never did and was never able to write her. His other promise, however, remained foremost in his mind.

Chapter
17

CLYDE KNEW that Tommy Ries would pay for squealing. Because of Ries, Lester was dead, Barney was wounded, and Clyde had three broken ribs. A good chance of getting out of the Retrieve hellhole was gone, too. Whether Ries would pay for it with his life or just short of it, Clyde wasn't sure. But he was certain Ries would pay.

After they delivered Lester's body to the morgue, Barney was taken to the infirmary. Clyde wanted to visit the infirmary, too. His ribs hurt, and his head ached from the blackjack blow. With his fingers, Clyde could feel the three ribs popping in and out of place.

"H——, no! You ain't gonna visit no infirmary," the captain informed Clyde. "And you ain't gonna stand around here restin', either. It's time you went back to work. So start runnin'."

Clyde started jogging back to his squad, bent forward from the jutting pain in his ribs. The captain remounted his horse and galloped up beside Clyde, swinging the blackjack.

"Pick it up, Thompson."

Clyde ran faster.

"I said, pick it up, Thompson!"

Clyde was now running at nearly full speed, pain shooting through his body.

"I ought to kill ya and say ya tried to get away," the captain shouted angrily. "S—— of a b——, try to get away from me! But I think I'll just give ya a belly full of runnin' instead. Now let's pick it up!"

Clyde was forced to sprint the two miles back to his squad, feeling continual pain and gasping for breath. The captain was beside him all the way, swinging the blackjack. *Next time I try to escape, I'll have a gun in my hand. Then we'll see who does the runnin'*, Clyde inwardly vowed. Clyde hated the captain, Retrieve, and all the guards and building tenders. But most of all he hated Ries, the squealer.

When Clyde returned to the squad, he was put back to work chopping on a tree. Ries was still with his squad, but Clyde was too tired and painracked to say anything to him. He did notice that Ries was staying away from him throughout the day and in the barracks that night. When they returned to the barracks, Barney had already been released from the prison infirmary with a bandage on his shoulder. Clyde was surprised that neither of them was thrown in the hole or put on barrels.

The next morning Clyde's ribs hurt so badly that Barney had to help him put on his shirt. Barney wasn't any better off himself. One arm was immobile. Both knew better than to ask to be excused from working. They ate breakfast and fell in with their squad. Before going to the field, the captain pulled Clyde out of line and told him he had been reassigned to the number one hoe squad. Clyde knew this meant plenty of fast work.

The number one hoe squad was known as the hardest working group at Retrieve. All the men in the squad wore stripes. Most were convicted murderers who had been in trouble at one of the other work farms and sent to Retrieve. A few were like Clyde. They had been reassigned to the squad after running afoul of the guards at Retrieve. They were known to be able to accomplish a task with twice the speed of any other squad. They often hoed, but if they were caught up on hoeing, they were assigned other jobs on the farm. On the morning when Clyde joined them, the squad was digging a huge hole in which to bury a rusting steam locomotive that was beyond repair. The old engine stood on the spur running into the farm. The spur was used to transport crops grown on the farm to the main track some three miles away.

Counting Clyde, there were eighteen men in the squad. They started that morning by digging a hole right beside the old locomotive. Every time Clyde stooped down to pick up a shovelful of dirt, his three broken ribs would pop out of place, causing him to nearly double over from the pain. After ten minutes, Clyde was sweating heavily and feeling as though he was going to keel over.

"You sick?" asked the guard.

"Yes, Boss," Clyde answered. "Every time I bend over, these broken ribs start killin' me."

The guard over this squad was Cy Smith, a man in his mid-twenties who was known to have more education than most of his peers. "Why don't you just sit down and take it easy until you feel better," Smith told him.

Clyde could hardly believe his ears. A guard was telling him not to work and to sit down? Clyde did as he was told. Nearly an hour passed, and the captain rode by, making his rounds.

"Get back to work! What you doin' sittin' down?" he yelled to Clyde.

Clyde got up and started digging again. But as soon as the captain was out of sight, Smith told him to sit down again.

"I hate to do it, Boss," Clyde told Smith, "'cause I don't wanna cause you any trouble with the captain."

"I can cause about as much trouble as anybody around here can give me," Smith replied briskly. "Just sit down and take it easy if you don't feel like working."

Clyde gratefully did as he was told.

In less than an hour the captain rode up again. When he saw Clyde, he shouted, "You s—— of a b——! Yesterday you try to escape and today you're loafin' on the job. Get back to work!"

Clyde started to get up, but Smith pulled his horse between the captain and Clyde. "Stay put!" Smith ordered Clyde.

He calmly turned around to face the captain. "I ordered him to rest because he was sick, Captain."

"Who said he was sick, a doctor?" the captain countered.

"Nope," replied Smith. "I saw that he was sick and told him to rest both times. And I don't like for anybody to order one of my men to do something other than what I've told him to do."

"Okay, Cy," said the captain with a trace of resignation in his voice. He rode away.

Clyde couldn't believe what he had just seen and heard. As he sat there, he understood why Smith ran the fastest squad on the farm. Clyde felt like working his heart out for this guy. And in conversations with others in the squad, Clyde found that all the men felt the same way.

During his year at the farm, Clyde had never seen such a good working relationship as existed between Smith and his lead row man. Smith would rarely talk to the man to give him orders about what to do with the squad. The two seemed to have an unspoken communication.

Smith didn't rant at his men, as did most of the other guards. And he never swore at them. Rarely did one of the men in Smith's squad end up on barrels or in the hole.

It was a wonder, thought Clyde, *how Smith had taken the worst eighteen men at the farm and turned them into the sharpest squad there.*

About a week later, Clyde overheard the captain tell Smith to give Clyde a hard time to make him pay for his escape attempt. "I don't blame him a bit," Smith told the captain. "If I had life, I'd try to get away, too."

Smith sensed that Clyde had overheard the conversation. "I don't blame you for trying to escape from this place," he said to Clyde. "But I hope you never do it when you're working for me. I'd hate to kill you, and it is my sworn duty to stop you if you ever try to escape."

Clyde nodded that he understood. He still planned to escape, but not from Smith. Clyde worked as hard as he could in the days after the escape attempt. His broken ribs continued to pop in and out of place, but the pain gradually subsided.

Nearly a month passed. During that time Clyde never missed an opportunity to badmouth Ries to the other prisoners. Clyde wanted a confrontation.

Ries had heard reports of Clyde's threats. One night after supper he approached Clyde. "You'd better keep your mouth shut about me if you don't wanna get killed," he threatened.

"You'd better get out of here or get ready to do it!" Clyde countered.

Clyde and Barney had a friend who worked in the blacksmith shop. They asked him that night if he could get knives for them. He immediately produced a sharpened, stainless steel dinner knife and handed it to Clyde. He promised to make another for Barney the next day. Clyde tucked the knife into his boot.

On Sunday, February 12, when they were lining up for the noon meal, Clyde and Barney waited to fall in at the end of the line, as usual. Suddenly Clyde heard Barney shout behind him, "Look out, Clyde!" Clyde spun around to see Ries coming at him with a knife. Before Ries reached Clyde, Barney grabbed him from behind.

This was the chance for which Clyde had been waiting. It was his chance to show that you don't squeal on another con and get away with it—especially when it means the chance between freedom and prison, life and death.

Clyde quickly reached into his boot for his own knife. Ries broke free of Barney's grasp and started to come at Clyde again. Barney again grabbed Ries, pinning his arms with a bearhug from behind. Clyde stepped forward and rammed his knife into Ries's chest. Ries let out a high-pitched grunt and kept struggling. Clyde pulled out the knife and then drove it in again. Then again. And again. Ries struggled, but Barney kept his tight grip. Blood squirted all over Barney, Clyde, and the floor. Clyde kept stabbing until Ries quit struggling and let out a final moan. He slumped to the floor when Barney let him go.

Clyde knew there was a good chance that he and Barney would be killed immediately if they were caught by a building tender. Their chances of living would be a lot better if they turned themselves in to a guard.

"Pick up the knife, Barney, and let's get up here!" Clyde yelled, pointing toward the picket area. Barney obeyed, and they ran through the crowd of men who had surrounded them in the barracks. When they approached the picket guard, both covered with blood, the guard drew his gun. Clyde and Barney threw the knives on the floor. They were taken to the main prison office.

Ries died in the prison infirmary within a few minutes. The sheriff and district attorney from the town of Angleton were called. Clyde and Barney were arrested on the charge of murder and taken to the Brazoria County Jail at Angleton. The district attorney announced that he would seek the death penalty for both men. Clyde would be standing trial for his life for the third time.

In the days that followed, a newspaper published a story saying Clyde had started his life of crime at the age of eight when he purposely shot out the eye of a lawyer with a B-B gun. According to the newspaper, Clyde's father had kept him from going to reform school. In fact, Clyde had never owned an air rifle, nor had he ever shot out anybody's eye. *It's just another example,* thought Clyde, *of the newspaper being in cahoots with law officers, prison officials, and everyone else to get me.* Clyde again felt that he was against the rest of the world. And he was tough enough to take whatever they could dish out, whether it was the hole, another ninety-nine years, or the electric chair. What he really yearned for was freedom to be with his family and do the things he'd done before all his troubles started. But they wouldn't let him do that. All they wanted to do was push him around. Clyde sometimes felt like crying, but he wasn't about to show any vulnerability. Weakness on his part would show that they were the winners.

Rees Thompson continued to stick by his son. He secured the services of Frank Judkins, an Eastland attorney who had assisted Prosecutor Sparks in both of Clyde's earlier murder trials. Clyde and Barney were to be tried simultaneously. Both would receive the same verdict and sentence.

While they waited for the trial, Barney's quick wit and singing made the time pass faster. Clyde especially liked Barney's rendition of "Silver Threads Among the Gold." Clyde was sure Barney was good enough to sing on the Grand Ole Opry if he wasn't locked up. "Just don't sing 'The Music Goes Around and 'Round,'" Clyde pleaded.

"And it comes out here?" Barney replied. Both laughed.

When the trial started, fellow prisoners from Retrieve were called as witnesses for the state. They testified that they saw Barney holding Ries and Clyde stabbing him. They made no mention of the fact that Ries had first drawn a knife.

The testimony of his fellow inmates disturbed Clyde. *How could a con turn against another like that?* For their testimony, these men were probably offered better, easier jobs in prison. So they were just watching out for themselves. It made him wonder who he could trust. As in his previous trials, Clyde didn't take the stand in his own behalf. Judkins didn't want the prosecutor to get a chance to ask Clyde questions about the previous murder trials for fear that this might prejudice the jury against Clyde. Barney took the stand and told what had happened, how Ries had come at Clyde from behind with a knife. Two other inmates testified they had seen Ries with a knife.

Before the jury was charged, Judkins made a case for self-defense, while the prosecutor called it out-and-out murder. The jury returned after four hours with the verdict on a slip of paper. It said, "We the jury find the defendants guilty of

147

murder as charged and assess their punishment as life imprisonment." The jury was polled, and it was found that there was little problem in reaching a guilty verdict. The sentence had been the hang-up. Eleven of the jurors had voted to give Clyde and Barney the chair. The final juror could not be persuaded to change his mind about life sentences. Finally, the eleven had relented.

When the verdict was read, Clyde inwardly breathed a sigh of relief, but he didn't show it on the outside. In a way he felt some invincibility—the jury was too timid to send a con as tough as triple-murderer Clyde Thompson to the chair.

Judkins was given fifteen days to ask for a new trial while Clyde and Barney waited in the Angleton jail. It was decided not to appeal Clyde's conviction, since a new trial might result in a death sentence. The request for a new trial was made on Barney's behalf and denied.

At the conclusion of the fifteen days, the captain and a guard rode their horses into Angleton to pick up Clyde and Barney. They were forced to run the seven miles back to the farm. But Clyde knew he was tough enough to take it. Besides, the time in jail had healed his ribs enough so that they no longer hurt when he moved.

Chapter

18

It WAS SUMMER, 1933, and new men were being sent to Retrieve from The Walls. One of these was Roy Thornton, husband of Bonnie Parker. He had been sentenced to fifty years for robbery. He was assigned the bunk beside Clyde's, and the two hit if off almost immediately, although Clyde did most of the talking. Thornton was a quiet man, sometimes given to brooding. He was a year and a half older than Clyde and about the same size. Thornton had dark hair, dark eyes, and several tattoos, one of which was a nude woman on his forearm. Thornton and his wife had been married as teen-agers. They would fight, separate, and then get back together again. During one of their separations, Bonnie had joined Clyde Barrow.

Barrow had first been arrested in 1930, and Bonnie had smuggled a gun into the jail, allowing him to escape. He was subsequently caught and sent to the Eastham prison farm, where he cut off his toe with an ax. He and Clyde Thompson had met in early 1932 at The Walls, shortly before Barrow was paroled from prison.

Teamed with Raymond Hamilton, Bonnie and Clyde made newspaper headlines in the summer of 1932. They committed several robberies and murdered a deputy outside a dance hall in Oklahoma. Newspapers weren't allowed inside the prison, but word of the escapades of Bonnie and Clyde spread quickly among the prisoners. This news grated on Roy Thornton, because he and Bonnie were still legally married. He vowed to kill Barrow if he could ever escape from prison. Barrow must think of him often, he said, because the names "Bonnie and Roy" were tattooed on Bonnie's thigh.

Roy was not good at farm work. He was often behind and ended up standing on barrels. In frustration, he swung at a guard. Instead of being sent to the hole, he was made to stand on a barrel for seven consecutive days and nights. As the week passed, his legs swelled to twice their normal size, and then they turned black. But there was no relenting on the part of the guards. Finally, his legs burst open. He was taken to a hospital, where he spent two months.

After returning from the Angleton jail, Clyde resumed his work with the number one hoe squad. Clyde was a hard worker in the field and especially wanted to do a good job for Cy Smith. But Clyde had a reputation as a troublemaker. Although it was none of Smith's doing and wasn't true, the charge was levied against Clyde that he refused to work in the field.

Punishment for laziness was being hit with the "bat," a punishment Clyde had avoided since he arrived at Retrieve. The bat was a hard leather strap about thirty inches long, two inches wide, and a quarter inch thick. The chunk of leather was fastened to a one-foot wooden handle. Use of the bat was legal in the Texas prison system, but the law stipulated that a prisoner could not be hit more than twenty times. Further, a doctor had to be present during the administration of the punishment. By law, the beating had to stop if blood was drawn.

Clyde feared the beating. He had never seen a man take the bat without screaming because of the pain. Many had begged for the beating to stop. But fear of pain would show vulnerability and weakness. Clyde vowed to take his punishment without crying out. "If I say anything," Clyde related to Barney, "I'll tell 'em to keep on goin'."

"Boy, you sure got guts," Barney told him.

"They ain't gonna break me," Clyde vowed.

Clyde rolled a cigarette and licked it lengthwise to seal the paper as the captain called over three new men who had just arrived at Retrieve. Clyde knew that these men and Barney would have to sit on his arms and legs as a husky guard administered the bat. Their weight would keep him from squirming around. He didn't hold it against them. If they refused, they could receive the same punishment.

Clyde stuck the unlit cigarette in his mouth.

"I wanted you new men to see what happens to lazy prisoners here at Retrieve," said the captain. "And," he added, "you'll get to see a tough guy cry."

The three looked wide-eyed at Clyde as they stood outside the barracks. Others inside were looking through the bars. Several guards had assembled to see how Clyde would take his punishment.

"Awright, shuck 'em off, Thompson," ordered the captain.

Clyde glared at the captain, the unlit cigarette still in his mouth. He unbuttoned the dirty white work shirt, then kicked off his boots, and removed his pants. He stood naked in the midst of them.

"Hit the ground, Thompson," said the captain.

Clyde lay down on the ground on his stomach, feeling the sweat of anxiety on his face and body.

"Now you men sit on his arms and legs."

The four obeyed. Holding the cigarette in his lips, Clyde clenched his teeth for what he knew would be coming. From the way others had screamed, he knew it would be terribly painful. But he renewed his vow of silence.

"Go 'head," said the captain to the guard holding the bat.

The guard brought it down on Clyde's buttocks with all his might. The sharp whack echoed off the nearby building, and pain shot through Clyde's entire body. He then knew why so many others had cried for mercy. The pain of one blow had been nearly unbearable.

The second blow came sooner than he was expecting it, the shock of the bat registering pain from the point of impact to the top of his head. Clyde gritted his teeth almost to the point of breaking them.

The blows came every two or three seconds; Clyde kept count in his mind and remained silent. After each blow, Clyde found himself suddenly gasping for breath through the pain. The intensity of the pain mounted.

Six more to go! Clyde counted to himself.

Five more!

Four!

Three! I'll kill these s—— of b——!

Two!

Clyde took the twentieth lick and still hadn't uttered a sound. He thought it was over when the bat came down on his buttocks again. And once again. Then it was over. The men on his arms and legs rolled off. And Clyde lay there momentarily, pain racking his body. With shaking arms, he got to his hands and knees. Then he stood, dazed, on wobbling legs.

"What you got to say for yourself now, Thompson?" probed the captain.

Clyde still held the unlit cigarette between his lips. He looked at the captain, holding himself as steady as he could. "Got a light?" he managed.

The captain looked away in disgust. To the prisoners who witnessed the event, Clyde had become a hero.

Clyde was taken by the doctor who had witnessed the beating to the prison infirmary. Large chunks of flesh had been torn from his buttocks so that he would always bear scars. The doctor told him the flesh had not been ripped open until the

152

last two or three strokes of the bat. Blood hadn't shown until the very end, according to the doctor. And it was the first time, according to the doctor, that he had seen more than twenty strokes administered. Clyde writhed in pain as the doctor administered iodine to the wounds. In spite of the pain, he felt he had won. Once again they had tried to break him, and they had failed.

After Clyde was released from the infirmary, he limped back to the barracks, where he was approached by Chester Arnold, one of the new men who had sat on him during the beating.

"I don't see how you took that beating without a whimper," said Arnold. "If I ever get it, I hope I can prove half the man you were."

Clyde clasped Arnold's hand. "I'm sure you would do just as well or better," Clyde told him.

The next morning Clyde crawled painfully out of bed. It hurt to take a step. As he was expected to do, Clyde fell in line with his squad.

Temperatures exceeded 100 degrees daily; the humidity was nearly as high. Clyde and the others were accustomed to the hard work in the sweltering heat. It was difficult, but they survived.

But there was no breaking-in period for the new men. They were expected to do the same day's work as the veterans, even though the inmates coming from The Walls may not have been subjected to hard work for two or three years. By noon, Chester Arnold and the other two newcomers had suffered sunstrokes in the field. Arnold died that afternoon in the prison infirmary. When Clyde heard Arnold was dead, he cried.

Chapter
19

CLYDE NEVER INTENDED to stay long at Retrieve, but another eighteen months passed. He had been promoted to lead row man of the number one hoe squad. They were paving the road from Retrieve to Angleton in mid-January, 1935, when the captain rode up on horseback.

"Hey, Thompson, I've got some good news for you," he said.

Clyde looked up. Good news from the captain was scarce.

"The governor has commuted your life sentence to fifteen years," the captain said.

"Whhh—what?" asked Clyde.

"That's right, Thompson, we got word from Huntsville that Ma Ferguson reduced your sentence to fifteen years before she left office," responded the captain, referring to Texas Governor Miriam Ferguson. "It's a good deal for you."

"Why, I guess so," said Clyde, grinning. "It's a great deal. Thanks, Captain."

The captain knew the news was good for Clyde and could make him less defiant. With two life sentences, Clyde had no reason for hope and nothing to lose by trying to escape. With a shorter sentence, he had reason to try to be a model prisoner and accumulate "good time" that would reduce his sentence even more.

Clyde knew his father had hired a new attorney, Everett O'Dowd, but he didn't know what course the attorney was taking. Whatever course it was, Clyde didn't believe it would be successful. Now he had hope for the first time. He might be able to get out in the foreseeable future.

For the next few days, Clyde looked at life differently. Having already spent six years and four months as a prisoner, counting his time in local jails, Clyde might be able to get out legally in three or four more years. He would be only twenty-seven or twenty-eight years old. He could start life over again. Clyde started to pay more attention to the way he addressed the guards, and to his attitude in general. He started thinking about what life would be like on the outside. There was always the possibility of finding the buried gold. Then he could return, buy the stupid prison farm, and give 'em "what for."

Clyde's optimism was short-lived, however. A few days after the outgoing governor reduced his sentence, the attorney general ruled that the governor's actions applied only to the life sentence he had received for the murder of Web O'Dell. He still had to serve a life term for killing Tommy Ries.

"Is life plus fifteen years any better than two life sentences?" Clyde asked Barney angrily after a guard relayed the news of the attorney general's ruling.

"H——, no, it's not," Clyde snarled in answer to his own question. "It's just a part of their game—give ya good news and a reason to get excited, and then take it all away."

Working as the lead row man for Cy Smith, Clyde hadn't grown to like the farm, but he had been close to accepting his plight. Now, much of the bitterness and hatred returned.

"Here, take one of these," said Barney sympathetically as the two walked to the back of the barracks and stood near a barred window. "Maybe it'll help ya feel better."

Barney handed Clyde a cigarette he had rolled out of their own special harvest. It was marijuana, which grew wild on the farm. There had once been a shakedown for booze after the guards observed several prisoners rolling around on the floor, laughing. But no alcoholic beverages were found.

"Thanks," said Clyde. He lit the cigarette and took a long drag. "I'll pay 'em back, Barney. I'll pay 'em back."

One of the frequent topics of conversation in the barracks was sex. All the men bragged of past exploits with whores, girl friends, and other men's wives. Some boasted of several dozen conquests, or of the unusual sex act they had witnessed south of the Rio Grande in an old Mexico border town. After a convict would relate such an experience, it would inevitably be followed by statements of disbelief or by another story topping the previous one. Clyde at first felt left out of these conversations. He listened quietly, sometimes in amazement. Sure, he had heard sex talk before. But nothing like this. As for personal experience, Clyde had none, a fact he never shared—not even with Barney. Eventually Clyde would chip in an occasional tale of his past exploits. It was always one that he had heard earlier and varied slightly.

During daylight hours or when the lights were on, the sex talk centered on male-female relationships. But when the lights went out at night, the sex was man-to-man. While homosexuality was not rampant at Retrieve, it was common. There was the occasional inmate who had been a homosexual on the outside. Far more prevalent, though, were inmates who turned to homosexual behavior to relieve their sexual desires.

Younger prisoners at Retrieve had been transferred to other units because of publicity given to homosexual activities in Texas prisons. Most of the time it occurred between an older prisoner and a younger one who allowed himself or was forced to become a "punk." For this reason the younger prisoners were sent to units where there weren't as many older prisoners.

At age twenty-four, Clyde was the youngest man left at Retrieve. Prison officials had been hesitant to transfer him because of his bad record. Clyde hadn't participated in homosexual acts, and he vowed not to become anybody's punk. But it was difficult not to observe the bed-hopping that went on at night. A prisoner would yell, "Alley, Boss," and the guard would allow him to visit the toilet. Instead of returning to his own bunk, he would crawl in with another man.

Some of the younger prisoners had sex forced on them. If they ratted, it meant serious injury or death. Sometimes, older prisoners made arrangements to have their punks moved to a bunk beside or beneath their own.

Part of what protected Clyde was his reputation as a killer. He held his own in fights within the prison and hadn't backed down. But after the younger prisoners left Retrieve, there was a prisoner who said things that made Clyde bristle. "You're prettier than any woman I ever saw," Everett Melvin had once said to him as Clyde was leaving the showers. Clyde didn't reply; he simply glared at Melvin.

Clyde's friend, Floyd "Dago" Seay, warned him about Melvin. "He's going around sayin' that either you're gonna be his punk or you'll be dead," Seay confided.

Clyde didn't want to force a confrontation. But he was prepared for one. It came on May 29, 1935.

The men had already eaten their evening meal and were preparing for bed. Clyde walked down the alley and rounded the corner between his bunk and the next. Melvin was waiting there for him. Clyde was taken by surprise as Melvin grabbed him around the neck with a hand, attempting to force his head downward.

"It's about time you were my boy," said Melvin as he grabbed Clyde.

Clyde ducked his head and pulled away, instantly drawing a knife that he had obtained from the blacksmith shop. Melvin also had a knife in his boot. He reached down and pulled it, shaking it at Clyde.

"Two can play with shivs, boy!" he growled.

Melvin lunged at Clyde with the knife. Clyde darted to one side and, before Melvin could draw back, plunged the knife into his chest. Melvin had a surprised look on his face. He dropped his knife and started to run. Before he could get away, Clyde methodically sunk his knife into Melvin's chest four more times.

Spurting blood, Melvin ran into the walkway between the bunks. There, he collided with Ed Ebbers, a 6'4", 240-pound inmate who hadn't witnessed the stabbing. The surprised Ebbers thought Melvin was attacking him, and the two scuffled momentarily before Melvin could free himself. Melvin then ran in the direction of the picket and collapsed dead in front of the guard. Clyde ran up behind Melvin and threw his bloody knife down on the floor in front of the picket guard. "He tried to climb in bed with me, Boss!" exclaimed Clyde.

"Well, Cap, it looks like I'm in trouble again," Clyde was quoted in newspapers as saying to Captain Ike Kelley following the stabbing. Clyde was described by the Associated Press writer as a "tow-headed preacher's son with a lust to kill."

Both Clyde and Ebbers were charged with first degree murder and taken to the Angleton jail.

Chapter

20

Rees THOMPSON REFUSED to give up on his son. He again secured the services of Frank Judkins to serve as chief defense counsel. Brazoria County Prosecutor Bob Bassett announced that he would seek the death penalty.

Nearly two months passed before the trial got underway with jury selection on July 22, 1935. *The Houston Chronicle* printed an exclusive story saying that one of its reporters had received a tip in the case. The tipster claimed that the only reason Clyde had committed the murder was that he would have a better chance of escaping from the Angleton jail than from Retrieve. *If that was true,* thought Clyde, *I guess I would have gone ahead and escaped the last time I was here.* But the story was accepted by local law enforcement officials. Sheriff Jimmy Martin requested and received the assistance of Texas Rangers to guard Clyde and to keep a watch on the Retrieve prisoners who would be testifying at the trial. Rangers kept a vigil at Clyde's cell and escorted him to and from the courtroom.

Rees broke down in tears as he visited Clyde in the jail before the trial. The two embraced, and Clyde cried, too.

"Thanks for sticking by me, Daddy," Clyde tearfully told his father.

"I know you're a good boy, and I still believe in you. I always will," Rees replied through his own tears.

The two were seated in the cell.

"You know, Clyde," said Rees, regaining his composure, "a father makes plenty of mistakes when he's raisin' his young 'uns. And I just can't help but believe that some of the turmoil in my life caused you all this trouble."

Clyde looked questioningly at his father. "What do ya mean, Daddy?"

"This isn't easy for me to say. I guess it's hard for a man to admit he was wrong," Rees replied. "Well, there were a lot of problems when you were growin' up. My divorce from your mama and then movin' in with Alma and sayin' she was your aunt, leavin' the church and all."

"It's not your fault, Daddy. I had to kill those guys. It was self-defense."

"Yeah, it is my fault. I just can't help but believe that if I had raised you in the church, things would have turned out differently for you."

"Aww," said Clyde, "I don't know about that."

"Well, whether you believe it or not, I wanted to tell you that. And I wrote you some time ago," Rees continued, "that Alma and I went back to church."

Clyde nodded.

"Well, it's given us a real peace, Clyde. And I wanted you to know, too, that I've gone back to preachin'."

Clyde looked surprised.

"Yep," Rees added. "In Rising Star—south of Cisco."

"Well, how do ya like it?"

"It's a nice little church, Clyde, and I wish you could be there."

Clyde twisted in the bunk on which he sat. "I'm glad ya like it, Daddy, and if I wasn't in here, I'd sure go to hear ya preach. But I ain't changed my mind. Maybe religion is fine for you, but it ain't for me."

Clyde Thompson with his father during Clyde's first trial, in 1928.

Clyde (center) stands outside the Eastland jail during his second trial, in 1929. Flanking him are his father (left) and younger brother, Bentley.

"The Walls," the TDC's main prison in Huntsville, where Clyde spent much of his prison time.

Death row at "The Walls." The closed door at the far end is the green door leading into the death chamber. Clyde narrowly avoided walking "the last mile" through that door. Texas's death row inmates are now kept at the newer Ellis Unit.

Shirley Ann, the little girl who won the hearts of Clyde and Julia, at one year old in 1960. She became their only child.

Clyde and Julia at work in the Lubbock, Texas, jail in 1977.

Shirley's boys, the grandsons Clyde never saw. Joey (left) was born 1980, Jeremy in 1981.

Ron Goodman (left) and Luke Curtis, the men who took over the Huntsville prison ministry in 1977 when Clyde and Julia moved to Lubbock.

"Clyde, I feel so much better gettin' back to where I know I always belonged, and I think you would, too."

Clyde broke eye contact with his father and looked at the floor of his cell, shaking his head negatively.

"I sure wish you'd think about it, Clyde," Rees urged.

Through his talks with prisoners at Retrieve, Prosecutor Bassett felt he could make a good case of premeditated murder. A couple of inmates whom Clyde counted among his friends, Leroy Lamar Case and Dago Seay, agreed to be witnesses for the state.

A murder trial was rare in Angleton, a town of just over one thousand people. And since it was Clyde's second murder trial there and it was receiving a lot of attention from Houston newspapers, local people were curious. A standing-room-only crowd packed the small courtroom.

Case took the witness stand to say that he had overheard a conversation between Clyde and Ed Ebbers. Clyde had said, "We will kill Melvin and get off the farm," according to Case.

"You lie, and you know it!" shouted Clyde as he jumped to his feet. Rees quieted his son.

"We'll have no more outbursts like that in this courtroom," announced Judge M. S. Munson.

Case continued his testimony, saying that he saw Ebbers grab Melvin from behind while Clyde stabbed him to death. Clyde seethed inwardly while shaking his head in disbelief.

Seay was the next to take the stand. He had watched Clyde during Wise's testimony and decided he might be better off toning down the story he originally told Bassett. Ebbers and Melvin were standing together in the barracks "trying to settle a little ol' debt" when the scuffle broke out, according to Seay. After that, he saw Clyde standing there with a knife in his hand.

Though Seay's testimony wasn't as condemning as Wise's, Clyde was livid. Two of his friends were trying to hang a murder conviction on him. He vowed silently to kill them both.

Not all the inmates testified against Clyde. Some were defense witnesses. Judkins hoped that Clyde would be able to avoid the electric chair once again if he could show that Clyde was not of sound mind. He also hoped to build a case for self-defense.

Inmate Russell Brown testified that Clyde sometimes said peculiar things. "He's easy to be talked into anything," said Brown. "I think he's of an unsound mind."

On cross-examination, Bassett wanted to know what, in particular, Clyde had said to make Brown think he was of an unsound mind. Brown pondered for a moment before answering, then his eyes seemed to light up. "One time he said, 'If I was in Africa, I could make soap out of the natives,'" testified Brown, bringing laughter from the courtroom.

Herbert Stanley, a second inmate testifying for the defense, told of Clyde's idea to build an airplane out of farm implements and "go up in the sky and go to sleep."

"At some times he seems sound," added Stanley, "but at other times he talks like a ten- or twelve-year-old child."

After cross-examining Stanley, Bassett addressed the court. "I just wanted to call to your attention that this man is serving a ninety-nine-year sentence for murder, is not a doctor, and has never treated an insanity case."

Effie Webb, Clyde's aunt, traveled from her home in Guymon, Oklahoma. She was the sister of Clyde's mother, Dolly. Mrs. Webb testified that there was insanity on her side of the family. She described Dolly as having "nervous and jerky attacks."

"She is highly emotional, but at times she is very brilliant," Mrs. Webb said of her sister.

In his three previous murder trials, Clyde had never taken the witness stand in his own defense. This time Judkins advised him to testify in order to help build a case of self-defense.

The thought of facing the packed courtroom made Clyde edgy. But after the testimony of Wise and Seay, Clyde was eager to tell his side of the story.

After answering preliminary questions about his identity and age, Clyde called the testimony of Wise and Seay "a frame-up." He vehemently denied the reports that he had entered into a conspiracy with Ebbers to kill Melvin so that the two of them could get to the Angleton jail for an escape.

"Are you crazy?" probed Judkins.

"No," answered Clyde. "I think I am a pretty smart man." This response was not the way Judkins had advised Clyde to answer the question.

In questions concerning the murder of Melvin, Clyde admitted he had stabbed the man. "But I only did what anyone else would have done under the circumstances," he added.

"What circumstances were those?" asked Judkins.

Clyde looked out into the courtroom. He turned to the judge. "This is pretty personal stuff, your honor," said Clyde in a low tone. "I don't think this is the kind of stuff that a lady should hear. D'ya think ya could have the women leave the courtroom?"

The courtroom was full, and people were standing along the back wall. It was hot, and most in the gallery quietly fanned themselves as they watched the proceedings. Nearly three fourths were women. The judge looked out into the courtroom, paused for a minute, and then nodded his head affirmatively.

"At the request of the defendant, we are going to ask all ladies present to leave the courtroom."

The women in the court looked at each other, wondering about the sudden announcement and who would be the first to leave.

"That's right," said the judge, "all you ladies are going to have to leave."

A few women stood up, followed by the rest. There were the sounds of quiet murmurings and the rustling of skirts.

Once the last woman was out the door, the judge nodded to Clyde. Clyde told about the homosexual relations that took place in the prison. He said he had been warned by Seay that Melvin had intentions of either forcing him into a perverted act or killing him. "When he tried to force himself on me, I killed him," Clyde stated.

The trial lasted four days. After a stirring plea by Bassett for the death penalty, the jury was charged. They deliberated five and a half hours before finding Clyde guilty of murder and assessing his sentence as life in prison. Clyde was relieved. Rees sighed heavily before throwing his arms around Clyde and hugging him. Clyde thought he saw a look of dejection on Bassett's face when the verdict was read.

Throughout the trial, newspaper headlines had called Clyde the thrill-killer who had shot Web and Jake O'Dell just to see them kick while they were dying. Clyde was happy when the newspapers ran into legal difficulties in covering his trial.

Judge Munson had told members of the press they could cover the trial, but they could not report daily testimony. Munson said he didn't want the people of Brazoria County reading about details of the crime because that would automatically prejudice potential jurors for the upcoming trial of Ebbers. Reporters went against the judge's wishes, however, and were found in contempt of court. The matter was finally settled by the Texas Court of Criminal Appeals several months later; the higher court ruled in favor of the newspapers.

Following his conviction, Clyde was sent to The Walls at Huntsville for reprocessing. The murder charge against Ed Ebbers was dropped because testimony in Clyde's trial showed he had been an innocent bystander. Clyde was placed in the third tier of a cellblock adjacent to the one-story building housing death row. Just before Clyde stabbed Everett Melvin, the chair had finally caught up with Joe Palmer and Raymond Hamilton, partners in crime with Clyde Barrow and Bonnie Parker. Bonnie and Clyde had been gunned down in Louisiana the previous year. Blackie Thompson had been killed in a gunfight with police in Amarillo in late 1934. This Thompson, no relation to Clyde, had made a daring escape from death row with Hamilton and Palmer. It was the first and only escape from death row in Texas history. Another criminal who had gained notoriety and recently walked the last mile was Ed "Perchmouth" Stanton. Stanton had escaped from the Lubbock jail, killed the sheriff in Dickens, and led police on a long chase. He vowed he'd never be taken alive, but he was.

The authorities had finally been the winners against some of the toughest criminals in Texas. Clyde vowed that it was going to be different for him.

Instead of being sent back to Retrieve, in mid-August, 1935, Clyde was taken to the Central farm in Sugarland, Texas, another of the "lower" farms south of Houston. The unit had been set aside for youthful offenders who were being segregated from the older men in the prison population. At twenty-four, Clyde was one of the oldest prisoners there.

Compared to Retrieve, Central was almost a vacation. Clean clothes were issued twice weekly instead of once a week. The food was better. The men bathed twice weekly, and there was warm water. At Retrieve there had been only cold water, and Clyde could remember taking showers in the winter when there was ice in the shower room. The men at Central walked to the fields at a relatively slow pace. If there were more than three miles to walk, they were taken to the fields in mule-drawn wagons.

Another notable difference was that homosexual relations were rampant at Central. It seemed that about half the men were punks and the other half were "married" to them. Clyde vowed to stick to himself.

Clyde turned twenty-five, and winter came.

One morning the inmates were raking manure near the barn. It was sleeting, and the wind was blowing. Unless they had been sent gloves from home, prisoners didn't have them. Many prisoners started dragging a rake with one hand while sticking the other hand in a pocket. Clyde followed suit. But when he did, the guard yelled, "Get both of those meathooks on that rake handle, Thompson!" Clyde reluctantly took the other hand out of his pocket and kept raking. The other men quickly did the same.

After a while some of the men put a hand in their pockets again. The guard either didn't notice or didn't seem to mind, so Clyde did the same thing. As soon as he did, the guard yelled at him, threatening to throw him in the hole. Clyde and the rest grasped the rake with two hands again.

Another thirty minutes passed, and a few of the men again stuck one hand in a pocket while raking with the other. Clyde followed suit.

"D—— it, Thompson, you really don't pay much attention, do you?" the guard chided. "You really do want to go to the hole, don't you?"

Clyde threw the rake on the ground, put both hands in his pockets, and began to whistle. The other prisoners looked at Clyde with amusement, but none of them dared to imitate him. They all raked with two hands.

The guard didn't say anything; he simply shook his head. The field captain was standing with some prisoners about fifty yards away. The guard caught his attention and motioned for him to come over. The field captain had a quiet conference with the guard.

"Okay, Thompson, let's go!" the field captain ordered after a couple of minutes. He motioned with his hand in the direction of a line of solitary cells a few hundred yards away. Clyde started walking, with the field captain following.

When they arrived at the cells, the field captain said, "Take off your clothes."

Clyde turned around and glared at the man. "I killed the last man who told me to do that!"

About that time the captain of Central walked out the door of his office. He walked toward them and was met halfway by the field captain. Both men strode over to Clyde. The captain was a big man who treated prisoners fairly as long as they obeyed the rules. He did not go out of his way to cause trouble for anyone, and he seemed to have a hard time understanding why someone would run afoul of the regulations. He was known to stammer when he got excited.

He was angry when he approached Clyde. He grabbed Clyde by the hand and in his frustration sort of waltzed Clyde around in a circle, nearly crying. "G—g—gosh, d—d—darn you, ol' C—Clyde Thompson, y—y—you just can't stand p—p—prosperity, son!"

Clyde wanted to laugh at the absurdity of it, but he restrained himself. It was clear that the captain was angry, and if they had been at another farm, Clyde knew the captain wouldn't be dancing with him. Two big trustees were called to hold Clyde while the field captain undressed him. The captain put the handcuffs and leg irons on him. One notable difference from Clyde's experience at Retrieve was that the cuffs were put in front of him rather than behind his back. Clyde was given two blankets and thrown in the hole for a week.

The cold weather continued. Clyde was able to wrap up in the two blankets. It was still cold, but not the twenty-four-hour-a-day torture it had been at Retrieve. Clyde went back to work and stayed out of trouble after his week in the hole.

Several months passed, and the grapevine carried word that prison officials would open a new unit for the most incorrigible prisoners in Texas. Word filtered in through many sources, including visitors, prisoners coming from other units, and occasionally a guard. This new unit was being called "Little Alcatraz," and it was to be located on Eastham farm north of Huntsville.

One day early in 1936, Clyde walked up to a group of prisoners at Central who were talking about whether they would be sent to Little Alcatraz.

"I don't know about you guys, but I'm sure I will," Clyde told them. He was right. Within a week, Uncle Bud's wagon stopped to pick up Clyde for the trip north to Little Alcatraz.

Chapter
21

CLYDE HAD A PLEASANT SURPRISE when the back of the prison truck was opened for his trip to Little Alcatraz. Sitting there chained together were Barney, Ed Ebbers, Roy Thornton, and Raymond Hall, all from Retrieve. It was like a homecoming as Clyde was padlocked to the long chain and the truck headed for The Walls. There, they picked up escape artist Charlie Frazier, David Sedlock, Jack Rice, Richard Sparks, and Tim Roberts. When these ten arrived at Eastham, they were greeted by Austin "Pinky" Avers, Forrest "Goodeye" Gibson, and Robert "Red" Massey.

Clyde liked the new setup. He was included with what were supposed to be the thirteen toughest cons in the Texas prison system. They all had long sentences and hoped to escape. Security would be tougher, but these prisoners had a common goal, and they would work together to accomplish it.

Of the twelve others, Clyde was most intrigued by Frazier, a genuine tough guy who was older than most of his fellow prisoners. Frazier was clever, and he was always happy to discuss his past exploits. He had served time in Texas, Louisiana, and Arkansas, some of the toughest prisons in the country. He was first sent to prison at Huntsville in 1917, when Clyde was only six years old. In the years since then, Frazier had escaped from prison eight times. He had first been convicted for armed robbery and burglary. He later received a life sentence for murder in Arkansas. In Louisiana he had been convicted of shooting with intent to murder and given life plus eighteen years. In September, 1933, Frazier and eleven others had escaped from the Angola State Prison in Louisiana, killing several guards and the warden in the process. He was captured in Texas and returned to the Texas Department of Corrections in November, 1933.

In July, 1934, Frazier had masterminded the escape from death row of Raymond Hamilton, Joe Palmer, and Blackie Thompson. Frazier stood at the bottom of the ladder on the inside of The Walls and let the three with death sentences climb out ahead of him. The fourth man up was shot and fell back on Frazier, and then Frazier, too, was shot. With no treatment for his bullet wound, Frazier was locked in a cell on death row, and the door was welded shut. Lee Simmons resigned as general manager of the TDC in November, 1935, and the day before he left his post, he had the door to Frazier's cell opened. Frazier was given his first bath in sixteen months, and his long beard was cut off. Dave Nelson, who replaced Simmons, had Frazier sent to Little Alcatraz when it opened in 1936.

All the men in Little Alcatraz laughed when Frazier told how he and some partners had returned home one night after robbing a bank to find their house on fire. Neighbors gathered, not knowing that Frazier and the others were bank robbers. There was a lot of ammunition in the house, and Frazier knew it would explode. He explained to the neighbors that they had just stocked up on canned goods. When the explosions from the bullets started, Frazier shook his head in mock dismay and told everyone, "Oh, no, there goes all our canned goods!" The sympathetic neighbors later brought over food for the bank robbers to eat.

Avers, thirty-five, had been one of Frazier's partners on the outside. A slim five feet ten inches, Avers was known as Pinky because of his peaches-and-cream complexion. The fair complexion didn't tell anything about the man, however. His record went back to 1919, when he served five months in Oklahoma for cattle rustling. He later got five years in Oklahoma for car theft.

Since then, Avers had escaped from prison three times in Oklahoma and four times in Texas. After an escape from a Texas prison in 1934, Avers robbed the Metropolitan Hotel in Fort Worth. For this, he was given ninety-nine years. It was known that Avers had driven the getaway car in the death row break. The authorities also believed that he smuggled the guns into The Walls that Frazier and the others had used during the break.

Forrest Gibson was known as Goodeye because he lost an eye in a free-for-all at the Eastham farm in 1932. In the fracas, Gibson had bitten off the left ear of the man who gouged out his eye. An infection set in where the man's ear had been, and the man died a few weeks later. The prisoners joked that Gibson had the bite of a rattlesnake.

The twenty-eight-year-old Gibson had served three years for theft starting in 1931. Two months after his release in 1934, he was found guilty of stealing a car and sentenced to ten years for a second offense of stealing over fifty dollars. Gibson had escaped four times from Texas prisons, and prison officials believed he would stop at nothing in his efforts to escape again. Gibson's last escape had been with Luke Trammel at the Retrieve farm after Clyde left. The two killed guard Felix Smith, took a shotgun and a pistol, and rode off on a horse and a mule. In the two weeks before they were recaptured, Gibson and Trammel had kidnapped several people and taken their cars.

Gibson was given sixty years for his part in the murder of the guard. Ten of the twelve jurors had voted to give him the chair.

His accomplice, Trammel, received the death sentence and was waiting on death row.

Raymond Hall was known as the prison poet. He had written many poems and songs about prison life. Earlier, Hall had jerked a guard from his horse at Retrieve and taken his gun in an escape attempt. He was captured and tried for the murder of a field captain during the aborted escape. Hall had eluded the chair but got another ninety-nine years added to his sentence.

Red Massey was a slight man, about five feet four inches tall and 115 pounds, serving time for robbery. Clyde first met him at Retrieve, where he had helped Red finish his work on many occasions to prevent his being punished. Red was a veteran of the war against the kaiser in Europe. The inmates believed that Red had been affected mentally by his war experience.

The prisoners in Little Alcatraz were divided into two squads for the same kind of work Clyde had been used to at Retrieve. The first squad consisted of those who authorities believed were the most desperate, including Clyde, Frazier, Gibson, Avers, and Hall. The remaining eight made up the second squad. Each squad was assigned its own guard. Additionally, a special high rider was stationed on horseback and kept about fifty yards away from where the men worked in the fields. The high rider, an expert shot, was armed with a high-powered rifle.

Little Alcatraz was a stone and concrete building connected to another wing in the Eastham farm by a picket. There were also a picket area inside Little Alcatraz and a door that led to a larger picket for the other wing. A commissary for prisoners was located in the larger picket, so that if prisoners in Little Alcatraz wanted to purchase something, their picket guard would unlock the door between the two areas and enter the larger picket to get it. A rope dangled down inside the larger picket from a bell hanging above. This bell was used to signal when it was time to get up, go to work, or go to the mess hall, located about forty yards away. The guards' arsenal in the bell tower contained shotguns, pistols, rifles, and ammunition. A stairway from the larger picket led up to the arsenal.

Besides the bunks, Little Alcatraz contained toilets and a shower area. A few days after the men arrived, one prisoner lit a cigarette and tossed the burning match toward the drain in the shower. An explosion followed, blowing the drain cover through the ceiling. The men were told that natural gas in the area would build up in the drain, and the match had ignited it. For a long time afterward the inmates discussed how to use the natural gas to blow a hole in the side of the building, but no means of doing this was ever found.

The prison grapevine carried word that TDC officials were talking with those at the Angola prison in Louisiana about Charlie Frazier. Louisiana officials believed that Frazier would get the death sentence there for murdering the warden at Angola. If it appeared certain that Frazier would get the chair in Louisiana, Texas officials would gladly drop the charges against him and allow him to be extradited to Louisiana.

Knowing this, Frazier had urgent reason to put together some escape plans. He arranged for an accomplice on the outside to hide guns beneath a bridge where the men would be working. The plan was that five men in the number one squad would find these guns, shoot it out with their guard and the high rider, and then escape. But this plan was thwarted when the high rider found the weapons just before the squad got to the bridge. It was several weeks before an alternative plan could be devised.

This time, hidden guns were to be picked up by John Reeds, a diminutive prisoner who drove the Eastham water wagon. Reeds would deliver the guns to Charles Chapman, a bank robber in one of the regular Eastham squads. With some of the men in his squad, Chapman planned to capture his own guard, then run over and take care of the Little Alcatraz guards as all the prisoners were working in the fields. Everyone would then make a run for it.

"This is the day," said Frazier to Clyde as they started work on the appointed day. "Are you ready to see what the free world looks like again?"

"Are you kidding? This is what I've been wanting to do for eight years," answered Clyde.

"Here's what we'll do," explained Frazier. "When Chapman and them come runnin' over, we'll take our guard. I'll take his shotgun, and you can have the pistol. [By this time TDC guards were wearing pistols again.] Then we'll blast our way outta here."

Clyde nodded anxiously.

As he hoed that morning, Clyde had a hard time keeping his mind on his work. It was his first good chance to escape since Lester was killed in the abortive attempt at Retrieve more than three years earlier. And teamed with Frazier, Clyde knew his chances were greatly improved. Every time there was any kind of unusual noise, Clyde would look at Frazier. Each time Frazier would shake his head or shrug his shoulders. Both knew that the real signal would be the sound of gunshots.

Lunch came. Still no shots. About a half hour after lunch, several shots rang out in quick succession. Clyde gave Frazier a quick look. Frazier nodded his head with a slight smile on his face. As the adrenalin pumped through his veins, Clyde could feel himself inwardly shaking with anticipation. He looked in the direction of Chapman's squad and saw nothing.

All the men in the squad stopped working and stared in the direction of the gunfire. A mounted guard yelled to the guard covering Clyde's squad, "Get those men back!" He then rode toward the gunshots.

"Okay, let's go!" ordered the guard, pointing in the direction of Little Alcatraz.

"Ya wanna just sit down and stay here?" Clyde asked Frazier in a whisper.

174

"Nope," Frazier answered dejectedly. "It wouldn't do any good. They ain't comin'."

Clyde's face slowly dropped. Either the guards had prevented Chapman and the others from coming, or there was a double-cross.

Clyde had been designated the lead row man in his squad. It was up to him to set the pace of the squad on the way back to the lockup. He trotted as slowly as he thought he could get away with. Clyde still hoped that Chapman and the others might show up. But even if they didn't, he wanted to give Chapman the benefit of the doubt and help his chances by keeping their guard away from the chase as long as possible.

"Pick it up, Thompson!" ordered the guard.

Clyde obeyed. He trotted the squad faster for about a hundred yards and then slowed down again.

The men were locked up. About an hour later, a pickup driven by a guard pulled up to the Eastham infirmary. The lifeless body of a convict was carried from the back of the truck. The inmates later learned that it was the water boy, Reeds. He had delivered the guns, as promised, and kept one for himself. He then tried to ride away on one of the mules that pulled the water wagon. The guards caught up with him in the woods.

Those who did escape included Chapman and two others. The prisoners at Little Alcatraz were kept locked up for the next three days to make sure the escapees weren't going to return to free them.

The night of the escape, the captain had stopped by. "I guess your little plan didn't work, did it, Frazier?"

Frazier pretended he didn't know what the captain was talking about. But he knew he'd probably be sent to Louisiana before another escape attempt could be organized.

The two other escapees had separated from Chapman as soon as they got away from the farm. Three days later they were shot by a farmer in Oklahoma. One was dead, and the other recovered and was returned to Texas. Chapman had headed for the hills of his native Arkansas and was slain a few months later in a gun battle with state police.

The grapevine proved reliable, much to Frazier's chagrin. On October 8, 1936, he was taken from Little Alcatraz to Louisiana to face trial. A few days later Frazier was shot six times by prison guards. The guards claimed the shooting occurred during an attempted prison break, but the word that came back via the usually reliable grapevine was that it was an execution attempt. Frazier bore the mark of powder burns from being shot at close range. Three bullets had hit him in the stomach, one had struck him in the back, one had hit his chest near the heart, and one had struck his hip. In spite of these injuries, Frazier lived. He stayed in the prison hospital about two weeks before he was released to face the murder trial.

He was found guilty of murdering the warden. But Louisiana authorities had guessed wrong about his sentence. Instead of the electric chair, Frazier was given another life sentence to add to the life plus eighteen years he had already been assessed.

Clyde really admired Frazier. When he left, Clyde knew his chances of escaping from Little Alcatraz were greatly diminished.

Chapter
22

NEW MEN WERE ADDED to bring the number of men
in Little Alcatraz to twenty. Big Ed Ebbers and one of the new
men, Jack King, were named as building tenders for the unit.
They were given blackjacks and long hunting knives, which
they wore in scabbards on their belts. With this power came
abuses of the other prisoners. Clyde watched as Ebbers
knocked crazy Red Massey to the floor and stomped on his
face, breaking his false teeth. Ebbers weighed more than
twice as much as Massey and stood a foot taller. The building
tenders had stayed clear of Clyde, but he swore that he would
kill them if they tried to strong-arm him.

One night the building tenders beat up Richard Sparks and
another inmate who had recently been transferred to the unit.
Clyde knew that crazy Red could do nothing to pay back Ebbers and King, but Sparks was not a man to be trifled with.
Clyde waited to see what would happen next.

Another recent transfer to the wing was a cousin of King, the
second building tender. This inmate was told to tell his cousin
to make himself scarce on a certain night because Ebbers
would be paid back. If King wasn't around, nothing would happen to him. On the appointed night, King was fixing some-

thing in the shower room when Sparks took the metal wagon rod that was used as a poker for the potbellied wood-burning stove. When Ebbers was out of sight of the picket guard, Sparks came up behind him, while a partner stood watch, and hit him soundly over the head with the poker. Ebbers didn't fall, so Sparks hit him again. Staggering, Ebbers grabbed the metal rod with his left hand and pulled his hunting knife from its scabbard with his right. He was too stunned to hold onto the knife, however, and dropped it to the floor. Sparks's partner picked up the knife and stabbed Ebbers five times in the chest. Ebbers continued to stand there for a moment, befuddled. Then he fell forward, hitting the floor with a force that seemed to shake the entire building.

Clyde walked over to the picket guard. "Hey, Boss, there's a dead building tender on the floor in here."

Within minutes, the captain and several guards came into the building, surveyed the situation, and dragged out Ebbers's body. The captain came back, took away King's blackjack and hunting knife, and told him to fall in with the rest of the men the next day. For many weeks thereafter, Little Alcatraz had no building tenders. When new building tenders were named, they were not armed, nor did they abuse the prisoners.

The security at Little Alcatraz was tight, but Clyde continued to seek a way of escaping. During the summer of 1937, he and Barney hit upon a plan. Every night the prisoners marched to the mess hall in a line, with each inmate placing his arm on the shoulder of the man in front of him. The guards from the small picket and the larger picket would walk to a picket outside the dining hall, from which they could observe the men. The two building tenders also went ahead to the mess hall, one counting the inmates as they marched through the door and the other counting them as they were seated.

If Clyde and Barney fell into the end of the chow line as they were leaving the building, they would be at the front of the line when they were returned. For the first minute or so, there would be no guard in the picket. They thought that if they could stick something in the lock on the picket to get an impression, they could make a key that would fit. Then they would ask the guard to get something for them from the commissary, and he would step through the door into the larger picket area. When he left, they would enter the smaller picket and capture the guard and his gun when he returned. With this gun, they could take the guard in the larger picket. Finally, they would go up to the arsenal with the guards as hostages and take all the weapons they would need for an escape.

The plan was put in motion. One day Barney and Clyde, being the first to return from the mess hall, put a piece of soft pine in the lock to get an impression. This method didn't work the first time; they had to make several attempts before they got a piece of wood the right size and got an adequate impression on it. They then filed out a piece of metal for a key. Much to their disappointment, the first key didn't fit. The entire process had to be started over again.

Shortly after the failure with the key, Thornton and Gibson took Barney and Clyde aside. "You boys are making too much show without getting anywhere," said Gibson. "Somebody's going to stool you off, and a bunch of people will end up getting killed."

"You could be right," Clyde agreed. "Every man in here knows what we're doin', and if just one of 'em's a stoolie, the whole thing'll be ruined."

"Four of us have a pretty good plan, and if you boys just wait a little while, we'll all get outta here," Gibson told them.

The usually quiet Thornton spoke up. "I don't want to offend you, Clyde, but you have a killer instinct. If you take the lead in this, you'll probably kill a bunch of guards and then everybody's hand will be against us. Look what's happened to Clyde Barrow, John Dillinger, and Pretty Boy Floyd."

Clyde nodded. "Okay, Roy, you guys go ahead. We'll just sit back and watch. When you're ready, give us the word."

It was Sunday, October 3, 1937—two days before Clyde's twenty-seventh birthday—when Thornton took Clyde aside to tell him the break would be that night. Thornton explained that he was a cousin to one of the guards and that the lock to the picket had been switched. His cousin had given him a key that fit.

"How do you want me to help?" Clyde asked.

Thornton outlined the plan. Four of them would overtake the two picket guards and then use them as hostages to get to the arsenal upstairs. Clyde's job was to keep the prisoners in the adjoining wing quiet. The four would then return with guns from the arsenal. If there was any trouble, they would lower the guns to Clyde on the bell rope, and he would distribute them to anyone who wanted one. The plan was to go into effect right after sundown.

That night at supper Clyde sat with Thornton and a new man in Little Alcatraz, bank robber Roy Maloney. Out the window of the mess hall, Clyde watched a guard walking down the steps from the arsenal. That by itself was not unusual. But what caught Clyde's attention was that the guard was carrying a rifle. Rifles were ordinarily carried only by high riders during the daytime. At night guards would be armed with pistols or shotguns. If a guard had a rifle, it could mean he was onto something.

When they got back into Little Alcatraz, Clyde told Gibson about the guard. Thornton and Maloney had seen him, too. "I thought it was a rifle, but I've been in here four or five years and could be mistaken," said Thornton.

Maloney spoke up. "Yeah, and Clyde's been in a lot longer than that. By this time, he wouldn't know a B-B gun from a rifle. I'm sure it was a shotgun."

"You're really sure?" probed Gibson.

"Yep," replied Maloney.

Gibson looked at Thornton. "What do you think, Roy? Is that good enough for you?"

"Yeah, I guess so," said Thornton, shrugging his shoulders.

Clyde had lingering doubts. He was certain the guard was carrying a rifle, but he hoped he was taking it home for hunting.

Later, both Thornton and Gibson walked to the picket and gave the guard some money for an order from the commissary. The guard unlocked the door that separated the two picket areas and closed it behind him. He was out of sight. Thornton quietly slid his key into the picket and turned it. The picket door opened.

Thornton and Gibson entered and stationed themselves on both sides of the door through which the guard would be returning. When the guard walked through, Thornton grabbed him and pinned his arms to his sides. Gibson took his gun. The guard looked as if he was going to cry out. "Don't do it, ol' man, or I'll blast you in two pieces," Gibson said.

"Please don't hurt me," whined the guard quietly. "I'll do anything you ask."

Thornton grabbed the guard's hunting knife and ushered the guard to a corner of the picket area, holding the knife to his throat.

Gibson took the guard's keys and opened the door separating the two pickets. He walked into the larger picket, holding the pistol to the head of the guard, who was talking to prisoners in the other wing. The guard started to go for his gun. "Go ahead, if you want to die," stated Gibson.

The guard slowly raised his hands above his head, and Gibson took his pistol from its holster.

"Everything's okay over here," Gibson shouted.

Avers entered the picket. Thornton handed him the knife and put him in charge of the first guard. Thornton then joined Gibson in the larger picket and was given one of the guns. Clyde, Barney, and a third man entered the picket with the intention of walking into the other wing to keep the men quiet. Clyde carried a key but found that it wouldn't open the door into the other wing. All was quiet on the other side. All the prisoners there knew that a break attempt was in progress. They had quietly circled the picket, hoping they might also be able to escape.

Clyde continued to twist his key in vain. Thornton's voice broke the silence. "Forget it, Clyde. It looks like they'll keep mum." A couple of prisoners on the other side nodded their heads affirmatively.

Thornton and Gibson pushed their hostage into the smaller picket, where Avers still held the first guard at knife-point. Gibson yelled into Little Alcatraz, "Where is the man who's supposed to take this guard?" There were four inmates in on the plan, and three of them now stood in the picket with the guards. The plan was for two men to hold onto the guards with knives while the other two wielded the captured pistols.

Gibson shouted out again, this time with more impatience in his voice, "Where is the man who's supposed to go with me?" There was still no answer. Gibson, Thornton, and Avers stared through the doorway, waiting.

After a moment, Clyde spoke up. "I'll take 'em for ya, Good-eye."

Gibson seemed to ignore Clyde's offer and called out a third time. There was still no answer. The old guard who had been in the Little Alcatraz picket was now pleading, "Please don't kill me, boys. I've got a wife and six children to support."

"Do just as you're told and stop that d—— whining, and no one is going to hurt you," said Clyde. He then turned to Gibson. "I'll go, Goodeye."

Gibson nodded.

Clyde pulled the knife from the second guard's scabbard, took the older guard by the belt from behind, and held the point of the knife into the man's shoulder blade.

"Let's go to the arsenal," ordered Clyde.

"Yes, sir," the guard replied.

The old guard marched up the stairs first, with Clyde hanging to his belt from behind. Gibson marched directly behind Clyde, hanging onto Clyde's belt with one hand while grasping the pistol in the other. The second guard was behind Gibson. Avers held a knife to this guard's back. Thornton brought up the rear, also armed with a pistol.

When they reached the platform at the top of the stairs, Clyde stepped out from behind his hostage and reached around to open the screen door of the arsenal. As he touched the knob, Clyde was knocked off his feet by a blast that came from the other side of the door. The old guard fell down with him. Shots suddenly rang out around them. Clyde knew that he was hit but didn't know where. His eyes and face burned. Clyde could hear two shots from the .38 caliber pistol that Thornton carried.

Both Clyde and the guard started to get up, but the guard suddenly ducked. Another shot came through the screen door, passed Clyde's head, and struck Gibson. The explosion was so close that the concussion knocked Clyde off his feet again. There were more shots. His hostage ran inside the screen door, but not before Clyde stabbed him in the calf. Gibson shot twice toward the door, staggered, and fell forward. Clyde crawled to the door and opened it so that Avers and Thornton could go on in with the second guard as a hostage. He turned to see that both were lying in pools of blood. The second guard then rushed into the arsenal.

Clyde grabbed the .45 from the hand of the fallen Gibson and fired twice through the screen door. Bullets were still hitting around Clyde, and he turned to see that there were two or three guards with rifles standing forty yards away beside the edge of the mess hall. Clyde fired twice in their direction, and they leaped behind the building. He turned toward the arsenal again and squeezed the trigger. It snapped on an empty chamber. Clyde jumped over Thornton's body and scurried down the stairs. There was a light bulb along the railing about waist high at the bottom of the stairs. It exploded beside Clyde's hand from a bullet fired from the arsenal. The bullet ricocheted in the direction of the guards beside the mess hall. Thinking Clyde had fired at them again, those guards jumped back to safety while Clyde ducked back through the door and into the picket. He threw down the gun, ran into Little Alcatraz, and hid under a table, bleeding from the rifle shot and rubbing his eyes from the powder burns.

Chapter

23

THE CRICKETS WERE CHIRPING in the black south Texas night as Clyde looked mournfully at the naked and bloody bodies of his friends, Thornton and Avers. Thornton's eyes were still partially open. His brown eyes had teemed with excitement as they had discussed the escape plans but were now in a cold, blank stare. The two were laid out on an examining table at the Eastham infirmary. A prisoner who worked in the infirmary looked at the bodies while the doctor worked on the critically wounded Gibson across the room.

Clyde's right shoulder alternately throbbed and ached from the bullet that had hit him. He was unable to raise his arm. His eyes continued to burn. *What could have gone wrong?* Clyde wondered. Tears came to his eyes as he looked at the still-warm corpses; he mourned the loss of Thornton and Avers and his chance of freedom.

The prisoner working in the infirmary touched a bullet that protruded from the skin of Avers's stomach. "Look at this," he said to the doctor. "He was shot in the back. The bullet went clean through 'im and stopped here."

The doctor looked up from his work and shook his head negatively, indicating the steward should keep his mouth shut.

The steward obeyed. There was no further mention of where the bullets had come from. Clyde could see that Thornton was shot twice in the back. Avers had been hit once in the back. Gibson had taken a bullet in the side and one in the back.

A short while later, the guard who had been in the arsenal came into the hospital bragging about how he had killed three men with three shots. It was as if he had just returned from a big-game hunting trip.

For a couple of reasons, Clyde knew his claims weren't true. First, Gibson wasn't dead—at least not yet. Second, Clyde could remember all three shots that had been fired from the arsenal. The first had hit him in the shoulder. The second had whizzed by his head and hit Gibson in the right side. The third had exploded the light bulb at the bottom of the stairs.

Newspaper reporters showed up at the infirmary about a half hour later. A sheet had been draped over the bodies so that just their heads were showing. The guard related his story of how he had been dressing in the arsenal when he heard footsteps on the stairs. He had seen that they were convicts, so he had taken a rifle and fired three times, killing Thornton and Avers and critically wounding Gibson.

Clyde still resented the press's calling him the kick-killer and other things during his murder trials. *This just shows how stupid those newspapermen really are,* thought Clyde as he sat in an adjacent room with his shoulder bandaged. *If they're so smart, why don't they ask how four men were hit with three bullets?*

The guard was a big hero with the journalists, but Clyde knew the only truthful part of the man's story was that he fired three shots. Clyde realized the whole story wasn't being told. No mention was made of the guards with rifles who had fired from beside the cafeteria. Only the guard in the arsenal and the guards who had stood below knew the truth.

Apparently, someone had stooled off the escape plans, maybe the fourth man who had failed to show up when he was called. The guards had planned the ambush. If the captain had known about it ahead of time, he would have taken steps to prevent the escape attempt. As it was, the lives of two guards had been in jeopardy, not to mention the fact that four convicts were shot and two of them were already dead. It seemed likely to Clyde that the captain never would be told what really happened.

It was a wonder, too, that more prisoners weren't wounded or killed, thought Clyde as reporters took pictures of the corpses. After Clyde had run into Little Alcatraz and hidden under the table, several guards had come to the windows and fired repeatedly into the building. Miraculously, no one had been hit. The captain had made his way to the larger picket and yelled in, "Ever who has the pistol, throw it out!"

"There's no pistol in here, Captain!" a prisoner shouted back.

"Where is it then?" the captain asked.

"I think it's in the small picket," the prisoner called back.

The captain ordered the guards to cease firing and stuck his head through the door to see the .45 lying on the floor in the Little Alcatraz picket. With that, the captain had called for the guards to enter the building as he stepped through the doorway and picked up the pistol.

All the prisoners were ordered to strip and stand against the wall with their hands up. Clyde was still under the table, his shoulder bleeding and his eyes hurting. He climbed out and started to peel off his bloody shirt. "There's the one! There he is!" exclaimed the captain. "It was pretty hot out there, wasn't it, Clyde?"

"Pretty d—— hot," Clyde answered.

"Now don't you cuss," said the captain. "It's Sunday."

If Clyde hadn't been in such severe pain, he might have laughed. The same captain cussed at the prisoners all week long. But he went to church every Sunday and never cussed on Sundays. *Typical church-goer*, thought Clyde.

Gibson was barely hanging on to life, and Clyde would require surgery. Late that night they were taken to the prison hospital inside The Walls at Huntsville. Gibson was placed in a room usually reserved for dying prisoners; Clyde was one door down. Prison doctors worked on Gibson throughout the night, and he was still alive the next morning.

Clyde went into surgery Monday morning. The hole in his shoulder was about the size of a silver dollar. He was on the operating table for over an hour as a doctor probed out pieces of lead and bone from the powder-burned wound.

Three days later, Clyde still didn't have use of his arm, but he was feeling better. He heard a commotion coming from Gibson's room. He got out of bed to see that Gibson was trying to leave his room, while two prisoner-orderlies were trying to guide him back to his bed. Gibson was delirious with fever. Clyde went to the aid of the orderlies.

"Get back in bed, Goodeye," said Clyde. "These men are trying to take care of you."

Gibson quit fighting the orderlies and crawled back into his bed. In the meantime, a doctor had come to investigate the commotion.

"We've been havin' a h—— of a time with this guy, Doctor. Can't keep him quiet and in bed," complained one of the orderlies.

Before the doctor had a chance to say anything, Clyde spoke up. "How 'bout if I stay in here with him, Doctor? I've known 'im a long time, and I think he'll listen to me."

The doctor nodded his head. "If you think he'll listen. His only chance of pulling through is to stay quiet in bed." Pneumonia had already started to set in as a result of a bullet that had passed through Gibson's lung.

In the days that followed, Gibson's condition would improve, then take a sudden turn for the worse. Sometimes he sat up in bed and talked with Clyde, and at other times he mumbled nonsense in his delirium. During one of Gibson's down spells, the doctor examined him and told Clyde that it would take a miracle for Gibson to recover. Knowing this, Clyde wanted to find out who had betrayed the escape attempt.

"Who was it, Goodeye?" Clyde asked when Gibson was sitting up in bed. "I just want to make sure he gets what's comin' to 'im."

"Now, Clyde, you've been in enough trouble already, and I don't want to see you get in any more," Gibson answered. "That d—— stool pigeon will answer to me when I get well."

But from what the doctor had said, Clyde knew Gibson's chances of recovery were slim. Since Gibson wouldn't tell the name of the stoolie in his more lucid moments, Clyde waited until he was delirious. Clyde got Gibson to talk about the escape, but Gibson seemed to catch himself just before Clyde thought he would divulge the name. When he was conscious later, Gibson teased Clyde for trying to take advantage of him.

Gibson was the oldest of nine children who had grown up on a farm in Olitha, Texas. He hadn't caused any trouble until he was thrown from a horse at age twenty, his mother, Beulah, had told prison officials. After the spill, Gibson had crazy spells that were due to the spinal injury, according to his mother. It was shortly after being thrown from the horse that Gibson had broken into a store. Then he had married a part-Indian girl named Lottie from Victoria. The marriage lasted seven months before the two were separated. They were officially divorced two years later in 1931 when Gibson went to the penitentiary for the first time.

Gibson's family was notified of the escape attempt and the injuries he had suffered. He received a letter from his mother at the hospital unit. "We are coming to see you as soon as we can," her letter had said. But before she could make the trip, according to the letter, they had three or four more bales of cotton to pick. She closed her letter with the admonition, "Forrest, be a good boy."

The eleventh day after the shooting Gibson asked Clyde to get him a pencil and paper so that he could answer his mother's letter. When Clyde returned with the writing materials, Gibson said he was too tired to write. He would do it the next day.

That afternoon the doctor tried unsuccessfully to drain some fluid from Gibson's right lung. Gibson had already recovered from pneumonia, but a bullet had also pierced his liver. Now, fluid from the liver was filling his lungs. He seemed to rally for a while but went into a coma toward evening. A death rattle started. Clyde held Gibson's hand until he quit breathing around midnight. The family had been notified of Gibson's grave condition. His mother and a sister, Mary, entered the room a few minutes after he died. They wept bitterly over the body. Clyde cried as he tried to comfort them.

Several weeks later, Clyde was still in the hospital, because his shoulder wasn't healing. Pus continually ran out of the wound. And every time the dressing was changed, there were on the bandage small pieces of lead that had come out with the pus. After several days, Clyde got a prisoner-nurse to probe into the wound. His examination revealed that the steel wadding from the bullet was still in Clyde's shoulder. Once it was removed, the shoulder started healing, although Clyde would always carry fragments of lead from the bullet.

In the hospital unit, Clyde had plenty of time to think about what had happened. Three of his friends were dead. Why hadn't he been killed, too? With two life sentences plus fifteen years, what was the purpose in continuing? His only chance was to escape, but his chances now seemed worse than ever. He wanted to kill the guy who ratted on them. There were two or three possibilities. Should he kill them all or wait until the stool pigeon somehow reared his ugly head? Clyde also wanted to plant a bullet between the eyes of the lying guard who had ambushed them.

Chapter
24

BY MID-NOVEMBER Clyde's shoulder had healed enough so that he was sent back to Little Alcatraz. His shoulder was still too sore to swing a hoe or an ax. And he couldn't raise his arm above shoulder level. So instead of chopping trees, Clyde cleared brush.

He killed a rabbit with a stick—his usual method—but his shoulder ached for a week afterward. This put an end to Clyde's having more meat to eat than the other prisoners. The soreness in the shoulder continued throughout the winter.

At one point during the winter, a letter was smuggled into Little Alcatraz from Dago Seay, the prisoner who took the stand as a witness for the state in the murder of Everett Melvin. Begging Clyde's forgiveness, Seay said he had been promised a trustee's job in exchange for his testimony. He had escaped from Retrieve and was living in Kansas City. In order to get back into Clyde's good graces, Seay said he would plant guns at Little Alcatraz and help Clyde to escape.

Clyde doubted that Seay ever intended to plant any guns. And if Seay did plant the guns, Clyde vowed that his first bullet would be one to Seay's head. A few weeks later Seay was recaptured and returned to Retrieve.

In June, 1938, Barney and some of the others who had not caused any major trouble at Little Alcatraz were sent back to their original units. Several men would be returned to Retrieve. "Ya want us to take care of Seay for ya?" one of the inmates had asked Clyde.

"It's good of you to offer, but just leave him alone," Clyde answered. "I want to kill him myself."

Before the prisoners were taken away, Clyde said good-by to Barney. They had been locked up together for nearly six years. Besides Clyde's own father, Barney was the best friend Clyde had ever had.

Because of his seeming insanity, Red Massey had continually been in trouble with the guards and other prisoners—not because he planned it that way, but because he just didn't seem capable of doing any better.

Clyde watched one day as Massey antagonized David Sedlock. It was July 27, 1938. Clyde knew that Sedlock was a tough customer and that if Massey had control of his mind, Sedlock was a man he wouldn't cross. After returning from supper, Sedlock took Massey to the back of the building, out of the sight of the picket guard, and stabbed him to death. Sedlock hid the knife and returned to where Clyde and some other prisoners were standing. "Well," said Clyde. "That's another murder rap for me."

"Naw, they won't charge you with it," Sedlock replied.

But Sedlock was wrong. Three days later Clyde was indicted for Massey's murder. He had previously knifed two fellow inmates, and it made sense that they would charge him with the murder of Massey. Two inmates said they would testify that they saw Clyde stab Massey. Instead of taking Clyde to the county jail, however, officials chose to leave him in the tighter security of Little Alcatraz. The trial was to be on October 21, 1938. Sedlock told Clyde that he would take the stand and admit he had killed Massey if it came down to it.

Facing his fifth murder charge, Clyde refused to go to work. He figured that they might shoot him down in the field and say he was trying to escape. Clyde knew that the bat was the penalty for refusing to work, but he had devised a plan to avoid it.

While he was still waiting for his trial, the order came through to use the bat on him. The others were working in the fields, and Clyde was the only prisoner in Little Alcatraz. He knew they would soon be coming for him, so he watched through a barred window. Shortly, Clyde could see the captain, doctor, a guard, and four building tenders walking toward Little Alcatraz. It was time for Clyde to put his plan into action.

He knew it was against regulations to beat a prisoner after blood was drawn. It was his plan to beat them to the punch. He had secured a piece of razor blade to use in drawing blood himself. That way they couldn't beat him. Clyde dropped his pants and methodically slashed in a checker pattern across his buttocks. The razor was sharp, so the pain wasn't as bad as Clyde suspected it would be. He could feel the gashes opening and the warm blood flowing down his legs. It formed a pool on the concrete floor beneath where he stood. He cut until the entire region had been thoroughly slashed.

Clyde concealed the razor blade when he could hear the group entering the picket. As they went in, he stood naked, waiting for them. "I'm waitin' for ya back here!" Clyde yelled.

Clyde bent over so that the first sight they would see would be his bleeding buttocks. He craned his neck to watch their expressions.

The captain had seen some grisly sights in his official duties, but the sight of the bent-over Clyde with slashed buttocks and blood running down his legs caused the captain to turn his head.

"Uhhh!" grunted one of the building tenders, dropping his head and raising a hand to cover his eyes.

"Put it right here, Captain!" taunted Clyde, still bent over. The doctor stood there, shaking his head in disbelief.

The group stood for a moment in shocked silence. The captain was the first to break the silence. "You just might get your wish, Thompson."

The captain walked toward Clyde, while the others followed. "Hold him down, men," ordered the captain.

Clyde started to struggle with the building tenders, but they quickly wrestled him to the floor, face down, and sat on his arms and legs. Clyde screamed protests as the doctor took a cloth and wiped the blood away to see the extent of Clyde's self-inflicted wounds.

"You s—— of a b——, you can't do this!" Clyde shouted. "You can't hit a bleeding man."

A building tender pushed Clyde's face into the concrete.

"Here's a place he seems to have missed," said the doctor to the captain, pointing to an area on Clyde's buttocks a few inches square.

The captain nodded to the guard holding the bat. The doctor backed away. Taking aim at the place where the doctor had pointed, the guard smacked the thick leather strap against Clyde's skin. This time Clyde wasn't quiet as the twenty whacks were administered. He screamed in pain at the top of his lungs, while threatening to kill them all. They left him writhing in pain on the concrete floor of the building.

Even with the beating, Clyde steadfastly refused to work as the murder trial approached. Public sentiment was already strongly against him because of his previous record. But TDC officials were taking steps to give Clyde the maximum unfavorable publicity, apparently in an attempt to get him executed once and for all. The TDC general manager went on the radio to say that Clyde was the meanest man in Texas. A prison chaplain said Clyde was a man without a soul. The guard who had taken credit for single-handedly stopping the prison break the previous year told in a radio interview how he had prevented the meanest man in Texas from escaping.

Captain J. H. Hamilton, Eastham farm manager, was quoted by newsmen as saying that Clyde was "a born killer but a coward at heart."

"He will slay a fellow man for the love of the kill and without the slightest provocation," said Hamilton. "He thinks no more of killing a person than a normal person does of lighting a cigar. It's just an unimportant incident."

The proof that Clyde was a coward, according to Hamilton, was the way he had fled back into Little Alcatraz and dropped his gun during the ill-fated escape attempt. "A real fighter would have shot it out," Hamilton stated.

Although newspapers and radio were forbidden to prisoners, word got back to Clyde. He didn't feel like the meanest man in Texas, but he promised himself that he would try to live up to that title if he got the chance. If it meant slashing the throats of a hundred guards to escape, he would do it.

Three days before the trial, the district attorney showed up at Eastham to secure more witnesses. Instead of going directly to the fields that morning, the prisoners were lined up outside the warden's office to talk with the district attorney. They marched in individually.

Most of Clyde's fellow inmates said they wouldn't tell who actually killed Red Massey, but they would take the witness stand to say that Clyde Thompson didn't. After this turn of events, the two convicts who had promised to testify against Clyde got shaky. They knew that if he got the chance, Clyde would kill them. They were promised protection but knew it would do them little good if Clyde was really after them.

The day of the trial came, but Clyde was baffled when the county sheriff and Texas Rangers didn't come to pick him up. The doctor came to Little Alcatraz to examine the damage done two weeks earlier by the razor blade and bat. "I sure wish I could get away with murder like you can and not even be tried for it," said the doctor while examining Clyde's buttocks. That was Clyde's first inkling that the murder charges had been dropped. The captain confirmed it for Clyde during lunch.

That afternoon, a building tender came to Clyde with a message. "Hey, Thompson, come here," he said.

Clyde was lying face down on his bunk, since it had been impossible to sit down for the previous two weeks. He walked over to the building tender, who was holding a piece of paper in his hands.

"It says here your father died of cancer last week," the prisoner told Clyde.

Despair instantly shot through Clyde's mind and body. Then he wondered if it was a ploy on the part of prison officials to break him down. He looked suspiciously at the building tender. "Is this some kinda trick? You're fooling with me, aren't ya?" His voice was filled with desperation.

The building tender had told Clyde the news routinely but started feeling badly. He really hadn't thought the message would bother a con as tough as Clyde. "No. They buried him four days ago. I'm sorry." He reached out to touch Clyde's shoulder, but Clyde suddenly pulled away.

"Leave me alone!"

The building tender left, while Clyde sunk to his knees. He wept bitterly, calling out to his father, the one person he was sure had loved him and never given up on him.

With the death of his father, Clyde knew that any legal means of getting out of prison were also dead. There would be no one on the outside fighting for his release. His only chance of ever getting out would be through escape.

Clyde had seen some of the toughest cons granted a leave from prison when a loved one was gravely ill or had died. Prisoners had been allowed to go to the deathbeds of their mothers and fathers and to the funerals. But in Clyde's case, prison officials had made sure he didn't even know his father was sick, much less had died. Clyde hated them for this. He vowed even more deeply than before to live up to his reputation as the meanest man in Texas. He knew he would stop at nothing to pay them back.

Chapter
25

CLYDE BROODED BITTERLY over the death of his father while continuing to refuse to work in the fields. He was surprised when, after a few days, they no longer tried to make him work. Clyde figured they were waiting for his rear end to heal enough so they could beat him again. He kept a small piece of razor blade with him so he could repeat what he had done earlier, only more thoroughly.

Then one day Clyde got word that he was to be transferred to The Walls. He figured they would hold him there while he healed and then use the bat on him again. In early November, 1938, the black prison truck pulled up to Little Alcatraz, and the captain came into the picket and called out to Clyde. Clyde walked slowly to the picket with the razor showing in his hand, ready to drop his pants and start slashing.

"Please don't cut yourself again," the captain earnestly pleaded. "I'm not going to whip you. We're just sending you to The Walls."

"When I get in there, you'll have men grab me and beat me again," Clyde said bitterly.

"No, no, I swear," replied the captain. "Nobody is going to lay a hand on you."

"I'll take your word for it, Captain," Clyde warned. "But I promise I'll kill you if you beat me."

No inmate in his right mind threatened to kill the captain. It was something an inmate just wouldn't do, because he knew he'd suffer grave consequences for such a threat. But the captain knew Clyde was more than a desperate criminal. He was a mad killer. And the captain was willing to do whatever was necessary to get Clyde out of his jurisdiction once and for all.

"We're not going to beat you," the captain promised.

Clyde disappeared momentarily, concealing the razor in his mouth. He then returned to the picket for the trip to The Walls. The chain was wrapped around his neck with the padlock in front, as usual. In addition, Clyde was secured with handcuffs and leg irons.

When he arrived at Huntsville, there were several guards and the warden waiting. The truck drove directly to the small concrete building near death row that Clyde remembered as the prison morgue. The building had concrete walls, ceiling, and floor that were all approximately two feet thick. It contained six concrete slabs, protruding from the walls, on which to lay coffins. The slabs were bunk-style on three of the walls. The door was on the fourth wall. The only ventilation in the building came from two round holes, each measuring about three inches in diameter. The holes were six feet apart and high on the wall opposite the door.

A new morgue had been built, and the old one had been converted into a special solitary confinement cell for Clyde. When he got out of the truck, he knew exactly where he was. He had picked up papers in this area after he got off crazy row. The bodies of men who died in prison or those Clyde had seen walk the last mile on their way to the electric chair had been kept in the morgue in previous years. They would stay there until claimed by a relative or until taken for burial at Peckerwood Hill. One noticeable difference was that the wooden door had been replaced by a thick steel door.

The chain, handcuffs, and leg irons were removed. Then Clyde was stripped and searched. He kept the razor concealed in his mouth, and they didn't find it. Clyde vowed to keep the razor in case they got the idea of beating him again. A five-gallon bucket with a little water in the bottom would serve as Clyde's toilet. Still naked, Clyde was ushered into the concrete building, and the door was locked behind him.

From inside, the place was nearly pitch black. Clyde could barely see his hand in front of him from the little light that came through the two small airholes. He stood on one of the concrete slabs and peered through one of the holes. It was like looking through a tunnel, and all he could see was the cell-block behind the morgue.

"I wonder how long they're going to keep me in this hole?" Clyde said aloud. He knew that thirty days were usually the maximum for solitary confinement. After that, then what?

Clyde paced back and forth, then lay down on one of the slabs for a few minutes. He was restless, so he got up and peered through the other airhole—same view. Then he paced some more. When night fell, it became totally black inside the morgue. Clyde tried to sleep, but he was cold and the concrete seemed to tear into his naked body. He had nothing to use for cover. He would doze for what seemed like a minute or two, then wake up shivering. He tried to roll up into a ball but found that the skin would stretch tightly across his buttocks, putting pressure on the gashes.

The next morning he continued to shiver until the sun warmed the old morgue two or three hours after daylight. He began a routine of pacing, looking out an airhole, and then lying on one of the slabs. His stomach growled, and he craved food.

Toward evening of the second day, the captain came with an older prisoner, Jack Moore. Moore's job was to tend to some nearby rabbit hutches, and he also was to care for Clyde. When they opened the steel door, Clyde had concealed the razor blade in his hand. But instead of a beating, he received a glass of water and a piece of bread. Clyde hadn't had food or water since leaving Little Alcatraz the previous morning. Moore took the five-gallon bucket from the morgue, emptied it, and brought it back with a little water in the bottom. With that, the cell door was locked for another twenty-four hours, when he was given another piece of bread and a glass of water. The routine stayed the same for the next thirty days.

During this time Clyde vacillated between hate, grief, and dejection. He hated prison authorities and continually thought of different ways of killing guards, captains, and wardens. He also wanted to get even with the men who had testified against him at his murder trials. They had lied, and now Clyde was in his present situation. There were also the prosecuting attorneys who had tried repeatedly to get the death penalty for him and had nearly been successful.

Clyde still mourned for his father and hated prison authorities for not letting him know his father had been sick. His mind returned to his boyhood years before his mother and father had divorced. He remembered his father's preaching, telling them Bible stories, and praying with them. It was a comfortable time. Now his father was gone forever, and Clyde missed him. Clyde was lonely, not just because he was alone in his private dungeon, but also because there was no one really pulling for him from the outside. This feeling doubled his isolation.

What's the point of it all? Clyde asked himself repeatedly. He climbed to one of the top concrete slabs and kneeled at the edge. He might be killed if he fell on his head to the concrete below. Teetering there momentarily, he finally leaned backward. There was always the razor blade. Perhaps it would be better to slash his wrists. But these thoughts would ease into the resentment he felt for anyone connected with the TDC and for anyone else who wasn't locked in the old morgue.

Pacing in the darkness, Clyde wondered if this was the way

Ol' Rip felt. Ol' Rip was a horned toad who had made Eastland, Texas, famous seven months before the shooting of the
O'Dell boys. If the story was to be believed, Ol' Rip had lived
sealed up in the cornerstone of old Eastland Courthouse for
more than thirty-one years. When the courthouse was built in
1897, there was a special ceremony at the laying of the cornerstone. Bibles, newspapers, and other items of the day were
put into the cornerstone for future generations to see. But before the cornerstone was sealed, as the story went, someone
mischievously slipped in a horned toad.

The old courthouse was to be torn down in February, 1928,
and a few days before the old cornerstone was to be opened, a
man told about putting in the horned toad many years earlier.
An eager crowd, including many leading citizens, gathered as
the cornerstone was opened. Looking into the cavity of the
opened cornerstone, the Methodist minister spotted a dusty,
dried-up looking horned toad. Someone reached in, lifted the
toad out by a hind leg, and held him up for the crowd to see.
As he was held aloft, one of his legs moved. Then his eyes
opened. He was still alive, much to the delight of the crowd.

Newspaper reports carried the story throughout the world.
The toad got his name from Rip Van Winkle, and he was taken
to the St. Louis Zoo. Moving pictures were made of him in
New York, and he was taken to the White House for President
Calvin Coolidge to see.

The famed horned toad died in 1929, and his body was embalmed and put on display in a marble and glass container in
the new courthouse.

As he paced in his own darkness, Clyde remembered that
people had said Ol' Rip's horns were gone when they found
him. A scientist speculated that the horns had been worn away
from the toad's hitting his head against the concrete, trying to
get out of the cornerstone. Clyde knew how he felt and contemplated doing the same thing.

When he finished taking care of the rabbits, Moore would sometimes stop by the steel door and talk to Clyde. These brief conversations temporarily took Clyde beyond his dungeon world. But soon after Moore would leave, the hatred, fear, and isolation would return.

Clyde was continually hungry and thirsty. He was weak from his meager diet. He could barely stand and found it more comfortable to lie listlessly on one of the slabs. His beard grew, and his body itched from not bathing. His skin hung from his body, and his eyes were sunken into his head at the end of the thirty days.

Finally, when a month had passed, Clyde was taken from the morgue for a bath in crazy row. He was given prison-issue clothes and two blankets. Several letters had arrived from his mother, sisters, and one of his brothers. A little money was enclosed with which Clyde was allowed to purchase writing paper, envelopes, and stamps.

He was then returned to the morgue.

Compared with the deprivation of the past thirty days, the clothes were a real luxury. Clyde would double up one blanket and put it on the slab as a mattress. He would cover himself with the other. Meals came twice daily. He also was given another, smaller bucket of water every day for drinking.

But Clyde continued to live in darkness, and he also encountered a new problem. He was not given eating utensils, so he had to scoop up the food in his hands. Because he had no hot water, it was difficult to eat something like chili and get his hands completely clean afterward. The cold water he had wouldn't cut the grease, and the morgue was filled with cockroaches. They really hadn't bothered him too much before, but now when he went to sleep, he knew he would wake up to find them crawling on his hands and lips. He would sling the roaches against the wall in the darkness, but they would return before he could doze off again.

Clyde had always thought that bedbugs were a prisoner's

worst enemy. He had seen fellow inmates try to kill them with insecticides, torches, and hammers. But now he had second thoughts. Maybe bedbugs weren't as bad as the cockroaches that plagued him night after night.

It became apparent to Clyde that his stay in the morgue was going to be indefinite. He was taken from the morgue once a week for a bath. After another month passed, the captain permitted him to order other items from the commissary besides writing paper. The first two things he ordered were soap and talcum powder. The soap seemed to keep the roaches from crawling on him so frequently, and the talcum powder kept him from feeling sticky in the week between baths.

One day a prisoner with a blowtorch came to Clyde's cell accompanied by the captain. A one-foot square hole was cut in the steel door, just below Clyde's eye level, and flat steel bars were welded in a checkered pattern over the opening. Clyde could see out, and the opening illuminated his cell from about ten in the morning until three in the afternoon. For the first time, Clyde could see where he was walking. He also could see to write letters, and he used one of the concrete slabs as a desk.

Clyde was allowed to order ice cream on a stick and some canned goods from the commissary. He made a spoon from an ice cream stick and the top from one of the cans so that he wouldn't have to eat with his fingers anymore.

His hatred caused him to constantly think of ways of escaping and of killing guards. He knew his chances of getting outside from his present situation were minimal. It was a game of waiting and plotting. He hated everyone connected with the Texas Department of Corrections, but he tried not to tip his hand. He knew he was going to have to con them in order to win their trust. Then his conditions might improve, and that would be his only chance for escape.

Chapter
26

SOME 150 MILES NORTHWEST of Clyde's private dungeon, in Hillsboro, Texas, Julia Perryman cried out, "Mama, did you see the way those people looked at me? It's like I was some sort of animal that crawled out from under a rock!" Julia threw down the brown paper sack that contained the shirt she had just bought her father for Christmas and ran toward her bedroom with tears streaming down her face. "I can't stand it anymore! I just can't stand it!"

Myrtle Perryman pursed her lips and closed her eyes. Yes, she had seen the curious way that people at the department store had looked at her daughter. There had been the little boy, probably no more than six years old, who was walking behind them with his mother. "Look, Mama, look!" he had exclaimed. Myrtle didn't have to look. She knew the boy was pointing to Julia's spine, which was so misshapen that she appeared almost to be a humpback. The little boy didn't know any better, but Julia had cringed because she had heard him, too.

Then there had been the woman in her forties who did know better. "You'd think she'd be too embarrassed to go out in public," the woman had said to her shopping companion, loud enough for both Myrtle and Julia to hear.

Myrtle walked to Julia's bedroom to see her daughter standing in front of the mirror, her cheeks still wet from the tears. She put a comforting arm around her daughter's shoulder. "It's all right, honey," she said soothingly. "Some people are just pretty rude."

The two stood there for a moment, Julia accepting her mother's comfort. "What am I going to do, Mama?" Julia asked.

Myrtle looked at the reflection in the mirror. Julia stood only four feet nine inches tall, barely coming to her mother's shoulder. "You're a pretty girl, Julia, and you're doing lots of good in this world. Why, you teach Sunday school to the children, help me around the house and garden, do my hair and your sister's when she comes over. . . ." Her voice trailed off.

Julia pulled away. "Next month I'm going to be thirty years old. Thirty! And what can I do to make my way in this world? Not a blessed thing, as far as I can tell. What if something was to happen to you and Daddy? Then what would I do?"

"Don't you worry about that, honey. Nothing's going to happen to your father and me."

Julia turned so that her profile faced the mirror. "Look at that," she said bitterly. "I hate going places where people have to see me for the first time. The way they stare."

"You don't have to go anywhere, Julia," said her mother. "Just stay home with us, and it'll be okay."

Julia stared into the mirror.

"S—— of a b——!" muttered Clyde under his breath, throwing an empty bean can against the concrete wall with all his might. It clanged several times before spinning to a stop at his feet. "How in the h—— am I ever gonna get outta here?" At least at the farm there was something to do, a chance of escape. But here there was nothing. And there was no one to talk to.

With meals twice daily, Clyde was regaining his strength.

The self-inflicted wounds to his buttocks were just about healed. He felt better physically, which allowed him to focus his full attention on his plight.

Clyde's only human contacts were the twice-daily meal visits from Moore and the captain, the occasional conversations with Moore through the barred window, and the chats with the guys on crazy row when he went for a bath.

A cot and mattress had been brought into the morgue. Each leg of the cot was placed in a small can containing coal oil, which prevented the roaches from crawling up the legs of the cot and onto Clyde.

With his limited education, Clyde was a poor reader. To make matters worse, he hadn't done any reading since his stay on death row more than seven years earlier. There were magazines available in the commissary, but at this point, Clyde didn't think the captain would allow him to buy a magazine. But he thought he might be allowed to get a Bible. It wasn't that Clyde wanted to study the Word of God. Rather, he was dying from boredom and wanted something to do—anything. A Bible would show the captain he was improving. Maybe it would get him out of the hole. But God? No God would have allowed him to rot in an old morgue. Or slave his life away on a work farm. And a real God wouldn't take away his father, his only possible means of ever getting out legally.

On a conscious level, Clyde planned to show that the Bible was full of contradictions. He would find these contradictions, and then he could show the church-going Bible believers what fools they really were. Subconsciously, the Bible reminded Clyde of a time in his life when there was stability—the happier times before his folks were divorced.

When Moore dropped by for a visit one day, Clyde asked about the Bible.

"I think they have 'em at the commissary for a buck," he replied. "Wanna spend that much?"

"Guess so," Clyde answered. "Say, you don't reckon the captain would let me have a *Life* magazine, too?"

"I doubt it," Moore replied. "That'd be pressing your luck. I'm gonna have to get his permission just for the Bible."

"Okay," said Clyde.

Permission was granted for Clyde to obtain a Bible. Moore purchased a small New Testament plus Psalms and brought it with Clyde's meal the next afternoon. The captain examined the book and handed it to Clyde. By then there was no light in the morgue, so Clyde had to wait until the next morning before he could start reading.

With nothing else to do, Clyde read for the entire five hours that there was light in his cell. The reading went slowly because there were many words he didn't know. He would sometimes puzzle over the simplest words. After a few days of plodding along, Clyde didn't feel he was making much progress. He asked for and received permission to purchase a dictionary. There were some words that he found especially hard to spell. He would write them on the wall and try to memorize the spelling when he wasn't looking at the Bible. During the remainder of his waking hours, he would pace in his cell, sometimes contemplating what he had read.

During the cold winter days of January, 1939, the only way Clyde could keep warm was to stay under the covers all day. Then the captain built a wood-burning stove right next to the morgue. Moore kept it burning throughout the day and built up the fire before going to the cellblock for the night. This heat took the chill out of the cell so that Clyde could walk around instead of staying in bed all day.

In March, the captain installed a light fixture in the ceiling of Clyde's cell. Then Clyde could read and study as much as he liked. As a result, his reading improved. The list of words on the wall of his cell grew to more than four hundred within a few months. He memorized each of them, and he rarely ran across a word in the New Testament that he didn't know.

Clyde made a list of places where the Bible seemed to contradict itself. The list grew long at first, and he found satisfaction in looking at it. Maybe he would write a book itemizing them all. He continued to search for more. But as he read over a period of weeks and then months, he found Bible passages that clarified earlier apparent contradictions. For every new discrepancy he thought he found, he would have to cross out two or three of the old ones. Then with more studying, he also eliminated his new contradictions.

Is there a God, after all? Clyde asked himself. *Lots of people believe there is. Dad did. It's pretty much my opinion against theirs. Maybe they're right.*

Clyde paced and contemplated. He thought about his close brushes with death, starting with the lynching of Ratliff, then the chair, two more life sentences when he could easily have been executed, and finally the bloody failure of the Little Alcatraz escape attempt. "I should be dead," he found himself saying aloud. "But instead I'm here in this old morgue reading the Bible. Why?" He reasoned that maybe a lot of people were right and he, Clyde Thompson, had been wrong. Maybe there was a God. Maybe this God had spared his life for a reason. Maybe God had been on his side all along. After all, he was still alive, and by all rights, Clyde knew he should have been dead many times over.

But what about Jesus? *He got what I should have got,* Clyde thought to himself. *But yet He didn't deserve what He got. And I do deserve what I've got—and worse.*

For years Clyde had blamed everyone else for his troubles, but maybe he should have blamed himself. After all, no one had shot the O'Dell boys but him.

Clyde started to regard God as his Father—a heavenly Father—who wanted nothing but good for Clyde, just as his father had stuck by him and wanted nothing but the best for him. Clyde knew he had been wrong. He prayed and cried and read his Bible. He prayed often. And he cried often as he thought of what his life had been for the past ten years.

Clyde's belief in God was not instantaneous, nor did it come easily. On some days Clyde would look at his surroundings, feel lonely and isolated, and doubt the existence of God. He would become angry at the authorities and at all the events and circumstances that got him where he was. He would think of his studies as nothing but a con job. But then he would come back to the thought that it wasn't a prison guard who had pulled the trigger on Web O'Dell. Jake O'Dell hadn't died by the hand of God. Finally, Clyde would decide that the blame had been placed where it belonged, and that he was getting what he deserved. No, he hadn't received what he really deserved—the electric chair. He had been spared that.

When Clyde reached the point where his belief in God outweighed his doubts, he wondered what he was going to do about it. He became concerned about the condition of his soul. How could he be forgiven for what he had done? He had been baptized once. He wondered if he should repeat the act. But he decided against it. It was more a matter of asking for forgiveness and of believing that he could be forgiven for what he had done. Clyde read Jesus' story of the prodigal son, who returned to his father after squandering his inheritance in the faraway land. Clyde identified with the young man who came home sorrowfully. There also was the matter of not repeating his previous wrongs. In order to do this, Clyde felt he must get rid of the hatred that filled him.

Clyde knew there was nothing he could do to bring back the men he had killed. In spite of the heinousness of his crimes, Clyde felt he could be forgiven through Jesus.

He knew he had to clean up his language. But it wouldn't be an easy task. If he became angry, swearing came automatically. He soon found, however, that even though the swear words came into his mind, he didn't have to say them. After a long

210

time of not saying them, the words no longer came into his mind.

Clyde enrolled in two-year correspondence courses in both Bible and journalism from Lee College in Baytown, just west of Houston. He received certificates of completion for both courses. In addition to his studies, he began writing poetry, mostly of a religious nature. He would distribute his poems to the men he passed in crazy row on his way to and from his weekly bath.

The captain could see the change in Clyde and let him out of the old morgue for exercise every day. At first he would unlock Clyde's door for fifteen minutes daily. Then it was a half hour. Then an hour. Finally, Clyde's cell door was left open all day long and locked only at night. But Clyde didn't have time to roam the prison grounds. He made a point of leaving his cell for exercise, but for the most part he stayed in the old morgue to study and write.

His first poem written in the morgue was entitled "Love and Sorrow":

> I know the Fieldlark's cheerful song;
> I know why brooks so joyous sing;
> I know why stars all shine so bright;
> I know why things get mute at night;
> I know why flowers bloom along.
> I know why chimes so gladly ring,
> —For Love had taught me everything!
>
> I know the call of mourning doves;
> I know the windblown gallows tree;
> I know the rasp of hempen strand;
> I know hunger and lonesome's band.
> I know the sting of cruel shoves.
> I know how ruthless hearts can be,
> —For Sorrow also spoke to me.

Chapter
27

As CLYDE Thompson had reached to God for help, Julia Perryman also sought help to break away from the prison of her deformity.

October 17, 1940

President Franklin D. Roosevelt
The White House
Washington, D.C.

Dear Mr. President:

I'm writing this letter to seek your advice on an important matter. Since you do a good job of running our country in spite of the fact that you had polio and have lost the use of your legs, you seemed like you would be the best person to ask.

As a small child I was twice stricken with typhoid fever and then with scoliosis. At the age of 12 my spine quit growing properly. Instead of growing straight, it grew crooked. I have full use of my arms and legs, however. It's just that I am a small person with a crooked spine.

People seem to assume that because my body is de-

formed, my mind won't be right either. One time I overheard my aunt tell my mother that I should learn how to
play the guitar so that I could sit on the sidewalk with a tin
cup. Isn't there something that I can do besides that? I
was valedictorian of my high school class (though I gradu-
ated with my brother, who is two years younger, because
of my illness). He and I both attended Abilene Christian
College. I had to drop out after one semester because I
was unable to work after my scholarship ran out.

I'm now nearly 32 years old and am looking for something meaningful to do with my life. I feel that there must
be something I could do. But just what, I don't know. Any
suggestions you could give me would be greatly appreciated.

Sincerely,
Julia Perryman

Julia mailed the letter and waited. She knew the president
was a busy man and wasn't sure she would ever receive a reply.
But she was proud that she had taken a step in the right direction.

She was reading a book a few weeks later when her mother
brought in the mail. "Julia," her mother said excitedly, "you've
got a letter here from the White House. Washington, D.C.!"

Julia jumped to her feet and examined the envelope. Yes, it
was from the White House. Had President Roosevelt answered her? She ran to the kitchen and got a knife to use as a
letter opener. She didn't want to ruin the envelope when
opening it. She unfolded the letter and started reading. "It's
from the president's personal secretary, Mama."

"Why are they writing you, Julia?"

"Oh, I guess I didn't tell you that I wrote a letter to President Roosevelt a few weeks ago," said Julia as her eyes scanned

the letter. "It says here that there's a Mr. Kilpatrick in Austin who will help me find a job or get some kind of training."

She held up the letter for her mother's scrutiny, then got a pen and some paper to write the Mr. Kilpatrick who was named in the letter.

The answer to Julia's inquiry came while she was staying with Ruby, her thirty-three-year-old sister, in Waco nearly forty miles south of Hillsboro. Julia's only other sibling was a brother, James, who was a minister. In his reply to Julia, Mr. Kilpatrick set a date for her to meet him in Waco. By the time the letter caught up with Julia at her sister's, however, the date had passed. She wrote again, seeking another appointment. After another breakdown in communication, Julia was finally able to set up an appointment she could keep.

"Just what is it you want to do?" inquired Kilpatrick when they met.

Julia wrung her hands and stared at the corner of the desk separating them. This man hadn't seemed alarmed by her deformity. He hadn't even registered surprise. *But he's probably used to dealing with all sorts of odd cases anyway,* thought Julia.

"I'm just not sure, Mr. Kilpatrick," she said in a weak voice. "But I must be good for something."

"I'm sure you are, Miss Perryman. I'm sure you are. A person wouldn't write a letter to the president of the United States unless she really wanted to do something with herself."

"Well," she said a little more confidently, "my mother says I'm pretty good at doing hair. How about if I become a hair dresser?"

"Wouldn't that require you to be on your feet all day?"

Julia nodded and said, "I see what you mean. That could wear me down pretty good."

Next Kilpatrick discouraged Julia from trying to become a secretary, because she might be confined to a chair throughout the working day.

Julia thought again, and a sign of recognition suddenly registered on her face. "You know," she said, "we lived in Murfreesboro, Tennessee, from 1932 to 1937, and I got to watch my uncle who's a photographer. That sure was interesting work, and I would be glad to learn something like that."

Julia had finally hit on something to which Kilpatrick would agree. He told her that the state would finance her training and that he wanted her to learn every facet of the business. She was given the names of two photo studios in Waco where she could train. It was up to her to arrange her apprenticeship.

Julia held her head high as she walked away from the interview. But dread and uncertainty filled her mind as she contemplated an interview at a photo studio. She would meet people for the first time, and she could count on their looks of curiosity and pity. With a great deal of apprehension, she made the first appointment.

On the morning of her interview, Julia felt a hollowness in her stomach. She carefully applied a small amount of rouge and lipstick, took time in brushing her naturally wavy hair, and put on her best dress. When she arrived in front of the studio that morning, she wanted to walk away as fast as she could. Instead she approached the door. The knob slipped in her hand because of nervous perspiration. Once inside, she felt a measure of accomplishment.

A husband and wife team ran the business. Julia talked with both of them about her goals and ambitions before they left her and went to another part of the studio for a conference. She waited nervously. Had she done all right? Were they sickened by her deformity?

They came back with what at first sounded like good news. Yes, they would accept Julia for training with them. But the only training would be in darkroom procedures. Julia wouldn't be dealing with their customers. Julia knew they were concerned that her deformity would scare away their customers.

"Mr. Kilpatrick said he wanted me to learn the whole business," she said. "And I guess this would include shooting portraits, as well as working in the lab."

"I'm sorry," the man replied. "We don't need anyone to help us out up here."

Julia left, feeling defeated and rejected.

Fearing a second rejection, it took all the courage Julia could muster to call the second number Kilpatrick had given her. Two days passed before she made herself do it. This man's name was Emmett C. Lloyd, and Julia set up an appointment with him over the telephone. Feeling frightened and still hurting from the last rejection, Julia walked into the studio apprehensively. She was greeted by the owner, who towered above her at six feet three inches.

"Don't you think you're a little too old to start in something like this?" probed the man.

Julia knew this appointment could be a turning point. If she didn't connect with Mr. Lloyd, it might appear to Mr. Kilpatrick that she wasn't trying. There might not be any further appointments, and then what would she do? She spoke up as boldly as she could. "I can still learn anything that I want to learn," she shot back with determination in her voice.

Lloyd smiled and said, "Miss Perryman, I believe you can."

Arrangements were made for Julia to start a one-year training program under Mr. Lloyd's direction.

When Clyde had been living in the old morgue for two and a half years, a female member of the prison board visited him on an inspection tour. She examined the scars on his buttocks and looked into his cell to see the bucket he used as a toilet. Appalled, she told the warden to either install a toilet and sink in the cell or move Clyde to a new facility. Plumbers went to work the next day to give Clyde indoor plumbing. This improvement indicated to Clyde that prison officials had no plans of upgrading his status in the near future. He would continue living in the old morgue. But he was determined to make the best of it.

Clyde still visited with Moore, who told Clyde that he could buy him a radio for six dollars. The captain approved the purchase, and one of Clyde's sisters sent the money. A small antenna was placed on top of the concrete building, enabling Clyde to pick up radio programs from all over the United States. The radio was a real luxury for Clyde, and it was the first time he'd been able to listen to one on a regular basis since his time on death row. He was continuing his studies, however, and he disciplined himself not to spend too much time with his ear to the radio. But from the radio Clyde found that he had been mispronouncing many of the words he had learned.

At the same time, Clyde began writing articles for religious newspapers and corresponding with ministers.

When Clyde's friend, the captain, went out on sick leave, his replacement confined Clyde to the old morgue, never leaving the door unlocked. Although he felt some confinement, Clyde vowed to put his extra time to good use. The first captain returned after two months and restored the open door policy for Clyde.

The captain allowed Clyde to talk with the men in crazy row as he was going to and from his bath. Sometimes Clyde visited with these men a half hour or longer while the captain talked to a guard in the cellblock. Clyde started discussing his religious faith with the prisoners.

"A few years ago they called me 'the meanest man in Texas,'" Clyde related to a prisoner. "And I thought about nothing but escape."

"Yes, I know," said the prisoner, nodding his head. "Everyone in TDC knows about you."

Clyde was momentarily surprised at the extent of his reputation. "Well, that may be," he said, "but I'd like you to know that I wouldn't leave here illegally now if the walls fell down and all the guards disappeared."

"Awww," exclaimed the prisoner in disbelief. "Come on."

"No," answered Clyde, "it's true. I'm a slave to this state because I deserve it. And the Bible teaches even slaves should be as obedient to their masters as they can."

The inmate looked at Clyde with surprise. The fact that Clyde Thompson had "got religion" was nothing short of miraculous. During his weekly visits, he guided several prisoners in their studies of the Bible. Three of the men asked if they could be baptized.

Clyde found that as a prisoner, he would not be allowed to baptize them. So he wrote to a minister friend on the outside, who made arrangements to visit the prison. The old chapel where Clyde had been baptized had been torn down, and the new chapel didn't have a baptistry. The solution was to take the three men to the bathtub on death row, the same bathtub in which Clyde had taken what was supposed to be his last bath.

Clyde was allowed to accompany Minister Charles H. Wilson and the three prisoners to death row. Also present were the prison chaplain, the warden, and the captain Clyde knew so well. Clyde shook each man's hand as he rose from the water. After the last man was baptized, Clyde asked the warden if the men might be permitted to come to his cell for worship each Sunday. The warden hesitated while all present looked at him. Finally, he reluctantly agreed.

Clyde made arrangements with the Church of Christ in Huntsville to send in unleavened bread and grape juice for weekly communion. Services included singing, prayer, Bible reading, communion, and a sermon delivered by Clyde. More were baptized and started attending the "morgue church." Other men had earlier called themselves Christians but had lost their faith. Some of these rededicated their lives to Christ and started attending the church. Soon, there were twenty-two prisoners worshiping together. There weren't enough places for them to sit, so latecomers sat on the ground in front of the open door.

When he was by himself, Clyde watched a spider build a web in one of the upper corners of his cell. He welcomed the companionship and noted in amazement how quickly the spider closed in on a hapless fly that flew into the web. The battle was quickly won by the spider, and Clyde secretly congratulated the eight-legged creature. Soon, though, a small orange and brown moth flew into the web and was rapidly dispatched by the spider.

"Ought I not wring thy bloodthirsty neck?" Clyde questioned in a poem.

But in later lines of the same poem, Clyde answered his own question.

> But that is fate: how sad, how true,
> You must sip blood to pull you thru
> This bitter life
> Of mortal strife!

Later, Clyde watched a honey bee fly into the web. He moved quickly to extract the bee from the web, but the spider moved more quickly. He was too late. He watched sadly as the spider extracted the bee's body fluids. He pondered the fragility of life. *That's the way I did it to the O'Dell boys*, he said to himself. *Quickly and without thinking. At least the spider has an excuse—that's the way God made him.*

Clyde got word one day that Dago Seay had been stabbed to death by another inmate at Retrieve. Clyde had earlier dismissed thoughts of getting even with Seay. "If only I could have talked to him about God, it might have made a difference," said Clyde aloud.

Clyde had listened to the radio reports as the Nazis invaded neighboring European countries. He had heard the announcement that Pearl Harbor was bombed, as well as President Roosevelt's speech that followed. In the months and years following, some prisoners were given early-outs so that they could fight for their country. Clyde didn't want to kill anyone else—enemy or otherwise—but thought he might serve as a medic. When he inquired about this he was flatly turned down. He was disappointed, but he understood. Prison officials had seen many prisoners "get religion" and soon revert to their old ways. Clyde felt his faith was genuine, but he couldn't blame them for having doubts about him. He still had his meanest man reputation with most who worked for the TDC.

The captain who had befriended Clyde fell ill again, and this time he went into retirement. The new captain knew Clyde only by his violent record. Clyde's cell door was again locked on a twenty-four-hour basis. His Sunday morning church services were stopped so that he had to worship on Sundays by himself. Following breakfast, he would recite all the Bible verses he had memorized. He would stop during the evening meal and quote the Bible again until it was time to go to bed. It took two Sundays for him to quote all the Scriptures he had committed to memory.

During the week, Clyde continued his studies, wrote articles for religious publications, and corresponded with Christians on the outside.

Chapter
28

CLYDE'S RECORD had been spotless for more than five years. This achievement in itself seemed like a miracle. Some prison officials took notice. Although they were not about to release Clyde, they were interested in the method by which his change had occurred. If isolation had worked on a prisoner like Clyde Thompson, as a number of people in the Texas Department of Corrections had been saying, it might have the same results for other tough cases in the prison system.

A new isolation wing was started in a three-story cellblock adjacent to death row. Prisoners in the isolation unit stayed in their cells twenty-four hours a day. They had no jobs in the prison and were never free to mingle with prisoners from other cellblocks. They were given only brief exercise periods outside their cells. Six months after the isolation unit was opened, Clyde was transferred from the old morgue. It was early 1944. He was thirty-three years old and had been incarcerated for more than fifteen years, the last five and a half in the converted morgue.

Clyde took the move philosophically. He had to leave his radio behind. New rules limited prisoners to sending out only two letters per week. In a further curtailment of mailing privileges, prisoners had to make up a list of six persons to whom they would be writing letters, and they could send mail only to those individuals. Clyde had been corresponding with many Christian people on the outside as a result of his articles in religious publications. He explained in one of those articles that he was no longer free to correspond with everyone who wrote to him.

Clyde had missed the church services in the old morgue, and in the new isolation unit he was happy to be able to talk about his faith with the men in the other isolation cells. The cells were about the same as those on death row; fellow prisoners could be heard but not seen. Clyde tried to talk about God and the Bible as much as possible. The lights were dimmed at 9:00 P.M. After that, there was no talking from cell to cell. But no one minded if someone whispered to the man in the next cell, as long as it didn't disturb the others. Clyde often talked to fellow inmates about the status of their souls until after midnight.

During his time in the old morgue, Clyde had corresponded with a woman who had two sons in prison. Clyde had earlier served time with Pete Norris, the older of the brothers, and now found himself in a cell beside Gene Paul Norris.

Pete had been convicted at age twenty-four of killing a Houston night club operator. Sentenced to life in prison, he had been sent to Little Alcatraz at the Eastham farm. It was there that Clyde had met him. Clyde remembered when he and Pete had encountered a deadly snake in the fields and how Pete had wanted to take it back to the barracks to see if he could get it to bite one of the guards. Clyde chopped off the snake's head before Pete could catch it. Pete was later sent to Retrieve.

Pete had escaped from Retrieve and joined forces with Gene Paul. The pair had then gone on a crime spree that lasted nearly a year. They were finally arrested on federal charges. Gene Paul was sent to Leavenworth, while Pete went to Alcatraz (not the Texas version, but the one in San Francisco Bay). Gene Paul had been paroled out of his five-year federal term after three years and then was returned to Texas to face state charges. That was how he ended up in isolation with Clyde.

Clyde felt that both Gene Paul and Pete were among the most intelligent men he had met in prison. Clyde stayed up late several nights talking to Gene Paul about the Bible and his faith in Christ. Gene Paul seemed to be interested and asked many questions. But for some reason, he never committed himself. Clyde felt he had failed with Gene Paul. But twenty-seven others accepted Christ following Clyde's cell-to-cell Bible studies during two years in the new isolation unit.

It was in mid-1946 that inmates in Clyde's unit started complaining that the cellblock was dirty and that the prisoner who served as janitor was shirking his once-a-week mopping duties. As a protest, several prisoners stopped up the toilets in their cells and continually flushed them until water filled the floor of the area. Clyde didn't participate in the protest, but he did use a towel to mop up the water that had run onto the floor of his cell.

When the mess was discovered, the men who had taken part in the protest were put into solitary confinement. A guard saw the wet towel on the floor of Clyde's cell and accused him of trying to stop up the drain. So Clyde was included with those who were marched off to solitary on a diet of bread and water. Clyde was returned to the old morgue. The door with bars on the windows had been replaced with a solid steel door. *Are things any different than they were when they first locked me in this dungeon?* Clyde bitterly asked himself when the steel door clanged shut and the old morgue blackened.

"But I know I've got enough love to give this baby, and I know I'd make him a good mother," Julia protested to her mother.

"Oh, I think you'd make an excellent mother, honey. It's just that your father and I don't think you'd be able to do it by yourself."

"I've got my own business now and the apartment in the back. Why, I could keep him in a crib right in the studio. And any time he started to cry, I could drop my work and go pick him up."

"It'd just be too much for you, honey," said her mother.

"Besides," interjected Elvis Perryman, Julia's father, "I don't know that the state of Texas would look too favorably on a single woman adopting a baby. They want children to have homes with both a mother and a father. And don't forget, you're thirty-seven now, Julia. That's a bit old to start thinking about motherhood."

Tears came into Julia's eyes. "I'm not too old," she said with resignation in her voice. She knew they were probably right. It would be tough for her to keep a baby. Tough, but not impossible. But it might be impossible to convince the state adoption agency that she could do it. Julia knew that this would probably be her only chance at parenthood.

A woman in Meridian, where Julia operated the Mer-Texas Photo Studio, had given birth to the baby. Meridian was some forty miles west of Julia's parents' home in Hillsboro. The woman had married as a teen-ager and given birth to a daughter. Then her husband left her. She was working as a waitress in a cafe in Meridian, trying to support herself and her baby, when she met another man. They were married within a few weeks. After the marriage ceremony, her new husband demanded that she give up her baby daughter. She refused, and he left her two weeks later to join the army, not knowing his wife was already pregnant with his child.

The baby was born in 1946. Barely able to make a living for herself and her daughter, the woman decided to give up her infant son. Marvin Harper, minister of the thirty-five-member

Meridian Church of Christ where Julia attended, and his wife were keeping the baby until a suitable home could be found.

"Well, I guess I'd better go over to Marvin's," Julia said to her parents. By the time she drove past Lake Whitney on Highway 22, Julia was convinced that she should heed her parents' advice.

The baby smiled and seemed to reach out to Julia as she looked into the crib. "Don't do that," said Julia in a voice that cracked as tears streamed down her face. "I'm not going to be your mama."

Marvin's wife put a comforting arm around Julia's shoulder. Although they already had children of their own, the Harpers made arrangements to adopt the baby.

In the small apartment that the men at the church had built for her at the back of her studio, Julia cried herself to sleep every night for the next two weeks. It looked as though she would never be a mother.

"What good am I?" Julia questioned in her prayers. But as the initial pain passed in the following weeks, Julia knew she had a lot for which to be grateful. She had come a long way since writing to President Roosevelt. Following her year of training in Waco, she had opened a photo studio in Hobbs, New Mexico, not too far north of Eunice, where her brother served as a minister. She had stayed in Hobbs until fall, 1942, when she moved to Dallas to work as a darkroom technician. The next year she and a partner started the Mer-Tex Studio. The partner soon bowed out, leaving Julia on her own. But she worked hard and soon established a thriving business, shooting portraits and developing them in her own darkroom.

Clyde paced back and forth in the darkness, much as he had when he was first put in the morgue. "Why me, God?" Clyde asked. "I've been trying to do Your will for a long time now, and I end up in exactly the same place as when they thought I was the meanest man in Texas. What's the point of all this?

Have You forgotten about me? Aren't there any rewards for trying to do the right thing?" Clyde kicked at the concrete wall.

He continued to pace and think in the darkness. *But, no, it's not the same as when I was first put in here. I know this will only last a week. At least I don't have to stay in here for months or years. And I'm not boiling on the inside with hate and anger.*

Clyde knelt on the concrete and prayed aloud. "God, I don't know why I'm here when I don't deserve to be, but I pray that You'll help me to cope with this. I'm grateful that this is only temporary, and I'm grateful that You were here in this dungeon in 1938—I can't believe that it's been nearly eight years—to answer my questions and give me hope for the first time. Thank You, Lord, that I've been able to talk about You with other prisoners and I pray that You'll be with those other fellas who are also in solitary now and comfort them. Please guide my actions and thoughts. In the name of Jesus I pray, amen."

Clyde had the feeling that everything would be okay. Even though he was now in solitary on a bum rap, he vowed to show prison officials that he wasn't the same man they had first put in the old morgue in 1938. The morgue was the same, but he wasn't. He was determined to continue to act like a new man.

After a week in solitary, Clyde was taken from the morgue. He and six others who also had spent the week in the hole were put on a chain and taken in the prison truck to the Wynne farm, located just a few miles from The Walls. A new isolation unit had been constructed at Wynne, consisting of twenty-two cells. Six prisoners were already there when Clyde and the others arrived in spring, 1946. Each of the cells contained a toilet, a sink, and a concrete slab for a bed, built into the concrete wall. Straw mats were placed on the slabs for mattresses. Each prisoner was given two blankets. For the first few days Clyde found himself sore from sleeping on the thin mat.

There were no commissary privileges in the new unit. There was also a rule of silence. Prisoners could never talk above a whisper, and they could talk only to inmates in the cells next to theirs.

The third night Clyde was there, the men on both sides of him openly defied the rule of silence.

"This place stinks!" said the raspy-voiced man in the next cell.

"Well, we might as well talk as loud as we want," said the man on Clyde's opposite side in a normal tone. "The worst they can do is put us in solitary, and it can't be any worse than this place."

It was true that there was little difference between this isolation unit and solitary. In solitary, however, a prisoner would be locked in total darkness and given reduced rations.

A guard walked over to the front of the cell of the first one who had spoken up. "Shut up," he ordered, "or I'll throw you in the hole!"

"Go right ahead, Boss," the prisoner replied. "It'd probably be a vacation."

Clyde watched in horror as the guard suddenly pulled his pistol and fired twice into the man's cell. "I'm shot!" yelled the raspy-voiced prisoner. "He shot me!"

With the prisoner still yelling, the guard walked past Clyde's cell to the cell where the other prisoner had defied the rule of silence. He aimed into the cell, and his revolver sounded twice. The guard walked briskly away as the second prisoner started to yell.

My Lord! Clyde thought. *What kind of place is this?*

The first man stopped screaming and began cursing the guard. "My eyes!" he yelled. "You s—— of a b——! My eyes!"

The prisoner on the other side responded in like manner. "It's tear gas!" one of them yelled. Both men started coughing.

227

The gas made its way into Clyde's cell, burning his nostrils and making his eyes water. It seemed like an hour or more before the effects of the tear gas subsided.

Tear gas became a common punishment for inmates in the isolation wing and in solitary. It was never fired into Clyde's cell, but anytime it was used on the cellblock, it seemed to make its way into all the cells. After feeling its effects several times, Clyde learned to cover himself with a blanket when it was fired. This method usually worked to lessen the effects of the tear gas.

Gene Paul Norris, who had stayed in the isolation wing at Huntsville, was released from prison. Clyde despaired when he heard that Gene Paul had been shot and killed by Texas Rangers near Fort Worth in an attempted robbery of an army arsenal. God had made a difference in Clyde's life, and he knew that if Gene Paul had accepted Christ, things would have turned out differently for him.

From his days in the old morgue, Clyde had corresponded with a woman named Maud Harper. Clyde called her "Mom" Harper. She encouraged him in her letters, sometimes sent him a dollar to use in the prison commissary, and purchased for him a subscription to the religious publication *Firm Foundation*. When he had to curtail his writing, "Mom" was still included on his list. Little could Clyde have guessed what his connection with her would bring.

Chapter
29

"AND BEFORE WE CLOSE our service today, I wanted to mention one other thing," Minister Marvin Harper told the thirty-five who were gathered for Sunday morning church service. "There's a Christian prisoner in Huntsville who's doing a fine work of ministering to other prisoners. The reason I know about him is that my mother has been corresponding with him for years. With Christmas coming up, I know you would greatly encourage this man by sending him a card. In case you'd like to do this, I've posted his name and address on the bulletin board in the foyer. Now let's bow our heads for a closing prayer before we are dismissed."

"Thompson, here's something for you." The mail steward handed Clyde the envelope between the bars. Clyde looked at it curiously.

"Hmmm," he said to himself as he examined the return address—Box 453, Meridian, Texas. He knew that "Mom" Harper's son, Marvin, was a preacher in Meridian. But this wasn't Marvin's address. He opened the envelope to find a Christmas card with a short note enclosed.

The note read, "Merry Christmas, in appreciation of the

Christian work you are doing in prison. God can use us wherever we are. Keep up the good work. Sincerely, Julia Perryman."

Clyde smiled. It was nice that someone would remember him at Christmas, and Clyde was grateful to receive anything from the outside. Some prisoners never received any mail. Clyde had been allowed to purchase a few Christmas cards. He sat down and addressed one to Julia Perryman and enclosed a note thanking her for remembering him at Christmas.

On the second Sunday of January, 1947, Marvin Harper had selected for his sermon text a reading from Matthew:

> Then shall the King say unto them on his right hand, Come, ye blessed of my Father, inherit the kingdom prepared for you from the foundation of the world: For I was an hungred, and ye gave me meat: I was thirsty, and ye gave me drink: I was a stranger, and ye took me in: Naked, and ye clothed me: I was sick, and ye visited me: I was in prison, and ye came unto me (25:34–36).

The name of Clyde Thompson wasn't mentioned in the sermon, but the text, especially the last sentence of it, struck home with Julia. The previous year, she had gone with Marvin and a few others from church to the local jail. They had intended to sing some hymns to the prisoners. The jailer had practically laughed at them. "You won't be allowed in here," the jailer had said. "Why are nice folks like you wanting to mix with guys like this anyway?" They had left dejected, but at least they had tried.

Julia thought about the pleasing Christmas she'd had with her parents. Her sister and brother-in-law had visited, and her mother had cooked a turkey for the occasion. But what about the prisoner from whom she had received a Christmas card?

What kind of Christmas did he have? Maybe his wife had come to visit him. Or maybe he didn't have anyone on the outside.

Though she wasn't actually going to visit the prisoner, as the verse in Matthew indicated, she could drop him a note to see if there was anything he needed.

"Thank you for the nice Christmas card and note," Julia wrote. "I do not know what it is like to be in prison, so I don't know what your needs might be. Please let me know if there is anything I could send you. Sincerely, your sister in Christ, Julia Perryman."

Clyde had corresponded with a number of Christian women who had encouraged him over the years. The earlier card and now the letter contained no indication of how old Julia Perryman was, whether she was married, or anything else about her. But Clyde responded that he could use a pair of socks and some old magazines. Then he waited for a reply.

A big red-haired man, Buddy Marrow, was transferred into the isolation unit at Wynne with a fifty-year sentence for killing a man with his bare hands. He was quiet and seemingly humble, but he would go into an uncontrollable rage once or twice a week. He would curse the guards or anyone else nearby and throw things in his cell. After the period of intense anger, he would have a seizure. Following the seizure, he wouldn't remember anything he had said or done. It was in one of those periods that he had allegedly killed the man.

Whenever he was taken from his cell for a bath, Marrow would be accompanied by three guards and two prisoner-workers in case a seizure started. But in spite of the added security, Marrow had beaten up five men before having a seizure on his way to a bath. After that, Marrow was never taken from his cell. His hair and beard grew long. And Clyde watched as a guard repeatedly fired tear gas into Marrow's cell as he was about to go into a seizure.

Clyde asked to be moved into a cell adjoining Marrow's so

that he could talk to him about the Bible. The guards honored his request, but Clyde found Marrow a bitter man for having been sentenced to prison for committing a crime over which he had no control—a crime he couldn't even remember committing. Marrow wanted nothing to do with religion.

Nearly two months had passed since Clyde wrote the letter to Julia, and he hadn't heard anything from her. Had he said something in the letter that she found offensive? Clyde wrote her again.

March 8, 1947

Dear Sister Perryman,
   Did I say something in my last letter to offend you? I wrote to you in January and have not heard from you since. If I did say something offensive, please accept my apologies.

Clyde received the following letter in reply:

March 14, 1947

Dear Brother Thompson,
   No, you didn't say anything to offend me. In fact, I didn't get the earlier letter and can only assume it was lost in the mail. When you didn't answer, I thought you had already gone home. Please let me know if there is anything I can send you.

Clyde smiled when he read that she thought he had already gone home. And he noticed that Julia had signed her letter "Miss Julia Perryman." Clyde knew the chances were slim that the earlier letter had been lost in the mail. It was far more likely that it had never left the prison. The mail steward sometimes tore up letters for no apparent reason.

That afternoon, Clyde wrote a reply to the letter, explaining that he would probably never be able to go home. He told her that he was serving two life sentences plus fifteen years, and he explained why he had received those sentences. But Clyde didn't want her to think of him simply as a killer, so he told her of the change in his life many years earlier.

Clyde and Julia continued to correspond, the letters becoming less formal and more personal. In her letters, Julia didn't seem to mind that he had killed four men. She said that she was more interested in the type of man he was today. Clyde also learned that she was about a year and a half older than he and had always been single.

She seemed like a lovely person from her correspondence. Clyde wondered why such a thoughtful woman had never been married. He wanted to find out as much about her as he possibly could. Even though he was probably behind bars permanently, Clyde felt romantic interest. He wasn't sure if she felt it, but he knew he did.

Clyde asked her several questions in one of his letters and got the following reply in mid-April:

> . . . I don't know where to start answering. But before any of those, I want you to know that I'm handicapped. As a child I was twice stricken with severe cases of typhoid fever. After the second bout with typhoid, I also developed scoliosis. As a result, my spine didn't grow straight but twisted. I now have a bad case of curvature of the spine and am only four feet, nine inches tall. I'm sure that you wouldn't want to meet me in person, but I'd be glad to keep sending you things you need. . . .

When Clyde received the letter, he felt bad—not because of the disclosure of Julia's handicap, but because of the way she seemed to feel about herself because of it. He replied: "In spite of the handicap, I would love to meet you in person. The most beautiful souls I have known were those in handicapped

bodies. I really appreciate you sharing that with me, but, believe me, it doesn't make any difference. . . ."

With Julia's accepting Clyde's past and his accepting her
handicap, the relationship between them thrived through
their letters. They had a common religious faith, and both
were prisoners, he behind bars and she in an imperfect body.

Clyde was delighted with the new relationship. Julia was his
first real romantic interest since Ruth Welsey some seventeen
years earlier. Clyde had observed that many men had girl
friends or wives when they came into prison. But as a man
spent more time behind bars, the likelihood increased that his
wife would divorce him or he would receive a "Dear John"
letter from his girl friend. Prisoners like Clyde, who had spent
years behind bars and had no prospects of getting out, rarely
had many contacts on the outside, especially not with eligible
women.

Julia sent a picture she had taken of herself, and Clyde
proudly displayed it in his cell. She noted in her letter that she
had retouched the photograph to make herself look better.

She seemed to be a kind person. And from her picture, she
was good-looking. In June Clyde signed his letter, "Love,
Clyde." In July he told Julia he loved her. And in August he
proposed marriage.

The love was not one-sided. Julia felt it, too. From his letters, Julia sensed that Clyde was a considerate person. She
was impressed with his knowledge of the Bible.

Julia's relationships with men had been limited. She told
herself that most men were interested in only a sexual relationship. And Julia was determined that she would remain
chaste until she was married. Therefore, she had spurned ad-
vances men had made toward her. But also a strong consideration was her fear of a relationship with a man because of her
physical deformity. *No man would really want me,* her inner-
most self whispered. And Julia believed it. She had overcome
her handicap enough to live on her own and run a successful

photo studio. But the handicap still stood in the way of any relationship with a man.

With Clyde, however, she felt comfortable. They were having a relationship of their minds and hearts, but it was impossible for it to go any further.

As their hearts grew closer, Julia felt a nagging desire to push away because of her deformity. It was a fear of rejection. And to avoid the rejection, she felt it might be better to back off. "You really wouldn't want to be engaged to me," she wrote in reply to his proposal of marriage. "It would just be a burden for you."

In a letter dated August 26, 1947, Clyde answered: "You've asked me to reconsider my thoughts about marriage, Julia, because I would have to share the burden of your handicap. That makes me cry. Your handicap is no worse than mine, being a convict. So please don't talk like that any more. . . ."

Though he seemed to fully accept her condition, Julia still hesitated. She wanted to be his fiancée, but it would be silly to be engaged to a man she had never seen face-to-face. At the first meeting Clyde would see how bad she really looked. *That might change his mind in a hurry,* she thought. Before she could accept his proposal, therefore, she had to meet him in person. Arrangements were made for Marvin Harper to drive with her to Huntsville to visit Clyde four days after the Christmas of 1947.

If Julia had apprehensions and fears, so did Clyde. It had been more than ten years since he'd had a visitor other than a minister. Clyde wondered if he would know how to act. What if he couldn't think of anything to say? What if he said something stupid or offensive?

Both Julia and Clyde looked forward to their first meeting but at the same time dreaded it.

Chapter
30

THE VISITING ROOM at Wynne was large, with painted concrete walls and a gray concrete floor. It smelled of cigarette smoke. The room was filled with wooden benches that visitors and prisoners sat on together. Those coming in from the outside were routinely searched, then taken to the visiting room to wait.

Julia sat close beside Marvin Harper on a bench, twisting a handkerchief in her hands and watching a young couple sitting on a bench across from her. The girl looked something like a nineteen-year-old version of Betty Grable, the movie star. But the excessive make-up she wore and the uneven way in which it was applied showed that she was probably a farm girl. She had been crying, smearing her make-up and giving her face a sad, clownlike appearance. The girl sat tightly against a white-garbed inmate to whom she was probably married. *He's twenty-two at the oldest*, thought Julia.

Julia looked around the room to see several other couples that she considered to be odd-looking. *But I guess I'm a good one to talk*, she thought. *I'm probably the oddest-looking one of the bunch.* What if Clyde took one look at her and headed back to his cell? He was probably too considerate to do that.

He'd more likely visit for a while, then write her a polite note discontinuing their relationship.

Julia felt a gentle nudge of Marvin's elbow at her side. "This is probably him," Marvin said quietly.

Julia looked at an inmate being led into the visiting area between two guards. *He sure looks short,* said Julia to herself. The eyes of the inmate quickly scanned the visiting area and then focused on Julia. Marvin motioned for the man to come over. Both he and Julia stood. Clyde walked directly to Julia and kissed her on the lips. Julia was surprised but didn't step back. The two stared into each other's eyes for a moment, then Clyde and Marvin shook hands and introduced themselves. *He's not so short, after all,* thought Julia. She looked at the two guards who had been standing beside Clyde. Both were over six feet tall. Standing beside them, Clyde had looked short. But now that he stood by her, he seemed just about right.

The three sat down. Marvin and Clyde talked briefly about Mrs. Harper, Marvin's mother and Clyde's long-time pen pal and "Mom." Marvin then excused himself, saying he wanted to look around the prison grounds.

"I knew it was you when I first stepped in here," Clyde told her after Harper left. "You look just like the pictures you sent."

"And you're just the way I pictured you in my mind's eye."

"I hope that's all right."

"It's great," she said, smiling.

The two moved closer together on the bench.

"What about . . . ?" her voice trailed off, and she motioned backward with her head in the direction of her misshapen spine.

Clyde looked to where she motioned. She felt herself growing tense. "I told you, darling," Clyde said gently. "My handicap is a lot greater than that. Besides, you made it sound a lot worse than it really is."

"I didn't want to paint a rosy picture and then have you be disappointed."

"I'm not one bit disappointed. The only thing that would disappoint me would be to lose you."

"Now, now," she chided jokingly.

"That's right," he countered.

Apprehensions that either of them had about the visit vanished almost immediately. There were no moments of edginess or awkward silences. They seemed to pick up where their last letters had ended.

Julia confided to Clyde that this was the first time she had gone against the wishes of her parents. Her father hadn't objected to her correspondence with a convict, but he hadn't thought it wise to visit him in person. Clyde told her he understood her father's apprehensions and didn't want to cause any problem between her and her parents. But Julia, who still had second thoughts about not trying to adopt the baby even though she had let her parents talk her out of it, was now determined to do what she thought was right, even if her parents disapproved.

The two hours allowed for visiting passed quickly. The guard signaled Clyde and Julia that time was up.

"Just think," Clyde recalled, still sitting on the bench. "This all started with a Christmas card a year ago."

"Sure am glad I sent it," Julia replied.

The guard again reminded them that visiting hours were over.

"I love you, Julia," Clyde said earnestly. It was the first time in his life that he had said that to a woman.

"I love you, too, Clyde," Julia replied, somewhat shyly. It was the first time she had said that to a man.

"I may be in here for the rest of my life, honey, and I don't know if it's right to ask you to wait," he said. "But if I ever get out of here, I want you to be my wife."

"You mean you had to wait 'til the last minute to make your

proposal official?" she said jokingly to overcome her own nervousness.

"Yeah," Clyde answered. "I've been trying to get up my nerve."

The guard walked toward them. "Ma'am, you'll have to leave now," he said politely.

Julia looked up at the guard. "Okay," she said, standing up.

"You mean the answer's yes?" Clyde asked.

She looked back at him. "Yes," she said. Clyde was still sitting on the bench, somewhat awestruck. Julia kissed him lightly on the lips and headed for the door.

Prison reform had been one of the biggest issues during the 1946 Texas gubernatorial election. It seemed that all the candidates were in favor of doing something to improve the conditions in TDC. But Beauford H. Jester, the most reform-minded candidate, got the nod from voters for a two-year term starting in January, 1947. With his inauguration, gone was the idea that the prison system would be self-supporting. Prison reform would cost money, and Jester planned to spend some to clean up the prisons. A search was conducted for a new head of TDC, and the man who got the job was O. B. Ellis, a professional penologist from Memphis, Tennessee.

Each time a new general manager took over, there was talk of reform, although it was usually short-lived. But Clyde saw changes shortly after Ellis took over. The bat had long since been outlawed as a means of punishing prisoners, but Ellis did away with the routine use of tear gas. The straw mats on which the prisoners slept were replaced by mattresses. Clyde once again received commissary privileges. Radios were allowed on the cellblock. These small changes made a big difference for those in isolation.

An hour didn't go by, however, without Clyde's thinking of Julia. He would read a chapter in the Bible and wonder what she would say about it. Or he would hear a song on the radio and wonder whether she liked it. They corresponded regularly, and she made the more-than-three-hour drive to visit as often as her work would allow. They both listened to the same radio station and would write the station to request songs for each other.

Although it was still a year and a half in the future, Clyde would be coming up for parole for the first time in 1949. He knew his chances of being released from prison were negligible. And he rightly assumed that his possibilities of release would be much better if he was first moved from the isolation unit, which was reserved for the most incorrigible prisoners. Counting his days in the old morgue, Clyde had been in isolation nearly nine years.

Julia helped Clyde in his efforts to improve his situation within the prison system. She wrote letters on Clyde's behalf to anyone in the state who had anything to do with prisoners, starting with the governor. She also made an appointment to see Ellis.

Ellis lived in a large brick home, supplied by the state, just across the street from the red brick walls of the main prison in Huntsville. He had arranged to see Julia during the noon hour at his home prior to her visit with Clyde at the nearby Wynne unit that afternoon. Julia was somewhat apprehensive about meeting the man in person. For Clyde's sake, she wanted to make a good impression.

Mrs. Ellis welcomed Julia at the door and guided her to the living room. She then excused herself, and in a moment Mr. Ellis came into the room. The man didn't fit the image Julia had in her mind of a prison official. He appeared to be a kind man. As he greeted her warmly, her apprehensions disappeared.

Julia had written two earlier letters to Ellis on Clyde's behalf. Curious about the prisoner Clyde Thompson, Ellis had looked in Clyde's file, talked to other prison officials about him, and briefly met him on a tour through the isolation unit.

Ellis had then written a memorandum stating, "He [Clyde] is one of the ten most desperate men in the prison system and is a lock-up case for the rest of his life." The memorandum was for internal use only and was, therefore, unknown to Julia.

Ellis's face didn't show it, but he regarded Julia with a certain degree of pity. The pity was not for her deformity, because she seemed to get along quite well. But she differed little to him from many other extremely overweight or crippled women he had seen involved with prisoners both in Tennessee and Texas. They were women who became involved with prisoners probably because no man on the outside would pay any attention to them. Maybe a man behind bars was better than no man at all? Ellis had seen these women pine away their years waiting for a man who had no chance of release. Other women had love pledged to them from behind bars, only to be suddenly discarded when the prisoner was finally released. Ellis didn't want Julia to be disappointed.

"I guess you came here to talk to me about Clyde Thompson," said Ellis.

Julia nodded.

"Did you know that Clyde Thompson killed two men when he was seventeen years old and came pretty close to dying in the electric chair?"

"Yes, sir, he told me about that," replied Julia without flinching.

This surprised Ellis a bit, because inmates often hid the true nature of their crimes from the people with whom they corresponded. "Did you also know that he's tried to escape from our farms and has been convicted of murder twice more for stabbing inmates?"

"Yes, I know that, too, Mr. Ellis."

"This is a violent man we're talking about, Miss Perryman," Ellis countered. "He'd probably stop at nothing, including murder, to escape again."

Julia smiled. "Oh, no, Mr. Ellis, he's as gentle as a kitten."

"If it were up to you, we'd just open all the doors and gates and let them all out, wouldn't we?" probed Ellis.

"No, Mr. Ellis, I wouldn't do that," she answered. "You have some very dangerous inmates locked up here."

"Are you asking us to release the meanest man in Texas?" inquired Ellis.

"No, sir, that's not why I'm here."

"What is it exactly that you're here for, then?" he asked, starting to wonder whether he knew her true motives.

"Mr. Ellis," said Julia, "I know you must be a very busy man with the thousands of inmates who are under your control. And I know there is no way you can get personally acquainted with each one of them. But I sure wish you could make an exception here. The Clyde Thompson they first brought to prison is dead. It says in the Bible that when a man puts on Christ, he dies to his old self. And that's the case with Clyde. He's put on Jesus and is a new man. If you could put away his past record and observe Clyde as he is today, you'd see that he could get along. He'd be a hard worker if you would give him a chance. Sure, I'd like for Clyde to get out. But there's no possible way you'd parole him from an isolation unit. So, first he needs to be given a chance by being taken out of isolation and put in one of the regular prison units. Then he could prove himself."

Ellis listened intently. He didn't respond right away but closed his eyes momentarily, as if thinking.

"Miss Perryman, I know that you are a sincere person, and I feel very bad for you," Ellis said as he lifted his eyes to meet hers. "It sounds as if you really love this man. But, believe me, it would be best for both of you if you just went away and forgot him."

"Do you mean to say he'll never get out?"

"I didn't say that," Ellis replied. "It's not up to me to free a man. That's up to the board of pardons and paroles. Only if they ask me the possibility of a man's making good on the outside do I have a right to speak on behalf of an inmate."

Julia nodded. "Yes, I know that. But it would sure be helpful if you could acquaint yourself with Clyde."

Ellis agreed that he would visit Clyde the next time he was at the Wynne unit. But before Julia left, he told her again that she would be better off forgetting Clyde. After her departure, he wrote a note saying he hoped he hadn't disappointed her too much, but he felt it his responsibility to show her the true picture.

As she drove toward Wynne, Julia wasn't disappointed. She believed she had brought Ellis a little closer to seeing the true picture.

Chapter
31

"MR. ELLIS will be coming through here in a few minutes," the guard announced.

Clyde had been reading a newspaper but quickly put it down to make sure his cell was in order. Julia had told him the details of her conversation with Ellis during her visit two and a half weeks earlier. Perhaps one of the reasons for his visit today was to get to know Clyde better, as Julia had suggested. *The impression I make on him today could make a big difference,* thought Clyde. He waited expectantly at the front of his cell.

In about ten minutes, Ellis walked into the unit with C. L. McAdams, the assistant warden of Wynne. They looked into all the cells as they walked up the corridor and talked briefly with many of the prisoners. They stopped in front of Clyde's cell.

"Hello, Clyde," said McAdams. "Have you met Mr. Ellis?"

"Yes, sir, we talked briefly before," Clyde answered.

Ellis extended his hand through the bars. The two shook hands.

"I've looked at your records," said Ellis. "And my opinion is that you must be a Dr.-Jekyll-and-Mr.-Hyde character. Have you ever read that book, Clyde?"

"No, sir, I haven't," Clyde answered.

"Could you get him a copy of that book, Captain McAdams?" asked Ellis.

"Yes, sir, I sure can," the assistant warden answered.

The two continued to the next cell, while Clyde walked dejectedly to the back of his cell. He had hoped he would have the opportunity to get to know Ellis, but it was clear that the new general manager already had an opinion of him. And it was a negative opinion. Clyde hadn't actually read *Dr. Jekyll and Mr. Hyde,* but he knew about the story. And it saddened him to think that Ellis still thought he was capable of behaving as he had before his time in the old morgue.

McAdams didn't have a chance to follow through on his promise of bringing the book to Clyde. A few days later he was promoted from assistant warden of Wynne to warden of the Ramsey farm near Otey. Captain Mac, as he was called by the inmates, was well liked. He always seemed to go out of his way to be fair to prisoners, though he wasn't a soft touch by any means. He stood six feet, two inches, weighed about 250 pounds, and had started as a guard at the Wynne unit in 1935, then enlisted in the armed forces to fight in World War II. Following the war, he had returned to work for the TDC.

McAdams had the nickname, "Bear Track." He had once walked in on a group of prisoners shooting craps. One of the prisoners was reported to have said, "I think a bear just walked in here, and every time I look at him, he seems to get bigger."

The "track" part of his name was said to have come from the fact that McAdams left his mark (or tracks) at every unit to which he was assigned.

Before leaving for his new post, McAdams came through the isolation unit to bid farewell to the inmates.

"I sure would like to come out to Ramsey with you, Captain," Clyde told McAdams.

"I'd be glad to have you out there, as soon as you can get off isolation."

"Well, sir, as long as Mr. Ellis maintains his present opinion of me, I think my chances of getting off isolation are pretty slim."

McAdams shook his head, affirming Clyde's beliefs. "Let me get things going out at Ramsey, and I'll talk to him for you, Clyde."

Clyde smiled. "I'd sure appreciate that," he said.

For Christmas of 1947, Julia gave Clyde a blank one-year diary. Clyde made daily entries and copied poems that he thought Julia would like. A typical day's entry read like this:

> Up at 5:30. Had light breakfast. Read Gospel newspapers and Psalms. Worked Bible lesson. Read the *Houston Post*. Lunch. Finished *Post* and read two old *Fort Worth Star Telegrams*. Took nap. Read Almanac. Supper. Read more in Almanac about Panama, Mexico and other countries. Started letter to you and did shoework. [Clyde made slippers in his cell by weaving together the sackcloths in which tobacco came.] Wish I were with you, sweetheart. We would be happy, I know. Good night, honey. I love you and need you, dear.

For her fortieth birthday on January 15, 1949, Clyde gave Julia the diary. She read and reread it. They made a pact to think of each other at eight o'clock each night.

Julia's parents continued to object to their daughter's visiting a convict. "It's about time you call off that so-called engagement and quit seeing that man," Elvis Perryman had told her more than once.

"You'd better listen to your father, honey," her mother had said. "We only want what's best for you."

Unknown to Julia, her father visited the Wynne unit in August, 1948. But he didn't go there to see Clyde. He wanted to find out first-hand what kind of man his daughter wrote and visited and, even worse, was engaged to marry. The visit confirmed Elvis Perryman's worst fears. A prison official told him that Clyde Thompson was a psychopathic killer who was using his daughter. "If Thompson ever gets out of prison, he will take your daughter for everything she's got and then kill her," the prison official told him.

Mr. Perryman left word at the prison that his daughter was forbidden to see Clyde Thompson.

Julia wondered why there was a delay as she waited for Clyde in the visitors' area on her next trip to the Wynne unit. Usually it took no more than a few minutes for Clyde to join her after she arrived. After a half hour, there was still no Clyde. When she inquired about the long wait, she found what the problem was. The prison official with whom her father had visited was attempting to keep her from seeing Clyde. At the same time, another prison official was pointing out that Julia was no schoolgirl and that her father had no right to determine who she could or couldn't see. Julia got in the middle of it. She and the official who had taken her side finally prevailed. But Julia was in tears when Clyde came to the visiting area.

"I'm just going to sever all ties with my family," she sobbed. "They've been telling me what to do my whole life, and I'm sick of it. They've gone too far this time."

Clyde put his arm around her. "Please, honey, don't do that," he said quietly.

"Yes, I'm going to do it," Julia said with determination.

"I feel badly about it, too," he said. "It makes me sad that even though I've had a good record for years, they still feel that way about me. But, before that, I spent a long time earning my reputation. And it's taking me longer to live it down. Your dad's just doing what he thinks is best for you. And I sure hate to think that I would come between you and your family."

When she left, Julia was still angry. But she promised Clyde she wouldn't make any immediate decisions concerning her family. Clyde returned to his cell feeling sad that his reputation was causing problems for Julia.

Clyde really felt his reputation as a killer and the meanest man in Texas was history. He prayed, read the Bible daily, and continued talking to prisoners about religion. He had a fine Christian lady on the outside who loved him. His old life was a thing of the past. But an incident soon occurred that made Clyde wonder whether he'd made *any* progress since earning his bad reputation.

Inmate Ted Seals was considered a tough convict. He was serving forty years for robbery and attempted murder and had been in isolation for six years, longer than any prisoner except Clyde. Seals was moved to the cell beside Clyde's in the fall of 1948.

The two were not the best of friends, but neither had there been any trouble between them. Clyde had known Ted since his days in isolation near death row. They had both been transferred to Wynne on the same chain. Now Clyde noticed that Seals seemed to go on a tirade about once a week. He would berate prison officials, guards, and sometimes other prisoners. Clyde didn't know whether this weekly occurrence was due to some type of mental quirk or whether Seals was getting dope smuggled into him on a weekly basis.

One week Seals began his verbal abuse of the prison system, then started in on Clyde. The guard was in a different part of the cellblock, or he would have put a stop to it.

"You're a coward, Thompson!" he taunted. "And when we go out onto the exercise yard this week, I'm gonna beat the h——outta ya. Might even stab ya like ya did to those other guys. Then everyone 'round here will know your true colors."

Clyde's gut-level reaction was to yell back and take the challenge. But he restrained himself. He reasoned that arguing with Seals would only make matters worse.

Seals stopped momentarily and seemed to be waiting for a

reply. When there was no reaction from the next cell, he started again. "You're a punk for not talkin' back, Thompson," he said in a voice loud enough to be heard by prisoners up and down the line. "The only reason you have a reputation as a killer is because you've picked on unarmed men. You've never fought anyone fairly. But this week you'll have an armed man to deal with, and you'd better be prepared or not come out of your cell."

Clyde's heart was pounding, and his hands were trembling. He was confident he could take Seals with either knives or fists. But that was behind him now. That was not what he wanted. And Clyde knew that although his chances of ever getting out were slim, even those slim hopes would be dashed if he killed Seals.

Clyde paced back and forth in his cell, sat on the edge of the mattress, and prayed for guidance. Seals had quieted down. About the time Clyde was finished with his prayer, a note was passed from a man Clyde considered to be one of his best friends on the cellblock. "You're not going to let him get away with that, are you?" the note said. "I've got a knife hidden in my cell that I'll give you in the morning. And if I was you, I'd be waiting when Mr. Seals comes out of his cell and cut him to pieces."

Clyde wrote back,

Thanks for the offer, pal. If this had happened upwards of ten years ago, I'd do just as you have suggested. If I kill him, he'll go to hell, and I don't intend to send another man's soul to that place. Whereas, if he kills me, I'll probably go to heaven. So I'm not going to fight him. And I plan to let the chips fall where they may.

Clyde sent his reply down the line. In a few more minutes, he got another note from the same man. "You must be crazy!" it said. Clyde didn't feel he was, but he spent a restless night thinking about what would be the right thing to do. He couldn't go to the guard, because that would label him as a stoolie. If he did nothing and backed down from the inevitable confrontation, he would be a coward, and that was just about as bad as being a stoolie. At the same time, Clyde felt it would be almost certain suicide to go out in the yard unarmed.

The next morning the friend who had sent him the notes walked by Clyde's cell on his way to the prison barber. He paused in front of Clyde's cell and looked to see where the guard was. The guard had his back turned, talking to another inmate at the other end of the cellblock. The man pulled a knife from his pocket and tossed it between the bars onto Clyde's bed. Alarm registered on Clyde's face. Here was a knife he didn't want, but to be caught with it would be big trouble. He hid it in his cell.

The knife added a new dimension to Clyde's dilemma. Now he could fight Seals on even terms. Should he follow the code of the prison or what he had learned in the Bible about turning the other cheek? Clyde finally decided on a middle course. He wasn't going to be labeled a coward, but at the same time he didn't plan to kill Seals. If Seals wanted to fight him and pulled a knife, Clyde would try to disarm him with the knife he had been given. He would try to stab Seals in the hand, wrist, or arm. Clyde knew, though, that this course of action could really mean death for either of them.

Clyde wrote a letter to Julia, explaining that he had to defend his honor and that it could cost him his life.

Julia cried when she read the letter and spent a sleepless night thinking about what Clyde had said. The next morning she wrote a letter back to Clyde in hopes that he would get it before the fight occurred.

Because of my love for you, what happens to you also happens to me. If you get hurt, I get hurt. . . . This could ruin any chances of your ever getting out of prison and any chances of our ever being together. . . . Look how they treated the Son of God. He was ridiculed, tortured, and finally crucified for no reason. But yet he didn't find it necessary to defend himself. If Jesus didn't have to defend his honor, why should you? Besides, how much honor does a three-time convicted murderer have?

Julia sealed the envelope and drove it to the Meridian Post Office.

But before Julia's letter arrived, the men in isolation got their weekly yard privilege. Clyde's cell was unlocked ahead of Seals's, so, with the knife in his pocket, he walked directly to the middle of the prison exercise yard to wait, sweating and trying not to shake. Seals walked out the door with two friends, and they stood at the side, talking, laughing, and appearing not to notice Clyde. Clyde watched them for a while, waiting for Seals to make his move. When Seals didn't, Clyde stalked over to him.

"Here I am, Seals. Now let's see your knife!" challenged Clyde.

"Why, Clyde, I haven't got a knife," Seals replied, seemingly surprised that Clyde was confronting him.

"After all the popping off you did the other day and you come out here without a knife—you're a bigger fool than I thought you were, Seals!" taunted Clyde.

Seals didn't answer but stood with a puzzled look on his face. "Take your hands out of your pockets, boy!" Clyde ordered. Clyde's grip tightened on the knife in his pocket as Seals's hands came out empty. Clyde left the knife in his own pocket, doubled up his right fist, and sent it crashing into Seals's face. Seals staggered backward, and a friend steadied him. He charged at Clyde, and the two men went at it.

Seals landed a couple of solid blows to Clyde's face, but Clyde landed four or five to his opponent's eyes and nose. After exchanging these blows, both men were panting for breath. Neither was in very good physical condition after the years spent in isolation with little exercise. A guard saw the fighting and blew a whistle to alert the other guards. The two stopped fighting when the whistle blew. Before the guards arrived, Clyde concealed the knife in his hand and returned it to its owner. The knife was buried in the prison yard.

Clyde was tired, and he already felt sore by the time he got back to his cell. An hour and a half later he received the letter that Julia had sent; he read it with tears in his eyes. *But she doesn't know that it's already too late,* thought Clyde. *Now what will she think of me? Maybe she'll quit me altogether. And maybe her father's completely justified in not wanting her to see me.*

Clyde also focused his thoughts on the progress he had made since first being put in isolation. He had tried to let God run his life and had felt relatively successful about it. But now, in a matter of days, he had reverted to the madman they had put in the old morgue—a con ready to stab another at the drop of a hat. Had he really made any progress? What must God think of him now?

Then there was the matter of his case soon coming up before the board of pardons and paroles. If his chances were slim before, they were nonexistent now.

These thoughts ran through Clyde's mind for the rest of the day. He felt alone and hopeless. He cried himself to sleep that night.

Chapter
32

THE DAWNING of a new day did little to alleviate Clyde's negative feelings. His body was sore. And both Julia and any chance he had of ever getting parole were probably gone. He had blown it.

That morning Clyde and Seals saw the warden. Clyde wasn't sure what Seals told him, but Clyde assumed the blame for the fight. Since they were already in isolation, Clyde and Seals weren't thrown in the hole. Instead, their yard privileges were suspended for a month.

Clyde paced dejectedly in his cell, and he kicked at the back wall. Then he sat down to write.

Dear Julia,
Thanks for the nice letter, but it got here too late. The fight had already gone on. Thankfully, neither of us was hurt besides a few bruises. What hurts much worse is the fact that I've probably thrown away my entire future, maybe our entire future.

I know that you must be very disappointed in me. But I love you, Julia, and please don't quit me on account of this fighting. You have my promise that it will never happen again.

Love,
Your Clyde

Clyde addressed and sealed the letter; then he fell face down on his bunk. Still in the same position thirty minutes later, Clyde prayed. Then he evaluated the way he had reacted to Seals's threats. Instead of behaving like a Christian, he had followed the code of the prison. Instead of doing what he thought was right, he had done what just about any other incorrigible prisoner would have done—he fought over some mistaken notion of honor. Clyde had allowed himself to stew over Seals's threats; he had lost his head and punched Seals. No matter what Seals had said, Clyde had no excuse for throwing the first punch. Clyde knew that he, Clyde Thompson, had been wrong.

A few days passed as Clyde thought through what had happened. He received a letter from Julia with a mild scolding for fighting. But she promised to stick with him as long as he lived up to his promise to not let it happen again. Clyde was relieved and grateful. He didn't know what he would do without her.

Then there was the matter of mending fences with Seals. One of the favorite items from the commissary was a Cho-Cho, ice cream with a chocolate and nut topping that came in a cone. A Cho-Cho cost a nickel. Clyde regularly ordered them for himself, and since he had money sent to his account from Julia, his mother, brother, and a sister, he often bought ice creams for other prisoners. The next time he ordered from the commissary, he ordered a Cho-Cho for Seals. In the coming days, they settled their differences and jointly wrote a letter promising it wouldn't happen again. The two became good friends after that. They regained their yard privileges when the month was up.

Throughout his confinement, Clyde had corresponded with

his mother. He had last seen her thirteen years earlier in 1936, when he was at Retrieve. After Clyde and Julia became engaged, Julia, too, wrote Clyde's mother who had relocated in Las Vegas, Nevada. The letters led to a visit. Clyde's mother stayed in Meridian with Julia, and they visited the prison together in April, 1949. It was a tearful reunion.

Clyde came up for parole for the first time in July, 1949, and he was routinely turned down. He was only mildly disappointed. He received a letter saying his case would be reviewed again in two years—mid-1951. He knew he could wait two more years.

The prison grapevine had long before carried news that a new isolation unit was going to be built at The Walls. This rumor had been confirmed by newspaper stories, which stated that the unit would hold more than 350 men. Shortly after Clyde had come up for parole, the new unit was completed, and he was moved back to The Walls. The new isolation unit was known as Shamrock.

When he arrived, Clyde was given a close-cropped haircut like a raw recruit in military basic training. His cell at Shamrock was similar to the ones at Wynne, although slightly larger. When a prisoner stepped out of line in the new unit, he was handcuffed with his hands sticking backward between the bars. This method cut off circulation, and the man's hands would turn blue. Then a guard would twist the man's fingers and hands. From the way they screamed, Clyde knew that the pain must be excruciating. The fact that prisoners were being tortured was unknown outside the unit, and it didn't fit in with the reforms instituted by Ellis.

Clyde hadn't been given any notice of the transfer and, therefore, hadn't been able to notify Julia. Nor had he been allowed to send out a letter during his first few days in the new unit. When the day came for her next scheduled visit, Julia drove to Wynne, only to find that Clyde had been transferred. From there she drove to The Walls.

Julia found that Shamrock had its own warden, and he was called in to talk with her. Visitors were allowed only once a month, compared to twice monthly at Wynne. Further, Julia was supposed to have written permission from the warden before coming to see Clyde.

"No one even let me know he was transferred, and I've driven a long way to see him," Julia persisted. "Since I didn't know about these rules, can't you let me see him today?"

The warden relented, but Julia did a double take when she saw Clyde. With barely more than stubbles of hair sticking out of his scalp, he didn't look like the same man.

Clyde was glad to see her. He was frightened at the cruelty in the unit, but he decided not to tell her about it. He was the first on the unit to have a visitor and knew the warden could make it tough on him if Julia went to higher authorities.

Clyde tried to be a model prisoner and avoided punishment. When walking in front of Clyde's cell, however, one of the guards regularly said, "There's ol' Clyde Thompson, the only man in Texas meaner 'n I am." Clyde was glad they respected him, but he was sorry it was for the wrong reasons. He also knew that as long as his old reputation was alive, it would be very difficult for him to be paroled or to be moved from isolation.

A month after her first visit, Julia visited Clyde again. This time, Clyde told her about the inhumane treatment to which some of the prisoners were being subjected. Julia wrote letters to the parole board and Ellis about it. Undoubtedly, the loved ones of others imprisoned at Shamrock were doing the same. There was an investigation, and a new warden, E. L. King, was named. He was a firm man, but he also seemed fair. These traits won him the respect of the inmates. The torturing of the prisoners ceased.

Under their new warden, prisoners were allowed to see a

movie once a week. It was the first time Clyde had seen a talking picture. And instead of weekly yard privileges, the men got to go in the yard three times a week for two hours each time. Prisoners were punished by the removal of their movie or yard privileges. Solitary confinement was still used, but sparingly.

Clyde was allowed to conduct weekly religious services in the prison yard. It was the first time he had been able to preach since his days at the old morgue. He felt more useful and spent a lot of time preparing his sermons. If he was ever released, Clyde hoped to be able to preach in churches on the outside.

After having a nearly spotless record for twelve years, Clyde was rewarded. He was put in a position of some responsibility and trust for the first time since he was the lead row man at the farms. He was given the job of serving meat in the prison dining room. Clyde and five others would dish food onto the men's plates from trays that were sent hot from the kitchen.

There was more to this job than simply putting a piece of meat on each dish. Clyde had to make sure that each prisoner got an equal portion. If one inmate got more than another, Clyde would be accused of favoritism. If he gave too-small portions and there was meat left over on the tray after everyone had been served, the prisoners would feel they had been slighted. If Clyde gave portions that were too large, prisoners at the end of the line wouldn't receive any.

Clyde took his new responsibility seriously. On the few occasions when he ran out of meat, Warden King didn't seem to mind if Clyde ordered more from the kitchen.

Inmates at Shamrock had once-a-week commissary privileges. A prisoner was given the job of taking orders from each man, picking up items from the commissary, and delivering them to the cells. With money sent to them from the outside, prisoners ordered writing materials, tobacco, gum, candy, and small personal items. The prisoner who took the orders made occasional mistakes, drawing the ire of prisoners, who complained to the warden. Since Clyde had done well for several months in the dining room, he was given the commissary job. About the same time, commissary privileges were extended to twice weekly. This new job was another promotion for Clyde, and it kept him out of his cell for long periods of time on commissary days.

Clyde was diligent about this task, as he had been with his earlier one. He knew how irritating it was to receive the wrong order from the commissary. A mistake meant that someone would have to wait three or four days before reordering. He took special care to see that the prisoners got what they ordered for the proper amount of money. Several inmates and guards praised Clyde's work to Warden King.

The commissary job also allowed Clyde to talk personally with each prisoner at Shamrock about his religious beliefs. He ordered religious booklets and distributed them to prisoners who were interested. As a result of these contacts, the number of men who were attending the religious services in the prison yard grew to fifty of the two hundred men in the unit.

In the meantime, Clyde's successor at the meat tray was not doing well in his new job. Apparently out of fear of running out of meat and displeasing the warden, he was giving skimpy portions. There was always a pile of meat on the serving tray after all the men had been through the line. Many prisoners grumbled that they left the dining hall still hungry. The problem came to a head one day as the thirty men on Clyde's wing were in the dining hall. Clyde and nine or ten others had been served and were already seated.

Clyde was taking a bite from his biscuit, listening to the familiar clatter of silverware, when he heard shouting at the serving line.

"Is that all you're going to give me?" a prisoner shouted at the man who served the meat. "I go to bed hungry every night, and it's 'cause you're tryin' to kiss the warden's a———."

There were shouts of agreement from those standing behind him in line. With this bit of encouragement, the prisoner threw his plate at the meat server. Others followed suit. The prisoner sitting beside Clyde heaved his portion of meat in the direction of the serving line. Clyde didn't want to be caught in the middle of it; he got up from the table and went off to the side as food and dishes sailed through the dining hall. An assistant warden was stationed in a picket area overlooking the hall, and he fired a volley of tear gas and called for help. The riot was soon quelled, and the men were taken back to their cells.

The five who seemed to be instigators were put in solitary for a month. The remainder who participated lost their writing, visiting, movie, commissary, and yard privileges for thirty days. Clyde was the only man on his wing not to lose his privileges. As a result, Clyde seemed to find even more favor with the warden.

At the conclusion of the thirty-day period, Clyde had prepared a sermon titled "Heavenly Hope" in which he related his personal testimony of how God had worked in his life. At the conclusion of the sermon, three of the men just released from solitary walked forward to confess their faith in Christ and asked to be baptized.

Clyde kept busy at Shamrock between his work with the commissary, the worship services in the prison yard, and his relationship with Julia. In early spring, 1951, an assistant warden visiting from the Ramsey farm walked through Shamrock with Warden King. When they got in front of Clyde's cell, King stopped and said, "This is Clyde Thompson, who is supposed to be the meanest man in Texas."

"Yes, I've heard of him," replied the assistant warden.

"He hasn't been mean around here," King related. "In my opinion he's the best prisoner in this unit."

Clyde smiled and nodded at the two men.

"I've heard a lot about you, Clyde," said the assistant warden.

"Well, I hope you've heard something good," Clyde replied.

"Just did," he said.

"How's Warden Mac these days?" asked Clyde.

"Busy, but fine."

"When he was leaving the Wynne unit, he promised to see about getting me out of isolation after he got settled out there. Do you think you could remind him of me?"

"Sure," replied the assistant warden.

In less than a week, Warden McAdams appeared at Clyde's cell. He apologized for forgetting his promise to talk with Ellis. Clyde didn't hold it against him, because he had seen a lot of positive things happen in his life since Wynne. And he had gained an ally in Warden King. McAdams and King went together before the three-member committee that determined whether prisoners would have a change in status. The committee consisted of Ellis and two other high-ranking officials in the TDC. Clyde tried not to get his hopes up. Ellis probably still thought he was a Dr.-Jekyll-and-Mr.-Hyde character, while the other two members of the committee were TDC old-timers who had known Clyde from his troublemaking days. Clyde was called before the committee. He answered questions about the black marks on his record dating back to 1932. He also told them about the change in his life that started in the old morgue.

"Do you think you deserved the punishment you received at the work farms?" probed Ellis.

Clyde nodded. "Yessir, I sure do. The punishments were tough—they used the bat in those days. But, somehow, we usually get what we deserve. I had a continually bad attitude. And I didn't miss too many chances to let people know about it."

Ellis nodded.

"Do you still think I'm a Dr.-Jekyll-and-Mr.-Hyde character, Mr. Ellis?" Clyde asked.

A sign of recognition came to Ellis's face. Although there were thousands of inmates in Texas prisons and he had talked with many of them, he remembered his earlier conversation with Clyde. He seemed to ponder the question. "I'm not sure, Clyde. I'm just not sure," he answered.

Clyde was returned to his cell to await the decision later that day. Had he said the right things? He wasn't sure. He had prayed about it beforehand. And he had tried to answer each question honestly.

Warden King came to the cell. "It's not good news, but it's not bad news either, Clyde," he said. "They've decided to postpone their decision for thirty days."

At least they hadn't turned him down flatly.

The thirty days dragged by. Once again, Wardens King and McAdams spoke to the board on Clyde's behalf. This time the board's decision was positive for Clyde. He was to be taken out of isolation and sent to the Ramsey farm with Warden McAdams in March, 1951.

As Clyde was getting his things together for the move, Ellis came to his cell and congratulated him.

"I'll bet he gets out of prison within a year," Clyde heard Ellis tell King. Clyde beamed inwardly. He knew his case would come before the board of pardons and paroles that summer. And he knew that he might finally have a chance of parole now that he was finally out of isolation. Thirteen years had passed since he first entered the old morgue.

Chapter

33

GOING TO THE FARM after nearly thirteen years of close confinement was almost like being completely released from prison. Clyde found that conditions had greatly improved since his days at Retrieve. The men worked eight hours a day, five days a week. They walked at a reasonable pace to and from the building each day. And if the work was more than three miles from the prison yard, they were given rides in trucks.

Ramsey was one of the "lower farms," located south of Houston near the Gulf coast. It had no barracks-type facility like the one at Retrieve. Instead, each man had his own cell. And instead of getting one bath weekly, as had been the case at Retrieve, prisoners bathed three times weekly.

Clyde was assigned to a hoeing squad, but Warden McAdams told Clyde to walk along with the squad at first and not to pick up a hoe until he had grown accustomed to being outdoors in the Texas sun again. Clyde could remember how many men died of sunstroke after coming from extended periods behind bars. He knew his muscles weren't in shape for the kind of work he had done at Retrieve, and he appreciated Warden Mac's giving him a breaking-in time.

As Clyde walked along with his squad, the guard would

often tell him to sit down and rest. Outside of Clyde's experience with Cy Smith, the guard at Retrieve whom he had respected, hearing this from a guard seemed unusual.

After a week of walking along with the squad, Clyde asked the guard for permission to start hoeing. The guard wanted to clear it with the warden. Later, Warden Mac told Clyde to get a hoe from the water wagon. "But don't hoe with it until I tell you. Just use it as a prop."

Clyde carried the hoe around for a few days, leaning on it occasionally. He was then given permission to "strike," which meant that he would pitch in with inmates who were behind the rest of the squad in their hoeing. After a week or two, Clyde was hoeing his own row and not having any trouble in keeping up.

A month passed, and a new guard, who had worked under McAdams at the Wynne unit, was transferred to Ramsey. Clyde was well acquainted with the new guard and had always thought him to be fair. The new guard was put in charge of the mess hall, and he asked Clyde to work with him. In his new duties, Clyde worked about two hours at each meal and was free to read, write, or rest in between.

Clyde and Julia wrote letters in preparation for the review of Clyde's case before the board of pardons and paroles. For the first time, Clyde had real hope of being released. He was no longer considered one of the incorrigible prisoners in isolation. His record was clear, and he had two wardens who he thought would give him favorable recommendations. He remembered what Ellis had said as he was leaving Shamrock. Perhaps Ellis would give him a favorable recommendation. The days seemed to pass slowly before the board in Austin would hear his case in July, 1951.

When the board finally made its decision, it was negative. They would reconsider his case in two more years.

Clyde felt defeated but not crushed. "Don't give up," said Julia on her next visit to a dejected Clyde. "You've come such a long way. And you know that I'll wait for you as long as it takes." She squeezed his hand.

"I know it could be worse," Clyde answered, returning the squeeze. "But I know I couldn't do it without you."

"Thanks, Clyde, but you were doing just fine before I came along," she reminded him. "The Lord was working in your life, and I guess He brought us together."

He nodded. "Warden Mac told me that my case will get a much more favorable review in 1953. He seemed to think the board didn't look favorably on the fact that I was just released from isolation a few months ago."

Clyde had reason to be grateful. His treatment was better than it had ever been in prison. He seemed to be well-thought-of, and as long as he kept a good attitude, his chance of release would be very good in 1953. His disappointment lasted only briefly.

There was a chaplain at Ramsey who ministered to the prisoners' day-to-day spiritual needs, but he preached at an outside church each Sunday. Services on Sunday were conducted by one of the inmates, just as Clyde had held services for prisoners at Shamrock. Clyde was among the twenty or so inmates who attended these services. When the prisoner who conducted the services was paroled, McAdams asked Clyde if he was willing to take over. Clyde agreed gladly. He taught Sunday school for about one hour. After that, he preached a sermon in the worship service. When he could, Clyde visited with his fellow inmates and discussed their spiritual convictions. Soon, the number attending Sunday services rose to fifty.

Just after Thanksgiving, Clyde was called in to see the warden. He waited in the reception area, thankful that he could wait without fear. In his old life, it would have meant trouble. But Clyde was curious about why Warden Mac wanted to see him. When he finally called Clyde into his office, McAdams asked Clyde to be in charge of the Christmas play for the inmates. He could pick forty prisoners with good work records to be in the show.

"I don't have any show business experience, but I would be glad to give it a try," Clyde answered.

Clyde picked mostly men who had jobs in the fields. Clyde reasoned that they would work harder in rehearsals because they would be grateful for the month's rest. Clyde decided on a nativity play. Fifteen of the men would act out parts in the play, while the remaining twenty-five would sing in the chorus. Clyde appointed two men who regularly attended Sunday services to lead the two groups. One directed the chorus, while the other directed the play. During rehearsals, Clyde split his time between them.

All went well, except for one minor problem. No one wanted to play the part of Mary. Clyde was beginning to think he would have to play the part himself when he mentioned the problem to the chaplain. If they could get the warden's permission, the chaplain thought he had a solution. The chaplain had an eight-year-old daughter who would probably be glad to play the part. The warden assented. The play went off without a hitch and was given a standing ovation by the prison population.

There were two building tenders to oversee the 120 prisoners in Clyde's wing of the prison. The job had changed since Clyde had first become acquainted with building tenders nearly twenty years earlier. It still consisted of acting as a type of internal policeman for the prisoners. Building tenders were also supposed to stop riots before they started, disciplining other prisoners by recommending loss of privileges. They also had the more mundane duties of making sure the cellblock was clean and beds were made. No longer did building tenders carry billy clubs and hunting knives. There was no more strong-arming of prisoners. Prisoners who broke rules were pulled out of line or taken from the mess hall and locked in their cells. Building tenders carried the clout of prison authorities, because prisoners knew they could be locked in solitary or put on a rock pile with a sledge hammer for not minding the building tenders.

One of the building tenders in Clyde's wing was paroled, and Clyde thought seriously about applying for the job. First, he went to Harry Charles, the other building tender, and asked whether he wanted him to apply. Harry thought it was a good idea. Clyde went to the warden and was immediately given the job.

There was also a guard in the wing, but the prisoners were directly responsible to Charles and Clyde. The two were responsible for inmates any time they were not on a work detail. The job began with opening the cells each morning. There was a control panel at the end of the cellblock for opening the cell doors. It contained a master switch for simultaneously opening all the doors and individual switches for each cell. As Clyde threw the master switch unlocking all the doors for the first time, he wondered how he would have handled the same responsibility in 1932 instead of 1952.

Either Clyde or Charles would accompany the inmates to the dining hall. The other would stay behind in the cellblock because, inevitably, there would be a few sick men who would stay in their cells. At night, the building tenders locked the men back in their cells and usually kept two men out for sweeping and mopping the cellblock. The building tenders also accompanied the inmates to the movies and to the recreation area. When the men were working during the day, there seemed to be enough to do to keep both Clyde and Charles busy.

Shortly after Clyde started in his new job, a television set was put in the recreation area. Clyde had read about television and was told about it by the new inmates, but this was the first time he had seen one. As a building tender, Clyde determined the program the majority of the men wanted to watch. "I Love

Lucy" was the favorite, followed by "You Bet Your Life" with Groucho Marx, Red Skelton's show, and "Dragnet." After their evening meal, the inmates were allowed to watch television until 9:00 P.M.

1952 passed quickly for Clyde. Julia came to see him every few weeks, making the long drive from Dallas, where she worked in a photo studio after selling her business in Meridian. Her parents had never accepted her relationship with Clyde and still tried to talk her out of it. She hadn't severed ties with them because of her father's earlier interference, but she steadfastly refused to bow to their wishes.

Having regular visits, Clyde was envied by other prisoners, many of whom never had a visitor. Clyde could empathize with these men because he had gone years without a loved one coming to see him. Around Thanksgiving of 1952, Clyde was permitted to put together another Christmas play. He worked hard and when it was finished, many said that it was even better than the previous year's event. Clyde also continued to conduct the weekly Bible study class and worship service. Attendance reached as high as eighty.

When a temporary position opened in a photo studio some fifty miles south of Houston near Freeport, Julia took it. She was just a forty-mile drive from the Ramsey farm. She visited Clyde as often as he was allowed to have visitors, twice monthly. Their love thrived, and they wrote each other nearly every day.

Clyde and Julia had high hopes that he would be released when he came up for parole in July, 1953. Clyde's brothers hired a lawyer to help his cause. Julia visited with prison officials in Austin on Clyde's behalf and wrote many letters to the TDC for him. Clyde's mother also joined in the letter-writing campaign.

Even if a prisoner was deemed fit to reenter society by the board of pardons and paroles, there were two stipulations. First, the parolee had to have a place to go when he was released. Second, he had to have a job waiting. Both of these were guaranteed for Clyde. In addition, the two prison officials, King and McAdams, would put in a good word for him. There was a chance that Ellis also might give Clyde a favorable recommendation.

Clyde had been behind bars since the age of seventeen. He was now forty-two and would be forty-three in October. Surely the board would look favorably on his request this time. His record had been nearly spotless for fifteen years and was exemplary for the nearly two and a half years he had been at Ramsey.

A few months before he was to come up for parole, Clyde's mother temporarily moved from Las Vegas to stay with Julia. She, too, visited Clyde twice monthly.

The weeks of waiting turned to days. Clyde was anxious. He prayed daily about his upcoming fate. He made petitions to God about being released, but was careful to add, "Thy will be done." Surely, after all the years, it was God's will for him finally to be released from prison and make a home with Julia.

The day came when the board would decide his fate. The decision was negative once more. His case would be reconsidered in two years.

Clyde was crushed. Would he be any worse off if he had not reformed? What would it take to show the board that he had changed? How could God allow this to happen to him?

In a letter to Clyde, the board said there had been a great change in Clyde's life—he had been rehabilitated. But members of the board thought Clyde had a low stress tolerance and, therefore, was not ready to be released into society.

When he was alone, Clyde wept silently. In a way he felt he had let down Julia, his mother, and his brothers. But there was nothing he could do about it. Julia had stuck by him for nearly six years, and what was she getting for it? Clyde wrote her a letter, telling her that he loved her and appreciated the way she had stuck by him. But, he continued, "as fine a Christian lady as you are, you won't have any trouble finding a nice man on the outside. There's no use in waiting for me, because it looks like I'll never get out of here."

Chapter
34

FOR THE NEXT FEW DAYS, Clyde walked around feeling lifeless. He continued his work as a building tender and did the best he could in preparing for Sunday's Bible study and worship service, but his heart wasn't in it.

McAdams took him aside. "Clyde," he said, "I know you must be disappointed."

Clyde stared blankly at the warden. He really wasn't in the mood for a pep talk.

"In fact," McAdams continued, "I probably can't appreciate the extent of your disappointment. You've been locked up a long time, and you've come such a long way. I just wanted you to know that I appreciate the work you're doing around here. As far as I'm concerned, you're the model prisoner for all of TDC."

Clyde listened carefully to the warden.

"Now, I know that you'd rather be on the outside, but I just wanted to encourage you to keep up the good work, because you're doing more good around here than you'll ever know." McAdams patted Clyde on the shoulder.

Clyde felt himself smiling for the first time since the board had turned him down. "Thanks, Warden," he said to McAdams. "It means a lot that you think so much of me."

That afternoon, Clyde received a letter from Julia. "There's only one man that I can ever love and that's you," she said. "And even if you have to stay in there for the rest of my life or yours, I'll always stand by you and love you."

Clyde started to feel much better. The board may not have believed in him, but some people did. And perhaps God hadn't let him down. Maybe God still had a purpose for his life.

In his sermon the next Sunday morning, Clyde told the story, from the book of Genesis, of how Joseph was sold into slavery by his brothers. As a slave in Egypt, Joseph gained a position of responsibility in the house of Potiphar. Potiphar's wife wanted Joseph to make love to her, but he refused. She then accused Joseph of raping her, and he was sent to prison. In spite of all the bad things that happened to him, Joseph never lost faith in God. After serving seven years on this bum rap, Joseph was released from prison because God gave him the gift of interpreting dreams. Joseph eventually became the "number two man" in Egypt and was able to assist the very brothers who had sold him into slavery.

Clyde hoped his sermon that morning did some good for the inmates. He knew it had helped him. Joseph hadn't deserved the imprisonment. In fact, he was punished for doing what he thought was right. Clyde did deserve to be in prison. He had killed four men. And even though the killings had occurred many years earlier, Clyde was still responsible and was still being punished for it. Because Joseph hadn't lost faith in God during low periods in his life, he was able to accomplish great things. Perhaps the same might be true for Clyde. He renewed a vow to trust that God was running his life and doing what was best for him, and he prayed for forgiveness of his doubts.

Julia visited on Sunday afternoon and confirmed in person the things she had said in her last letter. She mildly scolded Clyde for thinking she might want to give up on him. "After all," she said, "I've gotten more out of this relationship than you have."

"How?" he asked.

"Because of my handicap, I've always been really self-conscious," she confided. "I never wanted a man to get close to me. But because you were in prison, there was no way you could get close to me physically. First, we became close mentally, and now I don't mind being close to you physically." She scooted closer to him on the bench where they were sitting. He put his arm around her.

"In a way, I've been a prisoner, too," she continued. "A prisoner of my handicap. But God brought us together, and you've helped to set me free from my prison."

Clyde squeezed Julia gently and felt tears in his eyes. He hadn't realized how the relationship had helped Julia. He had assumed it was a one-way street, with her helping him, and this new understanding was comforting.

Because her job near Freeport was temporary, Julia returned to Dallas after eight months. With the much longer drive, she couldn't visit as often as before. But she continued to work quietly and methodically on Clyde's behalf, writing letters and making personal visits. She reminded herself of the New Testament story of the woman who was finally granted what she wished because of her persistence. She didn't want Clyde to stay in prison a day longer than he had to because she hadn't worked hard enough on his behalf.

The months passed. 1954 came and went. And the day came in July, 1955, for Clyde's case to be heard again. Julia requested that a collect telegram be sent to her as soon as the board had ruled in Clyde's case. She was certain the board would act favorably this time. Clyde's mother once again stayed with Julia so that she could be there when Clyde was released.

Julia rushed home from work on the day of the hearing to

find the telegram waiting for her. The word from Austin was negative. Clyde's case would come up for review in 1957. Julia was stunned. And she immediately felt the disappointment she knew Clyde would feel when he heard the news.

The telegram didn't state the reasons for denying Clyde's parole. However, the board had relied heavily on a psychological profile of Clyde that had been conducted earlier that year and had become a part of his records. Clyde had a "low frustration tolerance," according to the summary. The psychologist had given him a fifty-fifty chance of making it on the outside.

Julia and Dolly cried together. Julia felt more frustration than anger and spent a sleepless night, alternating between crying and trying to decide what was the best course of action. Giving up was not one of the alternatives.

Clyde, too, was disappointed when he heard the news. By praying about it and writing letters to the parole board, Clyde had done all he could. This time he was not crushed. He had made up his mind not to let his happiness be contingent on the actions of the parole board, something over which he had no control. He had decided to do the best he could each day, whether he was in prison or on the outside.

Julia spent a dreary day at work following her sleepless night.

When she got home, she wrote a letter to the board. In the letter Julia expressed her concern about Clyde's readiness to be able to make a readjustment to society. "He has already been behind bars for more than twenty-seven years. Will two more years in prison make this adjustment period any easier? If he spends much more time in prison, I'm afraid that it will make the readjustment period all the more difficult."

Julia also pointed out that Clyde had a place to live and a job waiting for him now. In two more years this might not be the case. Furthermore, Clyde's prospects for finding employment would be diminished, since he was approaching forty-seven years of age.

"Two more years will just further institutionalize him. Please give him a chance," Julia pleaded in closing her letter.

Not long afterward, Clyde received word that the board would consider his case again in three months—October, 1955—rather than in two years. Julia was as elated as he was when she heard the news. Clyde recalled that there had been a thirty-day delay in the decision on whether he should be sent to Ramsey, and that had ended up being positive. Also, there had been another case at Ramsey where a convict's parole decision had been postponed two months, after which the board had acted favorably. Clyde had hopes that the same thing would happen for him.

There was so much happening on the outside that Clyde wanted to experience firsthand. The world had changed a lot since he was first incarcerated in 1928. And there was Julia. Clyde wanted them to share all these things together. During the three-month period, Julia continued to work on Clyde's behalf. So did Clyde.

It was a Saturday night, October 23, 1955, and Clyde was in the cellblock helping a prisoner with some clean-up work before going to his cell for the night. Warden McAdams entered the cellblock and called to Clyde. As Clyde walked toward McAdams, he could see that the warden held a slip of paper in his hand. When Clyde was about halfway to him, McAdams spoke up, holding the piece of paper in the air. "It's a telegram from your wife! She says that the board has granted you a conditional pardon, and it's already been signed by the governor. Congratulations, Clyde!" The men in their cells joined in, some clapping and others yelling their own congratulations. The warden clasped Clyde's hand.

Clyde wondered if it was really happening as he stood there, shaking hands with the warden. With the other hand, McAdams gave Clyde the telegram from Julia. Clyde looked at it. "She's not my wife, yet, Warden, but she will be in a few days."

"You ought to be really proud of that little girl," McAdams said. "She wouldn't let anybody forget that she had faith in you and wanted you out of here."

"I sure am proud of her," Clyde replied. "I sure am."

McAdams told Clyde that it would take a few days for the papers to be processed in Austin and for arrangements to be made for his release. "Congratulations again, Clyde," he added. "You've done a fine job in here, and I know you'll do equally well on the outside."

Clyde thanked the warden and walked back to his cell. In a way it was the same way he walked to his cell on any other night, but this time he carried the telegram bearing news of his release. He was still in the same prison, but so much was different. Once in the cell, Clyde knelt beside his bunk and gave thanks to God.

The next morning Clyde preached what he knew would be his last sermon to the inmates at Ramsey. For the next three days he helped break in the man who would replace him as building tender. On Thursday morning he said his good-bys to the inmates and officials at Ramsey and was taken on his last ride in a prison truck from Ramsey to The Walls, from which TDC prisoners were processed and released.

Clyde was due to be released at 1:30 P.M. Monday, November 1. He spent four nights in a cell at The Walls. The nights were mostly sleepless as Clyde wondered what living in the outside world would be like after twenty-eight years without freedom. He had yearned for his freedom, but now he felt uncertain of what lay beyond the prison walls. If he wasn't ready, Clyde knew that God wouldn't allow him to be released. But at the same time, he wondered what the readjustment would be like. Readjustment? Perhaps the word should be *adjustment*. Clyde realized he had never been adjusted to the world to begin with or he wouldn't have ended up in prison. But to make this adjustment, Clyde knew he had some things going for him that he didn't have to begin with—faith in God and a woman who believed in him.

In his three days at Huntsville, Clyde talked at length with the parole counselor, who told him what kind of problems men leaving prison usually encounter. Clyde also spent time in prayer, seeking continual direction and help. He remembered that Paul had said, "I can do all things through Christ which strengtheneth me" (Phil. 4:13).

Julia arrived in Huntsville on Saturday night and rented a hotel room. The next morning she attended church in Huntsville, went out for lunch, and returned to her room. She sat on the corner of her bed, thinking. Clyde's release had been what she had been waiting for, but now she had some uncertainties about what lay ahead. Clyde had pledged his love to her many years before. He had vowed that they would get married if he ever got out. He had even tried to get permission for them to be married while he was in prison. But when he was actually released, would he really want to marry her? Julia felt she knew Clyde well enough to know he would follow through on his promise. He would marry her. But deep down in his heart, would he really want to? Would he want to be burdened by her deformity?

I've got to give him a way out, thought Julia. *If he takes it, then so be it. I'll at least know that I've helped a man get the freedom he deserves*. Julia knew she was setting herself up for what could be the greatest disappointment of her life, but she felt it was something that must be done—for Clyde's sake and for her own piece of mind. She had to be sure Clyde really wanted her, and there was only one way she could think of to prove it. Otherwise, she would always wonder.

She spent a fretful night, waking up several times to find that it was still dark outside. Finally, shortly after sunrise, Julia got out of bed. Her first stop after breakfast was at the prison to find out what time Clyde would be released. She asked if she could bring some new clothes for him to wear as he was leaving the prison. Yes, she could bring him clothing, and she was to have it at the prison at 12:30—one hour before he would step out as a free man.

Julia wanted Clyde to walk out of prison with the advantage of wearing nice clothes. Upon their release, prisoners wore a pair of khakis, work shirt, and shoes that were issued to them. They also received either fifty dollars or a bus ticket home and lunch money.

Julia drove to a men's clothing store in Huntsville, where she bought a new suit, white shirt with French cuffs, cuff links, tie, socks, underwear, and hat. By the time the slacks were altered and pressed, it was past noon. She had to hurry back to the prison, where she gave the clothes to the parole counselor.

There were seventeen other men being released from prison that day. Clyde found that he was the only one who would have someone to meet him as he left the prison. A couple of men said the first thing they were going to do was take the fifty dollars and celebrate with a bottle of booze and a broad. One of the stipulations for the parolees was that they had to avoid alcoholic beverages and nonprescribed drugs. With their plans of breaking parole the first thing, Clyde wondered how long it would be before these men would once again be on the inside looking out.

Clyde was excited when the new suit was brought to him. He'd never worn a suit in his life. O. B. Ellis was out of town, so Clyde went into Ellis's office with the parole officer to put on his new clothes. The parole officer left for a minute to attend to another prisoner. Clyde slipped on his new pants. They fit perfectly. And compared to the prison clothes he had worn for so long, these pants felt smooth and expensive. Then Clyde put on the white shirt with stiff collar. But he was alarmed that the sleeves came way down over his hands and that there were no buttons on the sleeves.

The parole counselor reentered to see Clyde appearing a bit frustrated.

"I sure am glad to see you," said Clyde. "Look at this shirt. It's way too long, and it doesn't even have any buttons on the sleeves."

The parole officer tried to hide a smile. "It's been a long time, hasn't it, Clyde?"

"What has?"

"Since you've dressed up and worn cuff links. I guess twenty-eight years is a long time behind bars."

"Cuff links?"

"Yes, cuff links. What do you have in your top pocket there?"

Clyde looked into the top pocket of his shirt. "Looks like Julia put some earrings in here."

"Well, take 'em out."

Clyde obeyed and held them in the palm of his hand for the counselor to see.

"Those are cuff links, Clyde. You use those instead of buttons on your sleeves."

"Aww," Clyde mustered, at first thinking the man was joking with him and then realizing he wasn't. Clyde knew this was just the tip of the iceberg. There was a whole lot about the ways of the outside world that he knew nothing about. And the cuff links were just one small example. Horses and buggies were still in widespread use when he entered prison. Now it wasn't uncommon to see jet planes overhead. There was also a lot of talk about the hydrogen bomb.

"Let me see your sleeve there," the counselor said. Clyde held out his hand, and the counselor took one of the cuff links. Clyde watched as the man inserted the cuff link through the holes that looked like button holes.

"That looks nice," said Clyde, holding up his arm. "Why don't you do this other side, too?"

278

Clyde knew he would also need help with the next procedure, putting on a tie. He had never worn a tie.

Once dressed, Clyde talked with the counselor for a while. Then he was taken to an office, where Julia was waiting for him. They embraced and kissed. Clyde turned and thanked the parole officer, and they were led to another waiting room, where the other parolees were sitting on benches in their prison-issued clothes. In a moment they were all released.

With his arm around Julia's shoulder, Clyde walked out the front door of prison a free man. They walked toward the lot where Julia's car was parked, while the other men went toward the bus station and stores just a few blocks away. If these men were typical, their first stop would be at a local clothing store to purchase a shirt and pants so their clothing wouldn't readily identify them as newly released ex-cons. They would then go to the bus station to wait for a ride home, if they had a home. Some men were known to get drunk, run afoul of the law, and end up in the city jail the very day they were released from prison.

"Which way y'all going?" one of the prisoners asked.

"Dallas," replied Julia.

"Mind if I hitch a ride with you?"

Clyde shook his head negatively. The man walked toward the bus station, and Clyde explained to Julia that as a part of his parole, he wasn't allowed even to talk with another ex-con.

Julia and Clyde got to her car. Clyde puzzled for a moment about how to open the door. The handles had changed since he last opened one for himself. But he figured it out, and from inside the car, he watched as the others walked briskly toward the bus station. "You know, I'd like for us to come back here and help men like that some day," Clyde remarked. "Maybe with some type of Christian ministry."

"Yes, that would be nice," Julia said, but she knew that before making any plans for the future with Clyde, she had something important to tell him.

Chapter
35

CLYDE LOOKED out the window as they pulled onto the street. After so many years of waiting, Clyde was finally free. It was the first time since 1928 that he had ridden in anything but a prison truck or sheriff's car. Clyde reached to feel the knot of his tie. Though the stiff white collar and tie were a bit uncomfortable, he was grateful to feel the knot instead of a padlock securing him to a chain.

Clyde and Julia's first stop was at the store where she had purchased his suit that morning. Everything fit perfectly except for the hat. The store didn't have one that fit, so Clyde exchanged the hat for a second pair of slacks.

They ate lunch at a cafe in Huntsville and agreed that before leaving Huntsville, they would visit the gravesite of the legendary Sam Houston, who had homesteaded in the Huntsville area. They got on the highway for Dallas at 3:30.

It was hot for November 1, even by Texas standards. For both it had been an emotionally tense day, and the heat was draining what little energy they had left. After an hour and a half, Julia pulled over at a roadside park. They held hands and walked in silence toward some trees where they sat down on a bench.

There were still prison authorities who believed Clyde would ditch Julia at the first opportunity—and perhaps might even kill her. Julia's parents were worried. But Julia had another concern.

"Clyde," she said, breaking the silence and then drawing a deep breath, "there's something I've got to tell you."

"What is it, darling?" asked Clyde, still feeling it was all too good to be true.

"You've been locked away for a long time and haven't had the opportunity to meet any nice girls." She paused, feeling the perspiration on the palms of hands that had suddenly become clammy.

Clyde looked concerned. "Have you gotten me out to tell me you don't love me?" he asked.

"No, nothing was said about love," she answered. "It's just that I'm not strong or healthy or beautiful." Her voice cracked, but she continued. "And there's a lot of nice-looking church girls who'd be glad to go on a date with an eligible guy like you. I'd help you meet as many nice girls as you want. Listen, I would have helped you get out anyway because you deserved to be out. You don't owe me anything in return."

"You love me, don't you, Julia?"

"Yes, I do."

"Well, I've got my girl, and I plan to marry her as soon as I can—that is, if she'll have me. That's what we've planned right along, and that's what I still want to do."

She smiled. "All you're going to do is trade one ball and chain for another."

"That's all right. This is one ball and chain of my choosing, and I've been looking forward to it."

Clyde knew Julia well enough by this time to guess her motives. As they walked toward the car together, Clyde put his arm firmly around Julia's shoulder and gently squeezed her.

Clyde and Julia were married at the home of Mr. and Mrs.

Charles Wilson at Rockwall, Texas, just outside of Dallas, on the following Saturday. Julia's parents refused to attend.

Clyde knew ahead of time that his transition from inmate to domesticated, married man on the outside would not be easy. He was accustomed to having prison doors opened for him by guards. He knew that on the outside it would look rude if he waited for Julia to open the doors. But this was an obvious change. There were many little things he could not anticipate. When he and Julia went into a store, for example, it would be filled with devices that he had never seen before. It was as if he had been a Robinson Crusoe.

Clyde would pick up an object in a hardware store or super-market and look at it with curiosity. "What's this?" he would ask quietly, or sometimes he would simply mouth the words, and Julia would lipread. It embarrassed him to have to ask, and he didn't want anyone overhearing him.

"Why, that's a can opener, honey," Julia replied. Julia never ceased to be amazed at Clyde's childlike qualities in regard to gadgetry or modern technology. Julia began to see that she took a lot of things for granted, since Clyde's view of the world for practically three decades had been limited to letters, maga-zines, newspapers, radio, and, in the last few years, television.

Clyde worked briefly as a salesman of staples and staplers before he and Julia obtained jobs at Southwestern Christian College, a predominantly black college just east of Dallas. Clyde worked in the woodworking shop, and Julia ran the mailroom.

While working at the college, within a year of his release, Clyde yearned to return to a location he had once visited. It had been thirty years since Clyde and his brother Bill had discovered the place where he thought the Mexican gold was buried. So many times he had thought about escaping from prison, digging up the gold, and living comfortably from then on. Now, he wanted to return once and for all to see if the gold was actually buried there.

Julia joined him on the drive to Cisco. When they arrived, Clyde found everything changed. An old road was gone and so were the houses that had been built alongside it. Cultivated farms had turned into goat ranches. Landmarks Clyde had used as a boy had disappeared. After searching for a few hours, Clyde gave up. But he wasn't disappointed. In the years since he had dreamed of being rich with gold, his definition of rich had changed.

The visit to Cisco, near the site of the murders of Web and Jake O'Dell, had rekindled a lot of memories—the months in jail, the years in prison, the death of his father, the murder of inmates, the escape attempts, and the years in isolation. He had sought freedom from prison, but he later found freedom through Christ long before he was released. He looked at Julia as they drove out of Eastland County. It had been a tiring day, and she had dozed off. He gently patted her hand, then focused his eyes on the road ahead.

Epilogue

CLYDE WAS GRANTED a full pardon by Texas Governor John Connally in 1963. And long before the pardon, Clyde was accepted as a son-in-law by the Perrymans.

After two years at the college, Clyde worked as a minister and salesman of Bibles and household products most of the time from 1957 to 1970. For nine months in 1960, Clyde served as the superintendent of the Navajo Indian Children's Home in Manuelito, New Mexico. While there, another dream came true for Clyde and Julia.

Clyde shared Julia's desire to be a parent. But by the time Clyde was released, it was too late for them to have a baby of their own. They tried numerous times to adopt a child but were told they were too old. While working at the children's home, they met a Navajo baby girl whose parents were unable to care for her. Clyde and Julia gave her a foster home, and after several months, they became the legal, permanent parents of Shirley Anne.

In 1970 the Thompson family moved to Huntsville to help prisoners. Through the support of churches, and under the direction of the Midway Church of Christ near Huntsville, Clyde opened the Prisoners Aid Center. It was a Christian ministry aimed at assisting convicts who were released from prison to reestablish themselves in society. Clyde went into the various TDC units to tell how the meanest man in Texas had been helped by God. Clyde's work in Huntsville lasted seven years. In 1977, the family sought a more arid climate to alleviate Julia's respiratory problems.

Luke Curtis, a former prisoner helped by Clyde, continued the prison ministry in Huntsville when Clyde, Julia, and Shirley moved to Lubbock, Texas. Sponsored by the Sunset Church of Christ, Clyde began a ministry to prisoners at the Lubbock County Jail and was named its chaplain.

Clyde summarized his story in a fifty-two-page book, *The Life Story of Clyde Thompson—Ex–83*, distributed in jails and prisons. The book contained highlights of Clyde's life and poems he had written as a prisoner. It was estimated that the story reached 250,000 prisoners.

Clyde's story became well known outside of prisons as well. He was asked to preach at churches throughout the United States and in foreign countries, and he held seminars on jail and prison ministries. Clyde spoke on the penal system at universities. He also was the guest on network radio and television programs in the United States, Canada, Mexico, and the West Indies.

One day in late April, 1979, Clyde and Bob Woodard, who had joined Clyde's ministry to prisoners in Lubbock, drove to the jail and prayed quietly together before entering. Following the prayer, Clyde suddenly grabbed Bob's arm with a firm grip, surprising Bob. "I'm not going to be around forever, and I have to make sure you're going to carry on this work," he said, staring intently at Bob.

"Yes," Bob answered, "I intend to stay with the jail ministry. But what on earth are you talking about? You're a healthy man."

"I just need to be sure of this," Clyde told him, starting to relax the grip on Bob's arm.

That scene was repeated in May, and then again in mid-June. At the time, Bob didn't place much significance on the questions. But unknown to Bob or anyone else, Clyde had been suffering from pains in his back with increasing regularity. He finally told Julia about them, and she urged him to visit a doctor. He did not heed her advice.

On the night of July 2, 1979, Clyde lay down on the floor of his living room, complaining of severe pains in his back and head. The pain was serious enough for Clyde to ask Julia to take him to the hospital.

Julia stayed with Clyde in the hospital room that night. They talked for a while the next morning. Then Clyde got out of his bed to go to the bathroom, and in a moment he was gasping, unable to catch his breath. Julia summoned help. As the doctors started to administer oxygen, Clyde looked up at Julia and seemed through his struggle for breath to be saying good-by to her with his eyes. He was pronounced dead of a cardiac arrest a few minutes later.

An autopsy revealed that Clyde was in the advanced stages of spinal cancer. Had he not succumbed to the heart attack, he would have lived, in pain, for only a few months longer.

Shirley married Jimmy McDonald on October 20, 1979. Julia now has two grandsons, Joey and Jeremy.